Machine Learning and Natural Language Processing

Student Edition

Kimberly Seefeld, EdD

Table of contents

Machine Learning and Natural Language Processing

Student Edition

By Kimberly Seefeld, EdD

Published under **DataJoyAI** imprint

Companion resources for this book are available at:

DataJoyAI

https://datajoyai.com

Edition: First Edition
ISBN: 978-1-969233-39-5

Chapter 1

Introduction to Applied Machine Learning

1.1 Learning Outcomes

1-1: Distinguish between supervised and unsupervised learning approaches and identify appropriate applications

1-2: Design and implement a complete machine learning pipeline from data preprocessing through model evaluation

1-3: Evaluate model interpretability requirements and implement bias detection strategies

1-4: Select and configure AI-assisted model selection tools to optimize performance

1.2 Introduction

Picture this scenario: You're scrolling through Netflix, and within seconds, the platform presents you with a curated list of shows that seem perfectly tailored to your taste. Meanwhile, your bank's fraud detection system is silently analyzing thousands of transactions per second, flagging suspicious activity before you even notice. In another part of the world, a radiologist is reviewing medical images with the assistance of an AI system that can detect early-stage cancer with remarkable accuracy. What connects these seemingly different experiences? They all represent the power of applied machine learning transforming how we live, work, and make decisions.

But let's step back for a moment. Before you even grabbed your phone this morning, you were already immersed in a world shaped by artificial intelligence. Your alarm clock learned your sleep patterns to wake you at the optimal time. Your coffee maker started brewing because it predicted when you'd wake up. Your car's navigation system analyzed traffic patterns to suggest the best route to campus. By the time you check Instagram and see posts from friends you actually care about at the top of your feed, you've already interacted with machine learning algorithms dozens of times.

This book focuses on understanding how machine learning moves from theoretical concepts to real-world business solutions. However, before we dive into advanced applications, we need to establish a solid foundation in the fundamental approaches that drive these systems. This opening module introduces the core concepts that every data professional must master: what machine learning actually is and how it fits within the broader landscape of artificial intelligence, the distinction between supervised and unsupervised learning, the systematic pipeline that transforms raw data into actionable insights, and the critical considerations of model interpretability and bias that determine whether our solutions succeed or fail in practice.

1.3 Understanding What Machine Learning Is

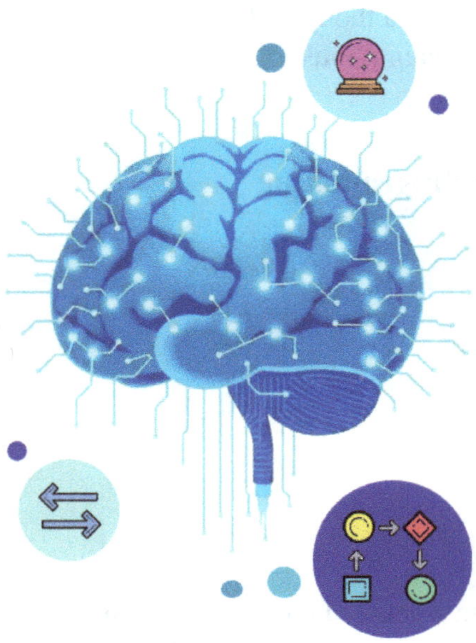

1.3.1 The Artificial Intelligence Landscape

Before diving into machine learning specifics, we need to understand where it fits in the bigger picture of artificial intelligence. Think of AI as a vast umbrella that covers any technology designed to make machines seem intelligent or human-like. Under this umbrella, you'll find several different approaches to creating smart systems, each with its own strengths and applications.

Artificial Intelligence represents the broad field focused on creating machines that can perform tasks typically requiring human intelligence. This encompasses everything from playing chess to recognizing speech to driving cars autonomously. While AI has existed since the 1950s, recent advances in computing power and data availability have transformed it from academic curiosity to practical business tool.

Machine Learning sits as a specific subset of AI, focusing on teaching computers to learn patterns from data without being explicitly programmed for every possible scenario. Instead of writing detailed instructions for every situation a system might encounter, we show the computer numerous examples and let it discover the underlying patterns. It's analogous to teaching a child to recognize different dog breeds by showing them thousands of photos rather than trying to describe every possible canine characteristic.

Natural Language Processing represents another crucial subset of AI, specifically

designed to help computers understand and work with human language. When you ask Siri a question, use Google Translate, or see autocomplete suggestions in your email, you're experiencing NLP in action. What makes NLP particularly exciting is that language sits at the heart of human communication and thought. Teaching machines to understand language opens possibilities for more natural interactions between humans and computers.

1.3.2 Machine Learning vs. Traditional Programming

Traditional programming operates like following a detailed recipe. You write specific instructions such as "If the customer purchases more than $100 worth of items, provide free shipping." The computer follows these rules exactly as written, but struggles when encountering situations you didn't anticipate. The system becomes brittle and requires constant updates as new scenarios emerge.

Machine learning fundamentally flips this approach. Instead of writing explicit rules, you provide examples of inputs paired with desired outputs. The system learns to recognize patterns and make decisions about new situations it has never encountered before. It's like having an exceptionally perceptive assistant who can figure out what you want even in novel situations, based on what they've learned from past examples.

This distinction becomes crucial when dealing with complex, dynamic environments. A traditional fraud detection system might use rules like "flag transactions over $10,000" or "alert if purchases occur in multiple countries within 24 hours." But fraudsters adapt quickly, finding ways around these static rules. A machine learning system, however, can identify subtle patterns in transaction behavior that humans might miss, adapting as fraudulent tactics evolve.

1.3.3 The Business Impact Revolution

The machine learning landscape has evolved dramatically in recent years. According to recent industry research, organizations implementing machine learning strategically report average ROI improvements between 10-20%, with marketing automation leading at an impressive 544% ROI . These aren't merely theoretical benefits—companies across industries are seeing measurable improvements in their operations and bottom lines.

Yet despite this tremendous potential, only 25% of companies successfully move beyond pilot projects to generate real business value . This gap between promise and performance often stems from a fundamental misunderstanding of how machine learning actually works in practice. Companies become excited about the possibilities but struggle with the practical challenges of implementation, data quality, and organizational change management.

Consider how different industries are leveraging machine learning today. Netflix uses sophisticated algorithms to recommend content, keeping viewers engaged and reducing subscription cancellations. Amazon employs machine learning for everything from product recommendations to warehouse optimization to fraud detection. Banks utilize these technologies to assess credit risk and detect suspicious transactions in real-time. Healthcare providers apply machine learning to analyze medical images and predict patient outcomes with remarkable accuracy.

These success stories share common characteristics that separate them from failed implementations. They begin with clearly defined business problems rather than technology-first approaches. They invest heavily in data quality and systematic processes. They implement robust monitoring and maintenance procedures. Most importantly, they recognize that machine learning is fundamentally about augmenting human decision-making rather than replacing human judgment entirely.

1.4 Understanding Learning Paradigms

The foundation of applied machine learning rests on understanding when and how to apply different learning paradigms. Like learning to drive a car—there are fundamentally different approaches you could take, and each has its place depending on your situation and objectives.

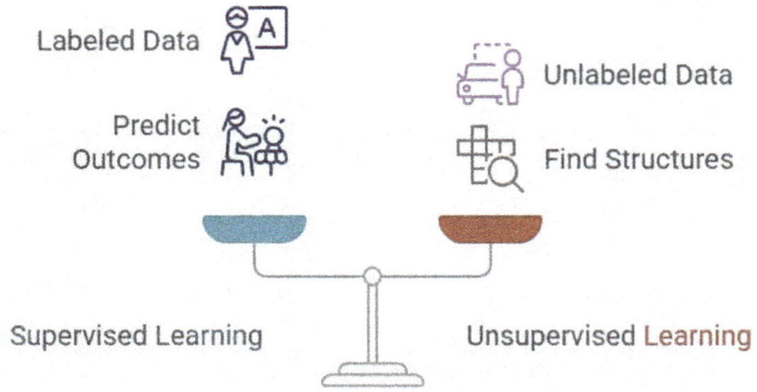

The first approach resembles learning with a driving instructor who provides constant guidance. "Turn left here," "brake now," "accelerate gradually." After hundreds of hours of this supervision, you develop the ability to drive independently. This represents supervised learning—you learn from examples where you know the correct answer.

The second approach would be like being placed in a parking lot filled with various vehicles and asked to identify how they naturally group together. You might notice that some cars cluster by color, others by size, still others by apparent cost or style. You're discovering patterns without anyone telling you what to look for. This represents unsupervised learning—finding hidden structures in data without predetermined answers.

This distinction between supervised and unsupervised learning fundamentally shapes how we approach business problems and determines the types of insights we can extract from our data. Understanding when to use each approach often makes the difference between project success and failure.

1.4.1 Supervised Learning: Learning from Examples

Supervised learning algorithms learn from labeled examples, where we provide both input data and the desired output. This approach excels when we have historical data with known outcomes and want to predict similar results for new situations. The "supervision" comes from essentially showing the algorithm thousands of examples of correct answers, allowing it to learn the underlying patterns that connect inputs to outputs.

Consider how Spotify's Discover Weekly playlist operates. Spotify possesses data on millions of users: which songs they skip, which they replay, which they save to playlists, and which they rate highly. The platform knows that when User A enjoys Song X and Song Y, they typically also appreciate Song Z. When a new user demonstrates similar taste patterns, Spotify can predict what they'll enjoy with remarkable accuracy.

The algorithm learned from examples where the outcome was known—whether people actually engaged positively with the recommended songs. This historical data serves as the "teacher," demonstrating which recommendations led to positive user engagement and which resulted in skips or negative feedback.

Amazon's recommendation system operates on similar principles but at an even larger scale. The company has accumulated millions of examples of customer purchases, ratings, and browsing behavior paired with actual buying decisions. This historical data serves as the foundation for learning, showing the algorithm which products customers actually purchased after viewing certain items. When you visit Amazon today, the system applies these learned patterns to predict what you might want to buy, creating those eerily accurate "customers who bought this item also bought" recommendations.

1.4.1.1 Classification vs. Regression Applications

Supervised learning divides into two primary categories based on the type of output we're attempting to predict. Understanding this distinction helps you frame problems correctly and choose appropriate evaluation methods.

Classification problems involve predicting categories or classes. Think of this as putting things into buckets or answering yes/no questions. Examples include determining whether an email is spam or legitimate, predicting whether a customer will cancel their subscription, diagnosing medical conditions from symptoms, or identifying fraudulent transactions. The output is discrete and categorical—you're essentially making decisions about which group something belongs to.

Regression problems, by contrast, involve predicting continuous numerical values. Examples include forecasting sales revenue for the next quarter, estimating house prices based on features like location and size, or predicting customer lifetime value. The output is a specific number that can take any value within a reasonable range, rather than a discrete category.

A practical example demonstrates this distinction clearly. Suppose you're working for a telecommunications company analyzing customer behavior. A classification approach might predict whether a customer will cancel their service within the next month—essentially a yes or no question. You'd analyze historical data from customers who did cancel and those who didn't, looking for patterns in calling behavior, data usage, payment history, and customer service interactions.

A regression approach to the same business context might predict exactly how much revenue that customer will generate over the next year—a specific dollar amount. This would involve analyzing similar historical data but focusing on spending patterns, usage trends, and service upgrades rather than cancellation events. Both approaches use the same underlying data but answer fundamentally different business questions.

1.4.2 Unsupervised Learning: Discovering Hidden Patterns

Unsupervised learning operates without labeled examples, instead seeking to discover hidden patterns, structures, or relationships within data. This approach proves invaluable when we don't know what we're looking for or when we want to understand the underlying structure of our data before applying other techniques. Think of it as being a detective with numerous clues but no clear idea what mystery you're trying to solve.

Instagram uses unsupervised learning to understand what types of content naturally group together. The platform might discover that certain combinations of hashtags, posting times, and image styles tend to cluster together, revealing trends that no human analyst would have noticed. They're not trying to predict anything specific—they're exploring to find insights that could guide content recommendation strategies or help creators understand what resonates with audiences.

1.4.2.1 Clustering and Pattern Discovery

One of the most common unsupervised techniques is clustering, which groups similar data points together without knowing in advance what those groups should be. Retail companies frequently use clustering to segment customers based on purchasing behavior, discovering natural groupings that weren't obvious from traditional demographic categories.

Target famously used clustering to discover that customers buying unscented lotion, cotton balls, and folic acid supplements were likely pregnant—even before they announced their pregnancy publicly. The algorithm identified a pattern that human analysts had missed, revealing a customer segment with specific needs and predictable shopping behaviors.

For instance, a grocery chain might discover through clustering that their customers naturally fall into groups like "health-conscious families," "convenience shoppers," and "bulk buyers," each with distinct purchasing patterns that cross traditional age and income boundaries. These insights enable more targeted marketing strategies and inventory management decisions. The health-conscious families might shop primarily in the organic section and respond well to nutrition-focused promotions, while convenience shoppers prefer ready-made meals and value quick checkout options.

1.4.2.2 Dimensionality Reduction and Feature Discovery

Another powerful unsupervised technique involves reducing the complexity of data while preserving its essential characteristics. This proves particularly valuable when dealing with high-dimensional data where traditional analysis becomes difficult or impossible.

Consider a manufacturing company monitoring hundreds of sensors on production equipment. Unsupervised learning can identify which sensor readings tend to change together, potentially revealing that dozens of individual measurements actually represent just a few underlying factors like "equipment temperature," "vibration levels," and "production speed." This insight dramatically simplifies monitoring and helps identify the root causes of quality issues.

Netflix might analyze viewing patterns and discover that people who watch cooking shows on Sunday afternoons also tend to binge-watch home renovation shows on weekday evenings. This insight could guide content creation and recommendation strategies, even though Netflix wasn't specifically looking for this connection. The algorithm revealed a hidden relationship between seemingly unrelated viewing behaviors that could inform content acquisition and production decisions.

1.4.3 Choosing the Right Approach for Business Problems

The decision between supervised and unsupervised learning depends on your business objectives and available data. This choice fundamentally shapes your entire approach to the problem and determines what kinds of insights you can expect to generate.

Supervised learning works best when you have clear goals and historical examples of success. If you want to predict customer churn, detect fraud, or forecast demand, and you have historical data showing what happened in similar situations, supervised learning provides the most direct path to actionable results. The key requirement is having labeled data—examples where you know the correct answer.

Consider a credit card company wanting to detect fraudulent transactions. They have millions of historical transactions labeled as either fraudulent or legitimate. Supervised learning can analyze patterns in transaction amounts, merchant types, geographic locations, and timing to learn what fraudulent activity looks like. The resulting model can then evaluate new transactions in real-time and flag suspicious activity for further investigation.

Unsupervised learning excels in exploratory scenarios where you're trying to understand your data better or discover unexpected patterns. When entering new markets, analyzing customer feedback, or investigating operational inefficiencies, unsupervised techniques can reveal insights that guide subsequent analysis. This approach is particularly valuable when you don't have clear success criteria or when you want to understand the natural structure of your data before building predictive models.

A company expanding into a new geographic market might use unsupervised learning to analyze local customer behavior and identify distinct segments that don't match their existing customer categories. This exploration could reveal cultural preferences, economic factors, or lifestyle patterns that inform product positioning and marketing strategies.

Many successful applications combine both approaches strategically. A retail company might start with unsupervised clustering to discover customer segments, then use supervised learning to predict which products each segment is most likely to purchase. This hybrid approach leverages the pattern discovery capabilities of unsupervised learning with the predictive power of supervised methods.

1.5 The Machine Learning Pipeline

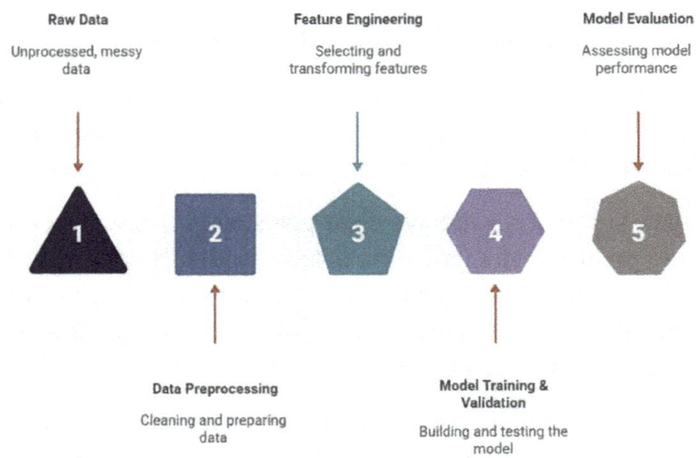

The journey from raw data to actionable business insights follows a systematic process that experienced practitioners call the machine learning pipeline. This structured approach ensures reproducible results, minimizes errors, and creates systems that can be maintained and improved over time. Understanding this pipeline is crucial because most machine learning failures occur not in the algorithms themselves, but in the systematic processes that support them.

Think of the machine learning pipeline like preparing a complex meal for important guests. You wouldn't just throw ingredients together and hope for the best—you'd follow a proven recipe, prepare ingredients properly, taste-test along the way, and present the final dish beautifully. The machine learning pipeline is your recipe for transforming raw data into business value, and like any good recipe, each step builds on the previous ones to create a successful outcome.

1.5.1 Data Preprocessing: The Foundation of Success

The preprocessing stage often determines the ultimate success or failure of machine learning projects, yet it receives less attention than the more glamorous modeling phase. Real-world data arrives messy, incomplete, and inconsistent. Effective preprocessing transforms this raw material into a format that algorithms can use effectively.

Let's follow Maria, a data analyst at a growing e-commerce company. She's been asked to build a system that predicts which products customers will buy. Excited about the project, she downloads the customer data and discovers a reality that's all too common in the business world. Fifteen percent of customer records are missing age information. Some customers have birthdates in the future, clearly data entry errors. Product categories are inconsistent, with "Electronics," "electronic," "ELECTRONICS," and "Tech" all referring to the same thing. Purchase amounts include obvious typos like $50,000 for a coffee mug.

This scenario illustrates the reality of real-world data. Unlike the clean datasets used in academic examples, business data is messy, and no algorithm can learn effectively from garbage input. The quality of your preprocessing directly impacts the quality of your final model, making this stage crucial for project success.

1.5.1.1 Data Quality Assessment and Cleaning

The first step involves understanding what you're working with through comprehensive data quality assessment. This means examining data distributions, identifying missing values, detecting outliers, and understanding the relationships between different variables. A financial services company analyzing loan applications might discover that income data is missing for 15% of applications, that some applicants report impossible ages, or that certain zip codes appear to be entered incorrectly.

Maria's approach demonstrates best practices for systematic data cleaning. Rather than making arbitrary decisions about how to handle problems, she creates visualizations showing data distributions and identifies patterns in missing values. She analyzes whether age correlates with other available information, which helps her make informed decisions about how to handle missing values. She creates rules for consistent category naming and applies them across all data, and she sets up checks to catch future data quality issues.

Cleaning strategies must balance thoroughness with practicality. Simply removing all records with missing data might eliminate valuable information, while imputing missing values incorrectly can introduce bias. The key lies in understanding why data is missing and choosing appropriate strategies for each situation. Sometimes missing data is random, but often it's systematic—certain types of customers might be less likely to provide age information, or certain products might have inconsistent category labeling.

1.5.1.2 Feature Engineering and Transformation

Feature engineering involves creating new variables that better capture the patterns relevant to your business problem. This process requires domain expertise combined with analytical thinking. Raw data rarely tells the full story, and the most predictive features are often combinations or transformations of the original variables.

Consider how a streaming service like Netflix approaches feature engineering. Raw viewing data includes timestamps, show titles, and user IDs. Through feature engineering, this becomes rich behavioral profiles including "prefers binge-watching," "watches across multiple genres," "sensitive to content ratings," and "likely to cancel after free trial." These engineered features often prove more predictive than the original raw data because they capture meaningful patterns in user behavior.

Maria discovers that while individual purchase amounts vary wildly, patterns emerge when she creates new features based on purchasing behavior. She develops features like seasonal purchasing patterns that capture whether customers buy more during holidays, brand loyalty indicators that measure consistency in brand choices, and shopping behavior features that distinguish between bulk purchasers and frequent small-order customers. These engineered features often prove more predictive than the original raw data because they capture meaningful business concepts.

1.5.2 Model Training and Validation Strategies

Once data is properly prepared, the training phase involves teaching algorithms to recognize patterns and make predictions. However, effective training requires more than simply feeding data into algorithms. It demands systematic approaches to ensure that models will perform well on new, unseen data.

Imagine teaching someone to evaluate job candidates by showing them hundreds of resumes alongside information about how those candidates actually performed in their roles. Over time, they'd learn to recognize patterns: certain combinations of experience, education, and skills tend to predict success. Machine learning training works similarly. The algorithm studies thousands of examples, gradually learning which patterns in the input data predict the desired outcomes.

1.5.2.1 Cross-Validation and Performance Estimation

The fundamental challenge in machine learning is ensuring that models generalize beyond the specific data used for training. This is like testing a job evaluator's skills on candidates from companies they've never seen before. They might seem accurate on familiar examples but fail miserably on new ones.

Cross-validation addresses this challenge by systematically testing model performance on data that wasn't used during training. This process helps identify whether a model has truly learned useful patterns or has simply memorized the training data—a problem known as overfitting.

A practical approach involves dividing available data into training, validation, and test sets. The training set teaches the model, the validation set helps tune parameters and select the best approach, and the test set provides an unbiased estimate of real-world performance. This separation ensures that performance estimates reflect what you can expect when the model encounters new data.

1.5.2.2 Hyperparameter Optimization

Most machine learning algorithms include settings called hyperparameters that control how the learning process works. These might include the learning rate for neural networks, the depth of decision trees, or the number of clusters in clustering algorithms. Optimizing these settings can dramatically improve performance, but it requires systematic experimentation rather than random guessing.

Modern approaches to hyperparameter optimization use automated search techniques that efficiently explore the space of possible settings. Tools like Optuna, Hyperopt, or cloud-based AutoML services can automatically test hundreds of parameter combinations to find optimal configurations. This automation allows practitioners to focus on higher-level decisions while ensuring that models are properly tuned.

1.5.3 Model Evaluation: Beyond Accuracy Metrics

Evaluating machine learning models requires understanding that different metrics matter for different business contexts. Accuracy, while important, tells only part of the story and can be misleading in many real-world applications.

Consider two fraud detection systems with different performance characteristics. System A achieves 99% accuracy by correctly identifying most legitimate transactions but only catches 50% of actual fraud cases. System B achieves 95% accuracy but catches 90% of fraud cases while flagging more legitimate transactions for review. Which system is better? The answer depends on your business priorities and the relative costs of different types of errors.

1.5.3.1 Business-Relevant Metrics

Effective evaluation starts with understanding what success means for your specific application and translating business objectives into appropriate metrics. In medical diagnosis, false negatives (missing a disease) might be far more costly than false positives (unnecessary additional testing). In marketing, the cost of contacting uninterested customers must be balanced against the revenue from successful conversions.

For a customer churn prediction model, traditional accuracy might suggest the model is performing well, but business-relevant metrics would examine whether the model identifies customers who can be retained through intervention, the cost of retention efforts, and the lifetime value of successfully retained customers. These business metrics often matter more than statistical performance measures.

1.5.3.2 Monitoring and Maintenance

Machine learning models require ongoing attention because the world changes over time. Customer behavior evolves, market conditions shift, and new competitors emerge. Models that performed well initially may degrade gradually as these changes accumulate—a phenomenon known as model drift.

Effective monitoring involves tracking both statistical performance and business outcomes over time. This might include monitoring prediction accuracy, but also tracking whether the model's recommendations are being followed and whether they're producing the expected business results. When performance degrades, systematic retraining processes ensure that models remain effective.

1.6 Model Interpretability and Bias Considerations

As machine learning systems increasingly influence important decisions, the ability to understand and explain these systems becomes crucial. The trend toward explainable AI reflects growing recognition that black-box models, regardless of their accuracy, may be inappropriate for high-stakes applications where people need to understand how decisions are made.

Imagine you apply for a loan and get rejected. When you ask why, the bank says, "The computer said no, but we can't explain why." This scenario is becoming increasingly common as AI systems make more important decisions, and it's simply not acceptable for many applications. People have a right to understand decisions that affect their lives, and organizations need to ensure their systems are making decisions for the right reasons.

The explainable AI market is projected to reach $20.74 billion by 2029 , driven by regulatory requirements and the fundamental need for people to understand decisions that affect their lives. This growth reflects increasing recognition that transparency isn't just nice to have—it's essential for building trust and ensuring accountability in AI systems.

1.6.1 The Interpretability Spectrum

Different applications require different levels of interpretability, and understanding this spectrum helps practitioners choose appropriate techniques for each situation. High-stakes applications like medical diagnosis, loan approvals, and criminal justice decisions require clear explanations that can be understood by domain experts and affected individuals. Medium-stakes applications like hiring decisions and insurance pricing should be somewhat explainable to ensure fairness and compliance. Lower-stakes applications like entertainment recommendations and advertising targeting can be more of a black box since the consequences of errors are relatively minor.

Some machine learning approaches provide natural interpretability. Linear regression models show exactly how each input variable influences the prediction, with coefficients that can be directly interpreted as the impact of each feature. Decision trees create explicit rules that can be followed step-by-step, making the decision process completely transparent. These approaches might sacrifice some predictive power for transparency, but they excel in situations where understanding the reasoning process is crucial.

For example, a bank developing a loan approval system might choose a decision tree approach specifically because regulators and customers can understand exactly why applications are approved or denied. The model might create rules like "if income exceeds $50,000 and credit score is above 650 and debt-to-income ratio is below 30%, then approve the loan." This transparency builds trust and ensures compliance with fair lending regulations.

When complex models are necessary for accuracy, post-hoc explanation techniques can provide insights into their decision-making processes. SHAP (SHapley Additive exPlanations) values, for instance, can explain individual predictions by showing how each input feature contributed to the final result. These techniques allow you to use sophisticated models while still providing explanations for specific decisions.

1.6.2 Identifying and Mitigating Bias

Machine learning systems can perpetuate or amplify existing biases present in training data or introduced through the modeling process. Addressing bias requires systematic approaches to detection, measurement, and mitigation throughout the development lifecycle. This isn't just an ethical imperative—biased systems can lead to legal liability, regulatory violations, and significant business risks.

Let's follow the story of TechCorp, a company building a hiring algorithm. They train their system on 10 years of hiring data, proud of their "objective" approach. But their historical data reflects past biases: engineering roles were predominantly filled by men, leadership positions went mostly to people from certain universities, and salary data reflected historical pay gaps. The algorithm learns these patterns as "success indicators," perpetuating and potentially amplifying existing inequities.

Bias can enter machine learning systems through multiple pathways. Historical bias reflects past discrimination embedded in training data. Representation bias occurs when training data doesn't adequately represent the population the model will serve. A facial recognition system trained primarily on images of light-skinned individuals might perform poorly on darker-skinned faces, not because of algorithmic limitations, but because of biased training data.

Systematic bias detection involves examining model performance across different demographic groups and identifying disparities in outcomes. Tools like IBM's AI Fairness 360 and Google's What-If Tool provide frameworks for measuring bias and exploring its impacts. These tools can automatically test for various types of bias and suggest mitigation strategies.

Addressing bias requires interventions at multiple stages of the machine learning pipeline. Data collection strategies can ensure representative samples. Preprocessing techniques can adjust for historical imbalances. Algorithm modifications can explicitly optimize for fairness alongside accuracy. One effective approach involves setting explicit fairness constraints during model training, ensuring that fairness considerations are built into the model rather than addressed as an afterthought.

1.7 AI-Assisted Model Selection Tools

The complexity of modern machine learning has led to the development of automated tools that assist practitioners in selecting and configuring appropriate models. These AI-assisted approaches, often called AutoML (Automated Machine Learning), democratize access to sophisticated techniques while helping experts work more efficiently.

Remember when creating a website required learning HTML, CSS, and JavaScript? Today, drag-and-drop website builders let anyone create professional sites without coding. Machine learning is experiencing a similar transformation through AutoML tools that handle much of the technical complexity automatically.

1.7.1 Automated Machine Learning Platforms

AutoML platforms handle many of the routine decisions involved in machine learning projects, from feature selection and preprocessing to algorithm choice and hyperparameter optimization. These tools don't replace human expertise but rather augment it by automating time-consuming tasks and exploring options that might be overlooked.

Imagine you want to predict customer churn but don't know which algorithm to use or how to tune it. With traditional approaches, a data scientist might spend weeks testing different algorithms, tuning parameters, and optimizing performance. With AutoML, you can upload your data, specify your goal, and let the system automatically test hundreds of algorithm and parameter combinations, often achieving performance that rivals manually tuned models.

Leading cloud providers offer comprehensive AutoML platforms that integrate with existing business systems. Google's AutoML, Microsoft's Azure Machine Learning, and Amazon's SageMaker AutoPilot provide end-to-end automation for common machine learning tasks. These platforms can automatically handle data cleaning, feature engineering, algorithm selection, and hyperparameter tuning, producing deployment-ready models along with explanations of their performance and limitations.

1.7.2 Balancing Automation with Understanding

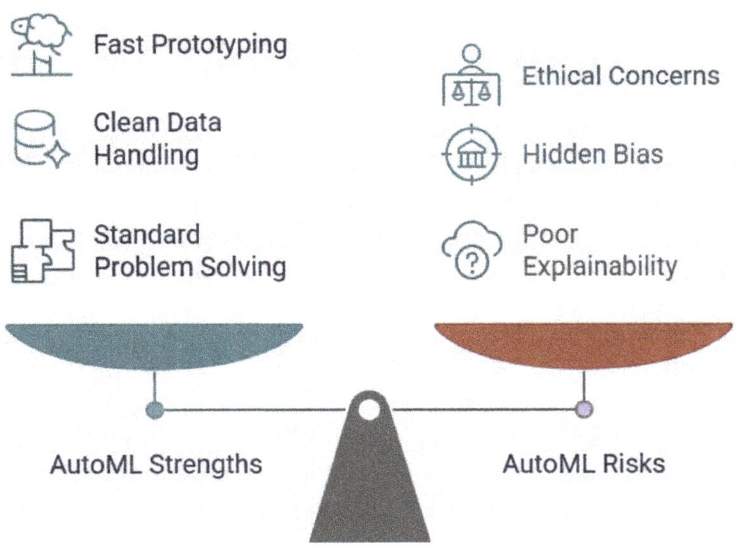

While AutoML tools provide significant benefits, they also introduce risks if used without proper understanding. Automated systems might select models that perform well statistically but fail to meet business requirements or ethical standards. Effective use of these tools requires maintaining human oversight and understanding.

AutoML excels in situations where you have well-defined problems with clear success metrics, relatively clean and structured data, need for rapid prototyping or baseline model development, and limited machine learning expertise. It's particularly valuable for standard business problems like customer churn prediction, demand forecasting, and fraud detection.

Manual approaches work better when problems are novel or highly specialized, complex business constraints must be incorporated, deep customization is required, or regulatory requirements demand specific approaches. High-stakes applications often require manual development to ensure that all requirements are met and that the solution can be fully explained and justified.

Successful AutoML implementation requires maintaining human judgment throughout the process. This includes validating that automatically selected models align with business objectives, ensuring that performance metrics reflect real-world requirements, checking for bias and fairness issues, and testing models thoroughly before deployment.

1.8 Conclusion

This introduction to applied machine learning has established the fundamental concepts that underpin successful data-driven decision making. We've explored how machine learning fits within the broader landscape of artificial intelligence, examined the distinction between supervised and unsupervised learning approaches, walked through the systematic pipeline that transforms raw data into reliable insights, and discussed the critical importance of interpretability and bias considerations in building trustworthy systems.

The distinction between supervised and unsupervised learning provides a framework for approaching new problems systematically. When you encounter a business challenge, asking whether you have labeled examples of desired outcomes immediately suggests which family of techniques will be most appropriate. This foundational understanding guides all subsequent technical decisions and helps you avoid common mistakes that derail machine learning projects.

The machine learning pipeline offers a structured approach to complex projects that ensures reproducible results and maintainable systems. By following systematic processes for data preprocessing, model training, and evaluation, you can avoid common pitfalls that derail machine learning initiatives. Remember that most failures occur not in the algorithms themselves, but in the processes that support them.

Perhaps most importantly, the emphasis on interpretability and bias detection reflects the growing recognition that technical performance alone is insufficient. As machine learning systems increasingly influence important decisions, our responsibility extends beyond accuracy to include fairness, transparency, and accountability. These considerations will only become more important as AI systems become more prevalent in business and society.

Looking ahead to the remaining modules in this course, you'll build upon these foundations to explore specific techniques for predictive modeling, natural language processing, and optimization. You'll learn to apply these concepts to real-world business scenarios, developing the practical skills needed to translate AI-driven insights into data-informed decisions.

The machine learning landscape continues to evolve rapidly, with new techniques, tools, and applications emerging regularly. However, the fundamental principles covered in this module provide a stable foundation that will serve you well regardless of how the field develops. By understanding these core concepts deeply, you'll be prepared to adapt to new developments and apply machine learning effectively throughout your career.

As you progress through this course, remember that machine learning is ultimately about solving business problems, not just implementing algorithms. The most successful practitioners combine technical expertise with domain knowledge and business acumen. They understand not just how to build models, but when to build them, how to evaluate their impact, and how to ensure they serve human needs effectively.

The journey from raw data to business value requires patience, systematic thinking, and continuous learning. But for those who master these fundamentals, machine learning offers unprecedented opportunities to create value, solve complex problems, and drive innovation across virtually every industry and application domain. The future belongs to people who can bridge the gap between human insight and machine intelligence, and you're now equipped with the foundational knowledge to be one of them.

1.9 Key Terms

Artificial Intelligence (AI) – The broad field focused on creating machines that can perform tasks typically requiring human intelligence, such as reasoning, learning, and problem-solving.

Machine Learning (ML) – A subset of AI that enables computers to learn patterns from data and make predictions or decisions without explicit programming for every scenario.

Natural Language Processing (NLP) – A branch of AI focused on enabling machines to understand, interpret, and generate human language.

Supervised Learning – A machine learning approach where the algorithm learns from labeled examples (input-output pairs) to predict outcomes for new data.

Unsupervised Learning – A machine learning approach where the algorithm finds hidden patterns or structures in data without labeled outcomes.

Classification – A supervised learning task that predicts discrete categories or labels (e.g., spam vs. non-spam emails).

Regression – A supervised learning task that predicts continuous numerical values (e.g., predicting house prices).

Clustering – An unsupervised learning technique that groups similar data points together based on inherent patterns.

Dimensionality Reduction – Techniques used to reduce the number of variables under consideration while retaining important information, often to simplify data analysis.

Machine Learning Pipeline – A structured workflow for building ML systems, including steps such as data preprocessing, feature engineering, model training, evaluation, and deployment.

Data Preprocessing – The process of cleaning, transforming, and organizing raw data into a format suitable for modeling.

Feature Engineering – Creating new variables or transforming existing data to better capture patterns relevant to the predictive task.

Cross-Validation – A technique for evaluating model performance on unseen data by partitioning data into training, validation, and test sets.

Hyperparameter Optimization – The process of systematically tuning algorithm parameters that control the learning process to improve model performance.

Model Interpretability / Explainable AI (XAI) – Techniques and practices that make machine learning models' decisions understandable to humans.

Bias in Machine Learning – Systematic errors in a model that lead to unfair or inaccurate predictions, often arising from historical data or underrepresented populations.

AutoML (Automated Machine Learning) – Tools and platforms that automate model selection, hyperparameter tuning, and other routine ML tasks, while still requiring human oversight for business alignment.

Model Drift – Degradation in a model's performance over time as the underlying data distribution changes.

1.10 Review Questions

1. Define artificial intelligence and explain how machine learning fits within the broader AI landscape.
2. Compare and contrast traditional programming with machine learning approaches.
3. Describe the differences between supervised and unsupervised learning, including practical business examples of each.
4. Explain the difference between classification and regression tasks in supervised learning. Provide a business scenario for each.
5. What is clustering, and why is it useful for unsupervised learning? Give a real-world example.
6. Define feature engineering and explain why it is critical in building effective machine learning models.

7. Why is data preprocessing considered the foundation of successful machine learning projects? Provide examples of common preprocessing steps.
8. Explain cross-validation and why it is important for evaluating model performance.
9. Discuss the concept of hyperparameter optimization and its role in improving model performance.
10. What is model interpretability, and why is it increasingly important in AI applications?
11. Identify common sources of bias in machine learning systems and describe methods to detect and mitigate it.
12. Describe the benefits and limitations of using AutoML platforms for model selection and deployment.
13. Explain model drift and why ongoing monitoring is essential for machine learning systems.
14. How can organizations ensure that machine learning solutions are both accurate and ethically responsible?
15. Summarize the machine learning pipeline and explain how each step contributes to generating business value.

1.11 Lab 1: Python Setup for AI/ML

1.11.1 Introduction

This lab will guide you through setting up Python for advanced AI and machine learning exercises.

Don't worry if you're new to some of these technologies—modern AI assistants like ChatGPT and Claude can help you focus on concepts while assisting with coding and implementation details.

This book **does not require a specific Python environment**. Instructors and students may use whatever Python platform works best, provided it supports the required packages and accessibility needs.

Python can be run in **local IDEs**, **cloud notebooks**, or **hybrid environments**, and accessibility considerations (screen readers, keyboard navigation, descriptive outputs) should be observed.

1.11.2 Choosing a Python Environment

Here are common Python options:

Environment	Description	Pros	Considerations
Local IDEs (VS Code, PyCharm, Thonny, RStudio)	Installed on your computer; supports scripts, virtual environments, and projects	Powerful, flexible, offline; full package control	Must be installed; setup may require guidance; check accessibility
Cloud Notebooks (Google Colab, JupyterHub, Binder)	Run Python in a web browser	No installation; easy collaboration; GPU access	Accessibility may vary; interactive outputs may need descriptive alternatives
RStudio with Python support	Primarily for R but can run Python alongside R	Useful for mixed-language labs or statistics-heavy exercises	Optional; adds complexity if Python-only work is sufficient
Other platforms	Examples: Repl.it, Anaconda Navigator	Beginner-friendly, easy access	Check package availability and save/share options

> **Instructor Note:** Students can choose any Python environment that meets the course requirements. Instructors should provide guidance for installation, accessibility, and usage based on local policies.

1.11.3 General Python Setup

Students will need:

1. **Python 3.9–3.11** recommended
2. **Core data science packages**
3. **Advanced AI/ML packages** for deep learning, NLP, and model evaluation

1.11.3.1 Core Data Science Packages

- `pandas`, `numpy`, `matplotlib`, `seaborn`, `scikit-learn`, `scipy`

1.11.3.2 Advanced AI/ML Packages

- `tensorflow`, `torch`, `torchvision`, `transformers`
- `spacy`, `nltk`, `gensim`, `textblob`, `wordcloud`
- `fairlearn`, `aif360`, `lime`, `shap`
- `pyLDAvis`, `umap-learn`, `plotly`, `dash`, `streamlit`

  Instructor Note: Installation commands differ by environment.
  - Local IDE: `pip install <package>`
  - Cloud notebooks: `!pip install <package>` or environment-specific commands

1.11.4 Package Requirements

1.11.4.1 Master Package List

Core Foundation:

- `pandas` - Data manipulation and analysis
- `numpy` - Numerical computing
- `matplotlib` - Basic plotting
- `seaborn` - Statistical visualization
- `scikit-learn` - Traditional machine learning

Deep Learning Frameworks:

- `tensorflow` - Google's deep learning framework
- `torch` (PyTorch) - Facebook's deep learning framework
- `transformers` - Hugging Face transformer models
- `datasets` - Hugging Face datasets library

Natural Language Processing:

- `spacy` - Industrial-strength NLP
- `nltk` - Natural Language Toolkit
- `gensim` - Topic modeling and document similarity
- `textblob` - Simple text processing
- `wordcloud` - Word cloud generation

Model Evaluation & Fairness:

- `fairlearn` - Fairness assessment and mitigation
- `aif360` - AI Fairness 360 toolkit
- `lime` - Local interpretable model explanations
- `shap` - SHapley Additive exPlanations

Advanced Analytics:

- `pyLDAvis` - Interactive topic model visualization
- `umap-learn` - Dimensionality reduction
- `plotly` - Interactive visualizations

1.11.5 Getting Help

1.11.5.1 When You're Stuck:

1. **Read error messages carefully** - Advanced libraries provide detailed error information
2. **Check documentation** - Each library has extensive documentation and examples
3. **Use AI assistants effectively:**
   - "ChatGPT, I'm getting this CUDA error: [paste error]. How do I fix it?"
   - "Claude, explain this transformer model architecture: [paste code]"
   - "Help me optimize this PyTorch training loop for better GPU utilization"
4. **Community resources:**
   - Hugging Face forums for transformer models
   - PyTorch forums for deep learning issues
   - Stack Overflow for specific implementation problems

1.11.5.2 Useful Prompts for AI Assistants:

- "Explain this advanced ML concept and provide a simple example: [concept]"
- "Debug this deep learning training loop: [paste code]"
- "How do I implement bias detection for this model: [paste model code]"
- "Optimize this NLP pipeline for better performance: [paste pipeline]"
- "Convert this TensorFlow code to PyTorch: [paste code]"

1.12 Conclusion

This introduction to applied machine learning has established the fundamental concepts that underpin successful data-driven decision making. We've explored how machine learning fits within the broader landscape of artificial intelligence, examined the distinction between supervised and unsupervised learning approaches, walked through the systematic pipeline that transforms raw data into reliable insights, and discussed the critical importance of interpretability and bias considerations in building trustworthy systems.

The distinction between supervised and unsupervised learning provides a framework for approaching new problems systematically. When you encounter a business challenge, asking whether you have labeled examples of desired outcomes immediately suggests which family of techniques will be most appropriate. This foundational understanding guides all subsequent technical decisions and helps you avoid common mistakes that derail machine learning projects.

The machine learning pipeline offers a structured approach to complex projects that ensures reproducible results and maintainable systems. By following systematic processes for data preprocessing, model training, and evaluation, you can avoid common pitfalls that derail machine learning initiatives. Remember that most failures occur not in the algorithms themselves, but in the processes that support them.

Perhaps most importantly, the emphasis on interpretability and bias detection reflects the growing recognition that technical performance alone is insufficient. As machine learning systems increasingly influence important decisions, our responsibility extends beyond accuracy to include fairness, transparency, and accountability. These considerations will only become more important as AI systems become more prevalent in business and society.

Looking ahead to the remaining modules in this course, you'll build upon these foundations to explore specific techniques for predictive modeling, natural language processing, and optimization. You'll learn to apply these concepts to real-world business scenarios, developing the practical skills needed to translate AI-driven insights into data-informed decisions.

The machine learning landscape continues to evolve rapidly, with new techniques, tools, and applications emerging regularly. However, the fundamental principles covered in this module provide a stable foundation that will serve you well regardless of how the field develops. By understanding these core concepts deeply, you'll be prepared to adapt to new developments and apply machine learning effectively throughout your career.

As you progress through this course, remember that machine learning is ultimately about solving business problems, not just implementing algorithms. The most successful practitioners combine technical expertise with domain knowledge and business acumen. They understand not just how to build models, but when to build them, how to evaluate their impact, and how to ensure they serve human needs effectively.

The journey from raw data to business value requires patience, systematic thinking, and continuous learning. But for those who master these fundamentals, machine learning offers unprecedented opportunities to create value, solve complex problems, and drive innovation across virtually every industry and application domain. The future belongs to people who can bridge the gap between human insight and machine intelligence, and you're now equipped with the foundational knowledge to be one of them.

1.13 References

[1] AMRA & ELMA Digital Marketing Agency. (2025). Top 20 Machine Learning Marketing ROI Statistics 2025. https://www.amraandelma.com/machine-learning-

marketing-roi-statistics/

[2] Machine Learning Mastery. (2025). 7 Machine Learning Trends to Watch in 2025. https://machinelearningmastery.com/7-machine-learning-trends-2025/

[3] SuperAGI. (2025). Mastering Explainable AI in 2025: A Beginner's Guide to Transparent and Interpretable Models. https://superagi.com/mastering-explainable-ai-in-2025-a-beginners-guide-to-transparent-and-interpretable-models/

[4] Cambridge Advance Online. (2025). Machine Learning Trend Analysis in 2025. https://advanceonline.cam.ac.uk/blog/machine-learning-trend-analysis

Chapter 2

Making Predictions from Data

2.1 Learning Outcomes

2-1: Understand what machine learning models are and distinguish between regression and classification problems

2-2: Identify the main types of regression and classification models and when to use each approach

2-3: Explain how basic recommendation systems work and why optimization matters in business

2-4: Understand the basics of model tuning and how to interpret what models learn from data

2.2 Introduction

Imagine you're the product manager at a streaming service, and your CEO walks into your office with a simple question: "How do we know which new shows to produce?" It's a million-dollar question—literally. Each new series costs millions to create, and picking the wrong ones could sink the company. But picking the right ones? That's how Netflix became a global entertainment powerhouse.

This scenario plays out across industries every day. Retailers want to know which products will sell during the holiday season. Banks need to predict which loan applicants might have trouble paying back their loans. Doctors want to identify patients who might develop health complications. Marketing teams need to figure out which customers will actually buy something if they send them an email.

Here's what makes this exciting: we're not just talking about making wild guesses. We're talking about using data and computer algorithms to make predictions that are often more accurate than human experts. Amazon's recommendation system drives 35% of their sales. Netflix keeps you watching for hours because their algorithms know what you'll enjoy. Your credit score is calculated by models that process millions of loan applications.

But what exactly is a "model" in machine learning? And how do these prediction systems actually work? This module will answer these fundamental questions and introduce you to the two main types of prediction problems that power most business applications.

2.3 What Is a Machine Learning Model?

Before we dive into different types of models, let's start with the most basic question: what exactly is a machine learning model? Think of a model as a mathematical recipe that takes information about something and makes a prediction about it.

2.3.1 Models as Pattern Recognition Systems

A machine learning model is essentially a pattern recognition system that learns from examples. Imagine you're trying to teach a friend to recognize whether a song is likely to become a hit. You might play them hundreds of songs and tell them which ones became popular. Over time, your friend would start noticing patterns—maybe songs with certain tempos, specific instruments, or particular vocal styles tend to become hits.

A machine learning model works similarly, but instead of a human brain recognizing patterns, it's a computer algorithm. You show the algorithm thousands of examples (songs and whether they became hits), and it learns to recognize the mathematical patterns that distinguish hits from flops.

The key insight is that models don't just memorize the examples you show them. Instead, they learn general rules that can be applied to new situations they've never seen before. A well-trained model can predict whether a brand-new song will become popular, even though it has never heard that specific song during training.

2.3.2 From Data to Decisions

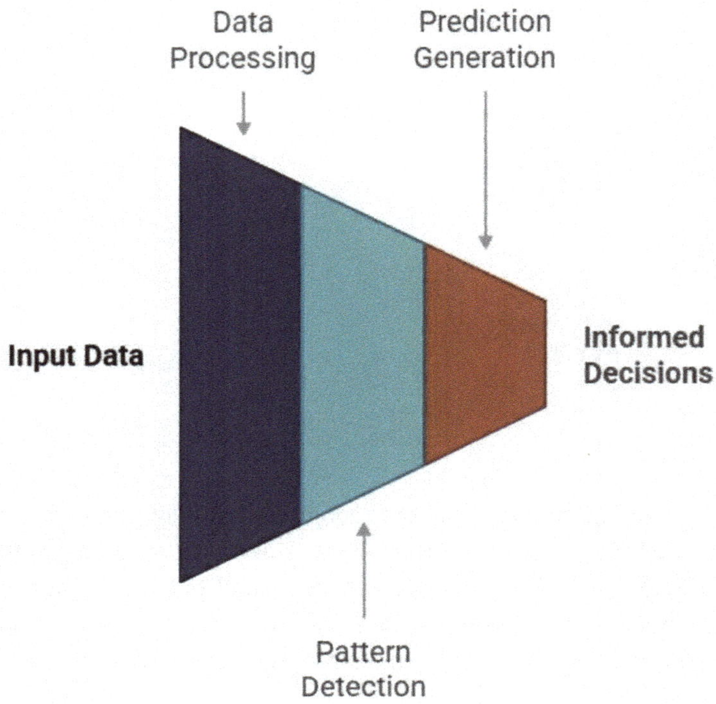

Every machine learning model follows the same basic process. First, you feed it input data—information about the thing you want to make a prediction about. This might be a customer's purchase history, a patient's medical test results, or the characteristics of a house you want to price.

The model processes this input data using the patterns it learned during training, then produces an output—its prediction. For a customer, the output might be "likely to cancel subscription." For a patient, it might be "low risk of complications." For a house, it might be "$347,500."

What makes models powerful is that they can process far more information than humans can handle, and they can identify subtle patterns that humans might miss. A human loan officer might consider 5-10 factors when evaluating an application. A machine learning model can simultaneously consider hundreds of factors and their complex interactions.

2.3.3 The Learning Process

The "learning" in machine learning happens during a training phase where you show the model lots of examples of inputs paired with the correct outputs. Think of it like teaching a child to recognize animals by showing them thousands of pictures labeled "dog," "cat," "bird," etc.

During training, the model starts with random guesses about how to make predictions. When it guesses wrong, it adjusts its internal rules slightly. When it guesses right, it reinforces those rules. After seeing thousands of examples and making millions of tiny adjustments, the model becomes quite good at making accurate predictions.

The beauty of this process is that you don't need to understand exactly how the model makes its decisions—you just need to provide good examples and let the algorithm figure out the patterns. This is why machine learning can solve problems that would be impossible to program using traditional methods.

2.4 Understanding Prediction Problems

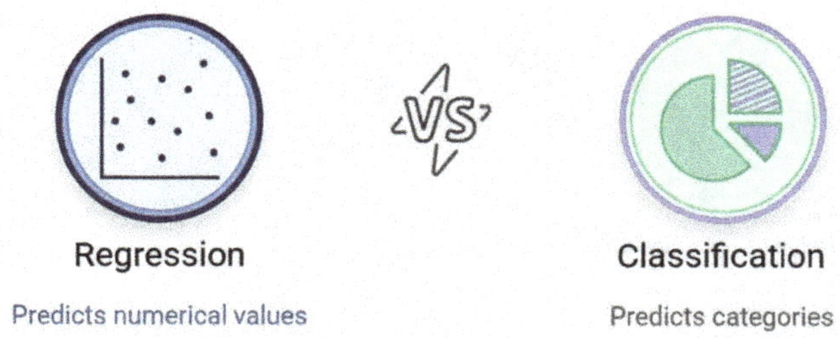

Now that we understand what models are, let's explore the two main types of prediction problems they can solve. The type of prediction you need determines which approach to use and how to measure success.

2.4.1 Regression: Predicting Specific Numbers

Regression models predict specific numerical values—exact amounts, prices, quantities, or measurements. When you want to know "how much" or "how many," you're dealing with a regression problem. The key characteristic is that the answer is a specific number that can vary continuously.

Think about predicting house prices. A regression model doesn't just tell you whether a house is "expensive" or "cheap"—it predicts the specific dollar amount the house will sell for, like $347,500. Small differences in the prediction matter because the difference between $340,000 and $350,000 represents real money.

2.4.1.1 Everyday Examples of Regression

You encounter regression predictions constantly in daily life, often without realizing it. When you request an Uber, the app predicts exactly how much your ride will cost and how many minutes you'll wait for pickup. When you shop online, websites predict shipping costs based on your location and package weight. When you apply for a loan, banks predict the specific interest rate to offer you.

Streaming services use regression to predict how many hours you'll spend watching different shows, helping them decide which content to license or produce. E-commerce companies predict how much each customer will spend over their lifetime, informing decisions about marketing budgets and customer service investments.

The power of regression lies in its precision. Instead of vague categories like "high value customer," regression can predict that Customer A will spend $1,247 over the next year while Customer B will spend $892. This specificity enables precise business decisions about pricing, resource allocation, and strategic planning.

2.4.1.2 Types of Regression Models

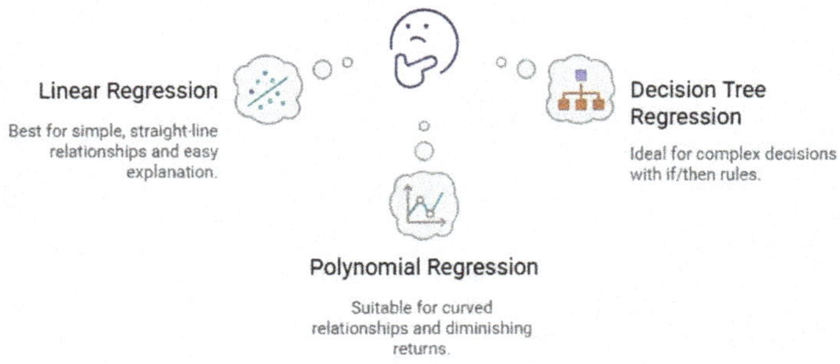

Different regression techniques work better in different situations. Linear regression represents the simplest approach, assuming that relationships between inputs and outputs can be captured by straight lines. If you're predicting sales based on advertising spend, linear regression might discover that each $1,000 in advertising generates $3,000 in additional sales.

Linear regression works well when relationships are genuinely straightforward and you need to understand exactly how each factor influences the prediction. A subscription business might use linear regression to understand that each new feature added to their product increases monthly revenue by $15 per user, while seasonal effects boost revenue by 12% during holidays.

Polynomial regression handles situations where relationships are curved rather than straight. Maybe the first $10,000 spent on advertising generates great returns, but additional spending has diminishing effects. Polynomial regression can capture these more complex patterns while remaining relatively interpretable.

Decision tree regression takes a completely different approach, creating a series of yes/no questions that lead to predictions. An insurance company might develop rules like "if driver is under 25 and lives in urban area and drives expensive car, then predicted claim cost is $8,500." These tree-based models excel when relationships are complex and you need to explain decisions clearly.

2.4.2 Classification: Predicting Categories

Classification models predict which category or group something belongs to rather than specific numerical values. When you want to know "which type" or "what category," you're dealing with a classification problem. The output is a label or category name, not a number.

Email spam detection represents one of the most successful classification applications. The model doesn't predict how "spammy" an email is on a scale from 1 to 100. Instead, it makes a simple decision: spam or not spam. The model analyzes features like sender reputation, subject line characteristics, and message content to place each email into one of these two buckets.

2.4.2.1 Binary vs. Multi-Class Classification

Classification problems come in different flavors. Binary classification involves choosing between two options—spam or legitimate email, approve or deny a loan application, fraud or legitimate transaction. This represents the simplest form of classification but often the most business-critical, since a single wrong decision can be expensive.

Multi-class classification involves choosing among three or more categories. A customer service system might automatically route support tickets to billing, technical support, or sales departments. A photo app might classify images as containing people, animals, food, or landscapes. A sentiment analysis system might categorize customer reviews as positive, negative, or neutral.

The distinction matters because different algorithms handle binary and multi-class problems differently, and the way you measure success changes depending on the number of categories.

2.4.2.2 Real-World Classification Examples

Classification powers many systems you use daily. When you deposit a check using your phone's camera, classification algorithms determine whether the image is clear enough to process. When you shop online, classification systems detect potentially fraudulent transactions and flag them for review.

Social media platforms use classification to identify inappropriate content, spam accounts, and fake news. Streaming services classify content by genre, age-appropriateness, and mood. Navigation apps classify traffic conditions as light, moderate, or heavy to suggest optimal routes.

Medical applications of classification can be life-saving. Algorithms classify medical images to detect cancer, classify symptoms to suggest diagnoses, and classify patients by risk level to prioritize treatment. These applications demonstrate why accuracy and explainability are so important in classification systems.

2.4.2.3 Types of Classification Models

Logistic regression serves as the foundation for many classification applications, despite its name suggesting it's a regression technique. It calculates the probability that something belongs to each category, then assigns it to the category with the highest probability. A credit card company might use logistic regression to calculate that a transaction has a 75% probability of being legitimate and 25% probability of being fraudulent.

The advantage of logistic regression is its interpretability. The model can tell you not just whether a transaction is likely fraudulent, but also which factors contributed most to that decision. Maybe transactions from certain countries, at unusual times, or for specific amounts increase fraud probability.

Decision trees for classification work like a flowchart of yes/no questions. A hiring system might create rules like "if candidate has relevant degree AND more than 3 years experience AND positive references, then classify as strong candidate." These rules provide clear explanations for decisions, which is crucial for legal compliance and fairness.

Random forests combine many decision trees to make more robust predictions. Each tree votes for a category, and the final prediction goes to the category that gets the most votes. This approach often achieves higher accuracy than individual trees while still providing insights into which factors are most important.

Support Vector Machines (SVMs) excel at finding the optimal boundary between different categories, especially when relationships are complex. Neural networks represent the most flexible approach, capable of learning extremely complex patterns when you have large amounts of training data.

2.4.3 Choosing Between Regression and Classification

The choice between regression and classification depends entirely on what type of answer you need. If you need a specific number—a price, quantity, time, or measurement—you need regression. If you need to assign something to a category or make a yes/no decision, you need classification.

Sometimes the same business problem can be approached either way. Consider customer value prediction. A regression approach would predict the specific dollar amount each customer will spend—perhaps $1,247 for Customer A and $892 for Customer B. A classification approach might group customers into categories like "high value" (over $1,000), "medium value" ($500-$1,000), and "low value" (under $500).

The regression approach provides more precise information for financial planning and pricing decisions. The classification approach provides simpler insights that might be easier for sales teams to act on—they can focus their attention on customers predicted to be "high value" without worrying about exact amounts.

Many successful companies use both approaches for the same problem. They might use regression models for detailed financial forecasting and classification models for day-to-day operational decisions.

2.5 Introduction to Recommendation Systems

Recommendation systems represent a special type of machine learning that focuses on suggesting items people might like based on their past behavior and the behavior of similar users. These systems power some of the most successful digital businesses and demonstrate how machine learning can create direct business value.

2.5.1 How Recommendations Work

The basic idea behind recommendation systems is surprisingly simple: find people who have similar preferences to you, then suggest items that those similar people liked. If you and another Netflix user both enjoyed the same five movies, you might also like other movies that person rated highly.

This approach, called collaborative filtering, works because people's preferences tend to be consistent and predictable. If you like action movies, you'll probably like other action movies. If you prefer indie music, you'll probably enjoy other indie artists. Recommendation systems identify these patterns across millions of users to make personalized suggestions.

Content-based filtering takes a different approach, focusing on the characteristics of items rather than user behavior. A music recommendation system might analyze the tempo, genre, instruments, and vocal style of songs you've liked, then recommend other songs with similar characteristics. This works well for new items that don't yet have user rating data.

2.5.2 Business Impact of Recommendations

The business impact of effective recommendation systems can be enormous. Amazon reports that 35% of their revenue comes from recommendations—that's over $100 billion annually. Netflix estimates that their recommendation system saves them over $1 billion each year by keeping subscribers engaged and reducing cancellations.

Spotify's Discover Weekly playlist has become one of their most popular features, introducing users to new music they wouldn't have found otherwise. This drives user engagement and helps record labels promote new artists. LinkedIn's job recommendations help people find career opportunities while helping companies find qualified candidates.

The key insight is that recommendations create value for both users and businesses. Users discover items they enjoy, while businesses increase sales and engagement. This win-win dynamic explains why recommendation systems have become so prevalent across digital platforms.

2.5.3 Simple Recommendation Approaches

The simplest recommendation approach is popularity-based: recommend the most popular items to everyone. This works reasonably well for new users who haven't provided much preference data, but it doesn't provide personalization and tends to reinforce existing popularity rather than helping users discover new items.

Similarity-based recommendations improve on this by finding users with similar preferences and recommending items those users liked. The challenge lies in defining "similarity" effectively. Do you focus on overall rating patterns, specific genres, or recent behavior? Different similarity measures work better for different types of products and user behaviors.

Matrix factorization techniques represent a more sophisticated approach that identifies hidden factors influencing preferences. For movies, these factors might represent genres, production quality, or cultural themes. By understanding which factors each user values and which factors each movie exhibits, the system can predict how much any user would enjoy any movie.

2.6 Basic Optimization and Business Applications

While prediction focuses on forecasting what will happen, optimization focuses on determining what should happen to achieve the best possible outcomes. Optimization helps businesses make better decisions by finding the best way to allocate resources, set prices, or organize operations.

2.6.1 Understanding Optimization Problems

Optimization problems involve finding the best solution from many possible alternatives, subject to various constraints. A delivery company wants to find the shortest route that visits all customers. A retailer wants to set prices that maximize profit while remaining competitive. A manufacturer wants to schedule production to minimize costs while meeting demand.

These problems share common elements: an objective (what you want to optimize), decision variables (choices you can make), and constraints (limitations you must respect). The art of optimization lies in translating real-world business problems into mathematical terms that algorithms can solve.

2.6.2 Real-Time Optimization Examples

Many modern businesses require real-time optimization as conditions change rapidly. Ride-sharing services continuously adjust pricing and driver allocation as demand patterns shift throughout the day. Online advertising platforms decide which ads to show in the milliseconds between when you load a webpage and when it displays.

Dynamic pricing represents one of the most visible applications of real-time optimization. Airlines, hotels, and ride-sharing services continuously adjust prices based on current demand, competitor pricing, and predicted future conditions. These systems balance multiple objectives: maximizing revenue, maintaining customer satisfaction, and ensuring adequate supply.

The algorithms powering these systems learn optimal strategies through experience. They try different approaches, observe the results, and gradually learn which strategies work best in different situations. Over time, these systems become remarkably sophisticated at predicting how customers will respond to different prices and adjusting accordingly.

2.6.3 Simple Optimization Techniques

Linear programming represents the simplest form of optimization, applicable when relationships can be expressed as straight lines. A food manufacturer might use linear programming to determine the optimal mix of ingredients that minimizes cost while meeting nutritional requirements.

Greedy algorithms provide another simple but effective approach for many optimization problems. These algorithms make the best choice available at each step, without worrying about future consequences. While not always optimal, greedy approaches often provide good solutions quickly and are easy to understand and implement.

More sophisticated optimization techniques like genetic algorithms and simulated annealing can handle complex problems with many variables and constraints. These approaches are inspired by natural processes and can find good solutions even when the mathematical relationships are too complex for traditional methods.

2.7 Model Tuning and Performance Improvement

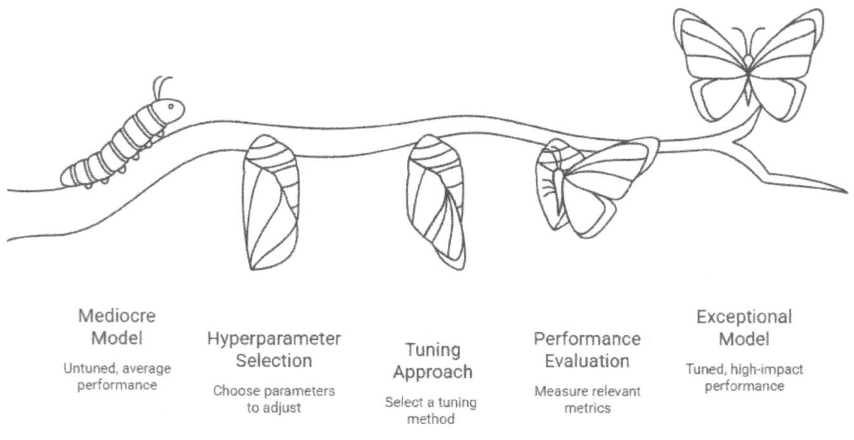

Even the best algorithms require careful adjustment to achieve optimal performance on specific problems. Model tuning involves adjusting various settings to improve accuracy, speed, or interpretability. This process can dramatically impact results, often making the difference between a mediocre model and an exceptional one.

2.7.1 Understanding Model Settings

Machine learning algorithms have many adjustable settings called hyperparameters that control how they operate. Think of these like the dials and switches on a complex machine—they determine how the machine works, but the machine itself learns the specific patterns in your data.

For decision trees, these settings include how deep the tree can grow and how many examples are needed before making a split. For neural networks, they include how many layers to use and how fast the algorithm should learn. The challenge is that optimal settings depend on your specific data and problem.

2.7.2 Simple Tuning Approaches

The most straightforward tuning approach is trial and error—try different settings and see which ones work best. While not sophisticated, this approach often works well for simple problems and helps you understand how different settings affect performance.

Grid search represents a more systematic approach, testing every combination of settings within specified ranges. While thorough, this can be time-consuming when you have many settings to adjust. Random search often achieves good results faster by randomly trying different combinations rather than testing everything systematically.

Modern AutoML tools can automate much of the tuning process, testing hundreds of setting combinations and often achieving performance that rivals manually tuned models. These tools save time and often discover setting combinations that human experts might not have considered.

2.7.3 Measuring Model Performance

Different types of problems require different ways of measuring success. For regression problems, you might measure how close predictions are to actual values on average. For classification problems, you might measure what percentage of predictions are correct.

However, simple accuracy measures can be misleading. A model that's 99% accurate at detecting fraud might still be useless if it fails to catch the 1% of transactions that are actually fraudulent. Understanding which types of errors are most costly helps you choose appropriate performance measures.

Business-relevant metrics often matter more than statistical measures. For customer churn prediction, you care more about whether you can successfully retain at-risk customers than about statistical accuracy. For medical diagnosis, you care more about patient outcomes than about mathematical precision.

2.8 Understanding What Models Learn

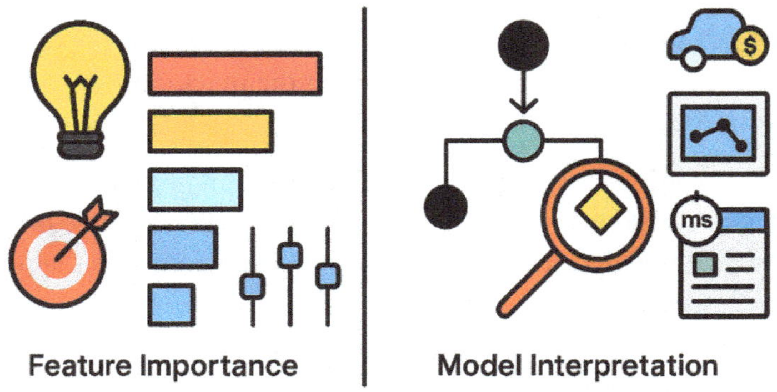

As models become more sophisticated, understanding how they make decisions becomes increasingly important. Feature importance analysis helps identify which input variables matter most, while model interpretation provides insights into the patterns the model has discovered.

2.8.1 Feature Importance and Variable Selection

Feature importance measures help you understand which variables in your data contribute most to accurate predictions. This information proves valuable for multiple reasons: it validates that your model is learning sensible patterns, identifies which data collection efforts provide the most value, and helps explain model decisions to stakeholders.

Different algorithms provide this information in different ways. Decision trees naturally show which variables are most useful for making accurate predictions. Linear models show feature importance through coefficient sizes, indicating how much each variable influences the prediction. Random forests aggregate importance across many trees to provide robust estimates.

Consider a model predicting customer lifetime value for a subscription service. Feature importance analysis might reveal that usage in the first month is the strongest predictor, followed by customer support interactions and initial subscription tier. This insight could guide product development and customer onboarding strategies.

2.8.2 Simple Model Interpretation Techniques

For simple models like linear regression and decision trees, interpretation is straightforward. Linear models show exactly how each variable affects the prediction, while decision trees provide clear rules that can be followed step-by-step.

For more complex models, interpretation requires special techniques. SHAP (SHapley Additive exPlanations) values provide a way to understand individual predictions by showing how much each input variable contributed to the final result. For any specific prediction, SHAP values show which factors pushed the prediction higher or lower.

Partial dependence plots show how changing one variable affects predictions while keeping other variables constant. These plots help you understand whether relationships are linear or curved, and whether the model has learned sensible patterns from the data.

2.8.3 Automated Interpretation Tools

Modern AI tools can assist with model interpretation, automatically identifying important variables and creating visualizations that help explain model behavior. These tools can test thousands of potential explanations and highlight the most important patterns.

However, automated interpretation requires careful validation to ensure that discovered patterns are meaningful rather than coincidental. The tools might identify relationships that work well on historical data but don't represent genuine causal relationships that will persist in the future.

The goal of interpretation isn't just to understand what the model learned, but to validate that it learned the right things for the right reasons. This becomes particularly important when models will be used for important decisions that affect people's lives or business outcomes.

2.9 Key Terms

Machine Learning Model – A mathematical system or algorithm that learns patterns from data to make predictions or decisions.

Pattern Recognition – The ability of models to detect trends, relationships, or regularities in data.

Regression – A type of prediction problem where the goal is to forecast a specific numerical value.

Linear Regression – A regression technique assuming a straight-line relationship between input variables and output.

Polynomial Regression – A regression approach for modeling curved or nonlinear relationships.

Decision Tree Regression – A regression method using a series of yes/no decisions to predict numerical outcomes.

Classification – A prediction problem where the goal is to assign items to discrete categories.

Binary Classification – Classification with two possible outcomes, e.g., spam vs. not spam.

Multi-Class Classification – Classification with more than two possible categories.

Logistic Regression – A classification method that calculates probabilities of category membership.

Decision Tree Classification – Classification using a flowchart of yes/no decisions.

Random Forest – An ensemble of decision trees that improves classification or regression accuracy.

Support Vector Machine (SVM) – A model that finds the best boundary separating categories in classification.

Neural Network – A flexible machine learning model capable of learning complex patterns from large datasets.

Recommendation System – A model that suggests items to users based on preferences and past behaviors.

Collaborative Filtering – A recommendation approach based on similarities between users' preferences.

Content-Based Filtering – A recommendation approach based on item features rather than user behavior.

Optimization – The process of finding the best solution to a problem, subject to constraints.

Linear Programming – A mathematical optimization method where relationships are linear.

Greedy Algorithm – An optimization approach that chooses the best option at each step.

Hyperparameters – Settings in machine learning algorithms that control learning behavior.

Model Tuning – Adjusting hyperparameters to improve model performance.

Feature Importance – A measure of how much each input variable contributes to predictions.

Model Interpretation – Techniques to understand how a model makes its predictions.

SHAP Values – A method to quantify the contribution of each feature to a specific prediction.

Partial Dependence Plot (PDP) – A plot showing the effect of a single feature on the model's predictions.

2.10 Review Questions

1. Define a machine learning model and explain how it differs from traditional programming.
2. Describe the difference between regression and classification problems and give a real-world example of each.
3. How does a model "learn" from data during the training process?
4. Explain the difference between linear regression, polynomial regression, and decision tree regression. When would you use each?
5. What is the difference between binary and multi-class classification? Provide examples of each.
6. Compare logistic regression, decision trees, random forests, SVMs, and neural networks in terms of use cases and interpretability.
7. How do collaborative filtering and content-based filtering differ in recommendation systems?
8. Why are recommendation systems valuable for businesses like Amazon or Netflix?
9. Define optimization in a business context and give two real-world examples.
10. What is a hyperparameter, and how does tuning hyperparameters improve model performance?
11. Explain why feature importance is important and how it can guide business decisions.
12. Describe SHAP values and partial dependence plots and their role in interpreting complex models.
13. When might a company choose a regression approach versus a classification approach for the same business problem?
14. What are some limitations of machine learning models that businesses should be aware of when making predictions?
15. How does understanding model outputs contribute to ethical and actionable business decisions?

2.11 Lab 2A: Classification and Regression Models

2.11.1 Introduction

Imagine you're working as a data analyst for a growing e-commerce company. Your manager walks into your office with two critical questions: "Can you predict how much each customer will spend next month?" and "Can you identify which customers are likely to cancel their subscriptions?" These questions represent the two fundamental types of prediction problems in machine learning: regression and classification.

The first question asks for a specific dollar amount - this is a regression problem where we predict continuous numerical values. The second question asks for a category (will cancel or won't cancel) - this is a classification problem where we predict discrete categories or classes.

Understanding these two types of problems is crucial because they form the foundation of most business applications of machine learning. Netflix uses regression to predict how many hours you'll watch a show and classification to determine if you'll like it. Banks use regression to predict loan amounts and classification to approve or deny applications. Retailers use regression to forecast sales and classification to detect fraudulent transactions.

In this lab, you'll get hands-on experience with both types of problems. You'll learn to build models, make predictions, and evaluate their performance using real-world scenarios that mirror what data analysts encounter in their daily work.

2.11.2 Demonstration

We'll work with a synthetic customer dataset that includes information about online shoppers. This dataset contains features like age, annual income, time spent on websites, and purchase history. We'll use this data to solve both regression and classification problems that are common in e-commerce analytics.

2.11.2.1 Step 1: Setting Up Our Environment and Data

First, let's import the necessary libraries and create our customer dataset:

```
# Import required libraries
import pandas as pd
import numpy as np
import matplotlib.pyplot as plt
import seaborn as sns
from sklearn.model_selection import train_test_split
from sklearn.linear_model import LinearRegression, LogisticRegression
from sklearn.tree import DecisionTreeRegressor, DecisionTreeClassifier
from sklearn.ensemble import RandomForestRegressor,
↪ RandomForestClassifier
from sklearn.metrics import mean_squared_error, r2_score,
↪ accuracy_score,
 classification_report, confusion_matrix
```

```
import warnings
warnings.filterwarnings('ignore')

# Set random seed for reproducibility
np.random.seed(42)

# Create synthetic customer data
n_customers = 1000

# Generate customer features
age = np.random.normal(35, 12, n_customers)
age = np.clip(age, 18, 70)  # Keep ages realistic

annual_income = np.random.normal(50000, 20000, n_customers)
annual_income = np.clip(annual_income, 20000, 150000)  # Keep incomes
 ↪ realistic

time_on_site = np.random.exponential(15, n_customers)  # Minutes spent
 ↪ on website
time_on_site = np.clip(time_on_site, 1, 120)

previous_purchases = np.random.poisson(3, n_customers)  # Number of
 ↪ previous purchases
```

This code generates two target variables for a dataset: monthly_spending for regression and will_purchase for classification. monthly_spending estimates a customer's monthly spending using factors like income, age, site activity, and past purchases, with added random noise and clipping to keep values realistic. will_purchase is a binary variable determined by a probability influenced by income, time on site, and purchase history, simulating whether a customer makes a purchase. Together, these variables create realistic behaviors for training or testing predictive models.

```
# Create target variables
# Regression target: Monthly spending amount
monthly_spending = (
    annual_income * 0.001 +  # Higher income = more spending
    age * 2 +                # Older customers spend slightly more
    time_on_site * 5 +       # More time on site = more spending
    previous_purchases * 25 + # Purchase history matters
    np.random.normal(0, 50, n_customers)  # Add some noise
)
monthly_spending = np.clip(monthly_spending, 0, 1000)  # Keep spending
 ↪ realistic
```

```
# Classification target: Will make a purchase this month (1) or not (0)
purchase_probability = (
    (annual_income - 20000) / 130000 * 0.3 +  # Income effect
    (time_on_site / 120) * 0.4 +              # Time on site effect
    (previous_purchases / 10) * 0.3            # Purchase history
 ↪  effect
)
will_purchase = np.random.binomial(1, purchase_probability,
 ↪  n_customers)

# Create DataFrame
customer_data = pd.DataFrame({
    'age': age,
    'annual_income': annual_income,
    'time_on_site': time_on_site,
    'previous_purchases': previous_purchases,
    'monthly_spending': monthly_spending,
    'will_purchase': will_purchase
})

# Display basic information about our dataset
print("Customer Dataset Overview:")
print("=" * 50)
print(f"Number of customers: {len(customer_data)}")
print(f"Number of features: {len(customer_data.columns) - 2}")  #
 ↪  Subtract 2 target variables
print("\nFirst 10 customers:")
print(customer_data.head(10))
print("\nDataset Summary Statistics:")
print(customer_data.describe())
```

Output:

```
Customer Dataset Overview:
==================================================
Number of customers: 1000
Number of features: 4

First 10 customers:
         age  annual_income  ...  monthly_spending  will_purchase
0  40.960570   77987.108732  ...        299.406879              0
1  33.340828   68492.673658  ...        289.840766              0
2  42.772262   51192.607398  ...        252.063199              1
3  53.276358   37061.264446  ...        174.312795              0
```

```
4  32.190160  63964.466272  ...        371.421389            1
5  32.190357  57869.707708  ...        523.918451            1
6  53.950554  67903.864401  ...        306.217770            0
7  44.209217  62703.436034  ...        428.144493            0
8  29.366307  70991.054306  ...        247.860371            0
9  41.510721  39295.295769  ...        154.158091            0

[10 rows x 6 columns]

| Stat |  Age | Annual<br>Income | Monthly<br>Spending | Will<br>Purchase |
| ---- | ---: | ---------------: | -----------------: | ---------------
: |
| N    | 1000 |             1000 |               1000 |             1000 |
| Mean | 35.5 |          51953.7 |              269.2 |             0.18 |
| SD   | 11.1 |          18839.5 |              101.4 |             0.38 |
| Min  | 18.0 |          20000.0 |               24.6 |             0.00 |
| Q1   | 27.2 |          37875.2 |              200.8 |             0.00 |
| Med  | 35.3 |          51261.5 |              262.6 |             0.00 |
| Q3   | 42.8 |          64577.6 |              329.7 |             0.00 |
| Max  | 70.0 |         113862.2 |              867.4 |             1.00 |


[8 rows x 6 columns]
```

2.11.2.2 Step 2: Exploring Our Data

Let's understand our data better through visualization and summary statistics. We start by examining the distribution of our regression target variable monthly_spending.

This histogram shows how much customers spend per month and highlights whether spending is evenly spread, skewed, or has extreme values. Understanding this distribution is important before building a regression model, because highly skewed targets may require transformation or special handling.

```
# Monthly Spending Distribution (regression target)
plt.figure(figsize=(8,5))
plt.hist(customer_data['monthly_spending'], bins=30, alpha=0.7,
    color='blue')
plt.title('Monthly Spending Distribution')
plt.xlabel('Monthly Spending ($)')
plt.ylabel('Frequency')
plt.show()
```

Next, we look at the relationship between annual_income and monthly_spending. This scatter plot helps us see if higher income customers tend to spend more each month. Identifying strong or weak correlations early informs which features are likely useful in predicting monthly spending.

```
# Income vs Monthly Spending (relationship check)
plt.figure(figsize=(8,5))
plt.scatter(customer_data['annual_income'],
 ↪ customer_data['monthly_spending'], alpha=0.5, color='teal')
plt.title('Annual Income vs Monthly Spending')
plt.xlabel('Annual Income ($)')
plt.ylabel('Monthly Spending ($)')
plt.show()
```

We also visualize the age distribution of our customers. While age is not the regression target, it can influence spending behavior. This histogram provides a quick overview of the customer demographics, helping us spot trends or unusual patterns.

```
# Optional: Age Distribution
plt.figure(figsize=(8,5))
plt.hist(customer_data['age'], bins=30, alpha=0.7, color='skyblue')
plt.title('Age Distribution')
plt.xlabel('Age')
plt.ylabel('Frequency')
plt.show()
```

Finally, we print simple statistics such as averages and percentages. These numbers summarize the central tendencies of age, income, time on site, monthly spending, and purchase behavior. Summary statistics complement the plots by providing exact values that help guide further analysis.

```
# Key summary statistics
print("\nKey Data Insights:")
print("="*50)
print(f"Average customer age: {customer_data['age'].mean():.1f} years")
print(f"Average annual income:
 ↪ ${customer_data['annual_income'].mean():,.0f}")
print(f"Average time on site:
 ↪ {customer_data['time_on_site'].mean():.1f} minutes")
print(f"Average monthly spending:
 ↪ ${customer_data['monthly_spending'].mean():.2f}")
print(f"Percentage of customers who will purchase:
 ↪ {customer_data['will_purchase'].mean()*100:.1f}%")
```

Output:

```
Key Data Insights:
==================================================
Average customer age: 35.5 years
Average annual income: $51,954
Average time on site: 14.9 minutes
Average monthly spending: $269.17
Percentage of customers who will purchase: 18.0%
```

The results reveal key insights about our customers. On average, they are 35.5 years old, earn about $51,954 annually, and spend roughly 15 minutes on the site. Their monthly spending averages $269, with higher-income customers generally spending more, indicating a positive income-spending relationship. Only 18% of customers are likely to make a purchase, highlighting that buying behavior is relatively infrequent. The age distribution and spending patterns provide context for modeling and show which features, like income and site activity, may be most predictive.

2.11.2.3 Step 3: Regression - Predicting Monthly Spending

Now, we turn our attention to our first predictive task: estimating each customer's monthly spending. Because monthly spending is a continuous numerical value, this task falls under the category of regression. To approach it, we will examine several regression models to determine how accurately we can predict spending based on key customer characteristics such as age, annual income, time spent on the site, and previous purchases. We identify these variables as our predictors (X), with monthly spending serving as the target variable (y). To assess model performance effectively, we split the dataset into a training set comprising 80% of the data, which we use to fit the models, and a testing set containing the remaining 20%, which we use to evaluate how well the models generalize to new, unseen customers. This approach ensures that our predictions reflect realistic performance on data the model has not encountered before.

```
print("REGRESSION PROBLEM: Predicting Monthly Spending")
print("=" * 60)

# Prepare data for regression
X_features = ['age', 'annual_income', 'time_on_site',
 ↪  'previous_purchases']
X = customer_data[X_features]
y_regression = customer_data['monthly_spending']

# Split data into training and testing sets
X_train, X_test, y_train, y_test = train_test_split(X, y_regression,
 ↪  test_size=0.2, random_state=42)
```

```
print(f"Training set size: {len(X_train)} customers")
print(f"Testing set size: {len(X_test)} customers")
```

Output:

```
REGRESSION PROBLEM: Predicting Monthly Spending
============================================================
Training set size: 800 customers
Testing set size: 200 customers
```

2.11.2.3.1 Linear Regression

Linear regression is the simplest model we try. It assumes a linear relationship between the features and monthly spending. After fitting the model, we calculate performance metrics such as Mean Squared Error (MSE), Root Mean Squared Error (RMSE), and R-squared. We also examine the coefficients to see how much each feature contributes to predicted spending.

```
# Model 1: Linear Regression
print("\n1. Linear Regression Model:")
print("-" * 30)
linear_reg = LinearRegression()
linear_reg.fit(X_train, y_train)
y_pred_linear = linear_reg.predict(X_test)

# Calculate performance metrics
mse_linear = mean_squared_error(y_test, y_pred_linear)
r2_linear = r2_score(y_test, y_pred_linear)

print(f"Mean Squared Error: ${mse_linear:.2f}")
print(f"R-squared Score: {r2_linear:.3f}")
print(f"Root Mean Squared Error: ${np.sqrt(mse_linear):.2f}")

# Show feature importance (coefficients)
print("\nFeature Importance (how much each feature affects spending):")
for feature, coef in zip(X_features, linear_reg.coef_):
    print(f"  {feature}: {coef:.4f}")
```

Output:

```
1. Linear Regression Model:
------------------------------
Mean Squared Error: $2565.91
R-squared Score: 0.792
Root Mean Squared Error: $50.65
```

```
Feature Importance (how much each feature affects spending):
  age: 1.7779
  annual_income: 0.0010
  time_on_site: 4.8766
  previous_purchases: 24.1113
```

2.11.2.3.2 Decision Tree

Decision trees split the data into regions based on feature values to make predictions. They can capture non-linear relationships that linear regression cannot. We limit the tree depth to prevent overfitting. After fitting, we check performance metrics and feature importance, which tells us which variables most influence spending.

```
# Model 2: Decision Tree Regression
print("\n2. Decision Tree Regression Model:")
print("-" * 35)
tree_reg = DecisionTreeRegressor(max_depth=5, random_state=42)
tree_reg.fit(X_train, y_train)
y_pred_tree = tree_reg.predict(X_test)

mse_tree = mean_squared_error(y_test, y_pred_tree)
r2_tree = r2_score(y_test, y_pred_tree)

print(f"Mean Squared Error: ${mse_tree:.2f}")
print(f"R-squared Score: {r2_tree:.3f}")
print(f"Root Mean Squared Error: ${np.sqrt(mse_tree):.2f}")

# Show feature importance
print("\nFeature Importance (0-1 scale, higher = more important):")
for feature, importance in zip(X_features,
↪   tree_reg.feature_importances_):
    print(f"  {feature}: {importance:.3f}")
```

Output:

```
2. Decision Tree Regression Model:
-----------------------------------
Mean Squared Error: $4230.26
R-squared Score: 0.658
Root Mean Squared Error: $65.04

Feature Importance (0-1 scale, higher = more important):
  age: 0.050
  annual_income: 0.037
```

```
  time_on_site: 0.737
  previous_purchases: 0.176
```

2.11.2.3.3 Random Forest Regression

Random forest regression combines many decision trees to improve accuracy and stability. By averaging multiple trees, it reduces overfitting and can capture complex patterns. We evaluate RMSE and R-squared again and inspect feature importance on a 0-1 scale. This model often performs better than a single tree or linear regression.

```
# Model 3: Random Forest Regression
print("\n3. Random Forest Regression Model:")
print("-" * 35)
rf_reg = RandomForestRegressor(n_estimators=100, max_depth=5,
 ↪  random_state=42)
rf_reg.fit(X_train, y_train)
y_pred_rf = rf_reg.predict(X_test)

mse_rf = mean_squared_error(y_test, y_pred_rf)
r2_rf = r2_score(y_test, y_pred_rf)

print(f"Mean Squared Error: ${mse_rf:.2f}")
print(f"R-squared Score: {r2_rf:.3f}")
print(f"Root Mean Squared Error: ${np.sqrt(mse_rf):.2f}")

# Show feature importance
print("\nFeature Importance (0-1 scale, higher = more important):")
for feature, importance in zip(X_features,
 ↪  rf_reg.feature_importances_):
    print(f"  {feature}: {importance:.3f}")
```

Output:

```
3. Random Forest Regression Model:
-----------------------------------
Mean Squared Error: $3391.70
R-squared Score: 0.726
Root Mean Squared Error: $58.24

Feature Importance (0-1 scale, higher = more important):
  age: 0.069
  annual_income: 0.046
  time_on_site: 0.708
  previous_purchases: 0.177
```

2.11.2.3.4 Comparing Models

We summarize the RMSE and R-squared for all three models in a table. This allows us to quickly see which model predicts monthly spending most accurately. Comparing models also helps us understand the trade-offs: simplicity of linear regression versus flexibility of tree-based methods.

```
# Compare all models
print("\n" + "="*60)
print("REGRESSION MODEL COMPARISON:")
print("="*60)
print(f"{'Model':<20} {'RMSE':<15} {'R-squared':<15}")
print("-" * 50)
print(f"{'Linear Regression':<20} ${np.sqrt(mse_linear):<14.2f}
↪ {r2_linear:<15.3f}")
print(f"{'Decision Tree':<20} ${np.sqrt(mse_tree):<14.2f}
↪ {r2_tree:<15.3f}")
print(f"{'Random Forest':<20} ${np.sqrt(mse_rf):<14.2f}
↪ {r2_rf:<15.3f}")
```

Output:

```
REGRESSION MODEL COMPARISON:
============================================================
Model                RMSE            R-squared
--------------------------------------------------
Linear Regression    $50.65          0.792
Decision Tree        $65.04          0.658
Random Forest        $58.24          0.726
```

The regression analysis shows how well different models predict monthly spending based on customer features like age, income, time on site, and previous purchases. Linear regression performed best overall, achieving an RMSE of $50.65 and an R-squared of 0.792, with previous purchases and time on site contributing most to spending. Decision tree regression captured non-linear patterns but had a higher RMSE ($65.04) and lower R-squared (0.658), relying heavily on time on site as the key predictor. Random forest regression, which averages multiple trees, offered a balance, reducing overfitting and achieving an RMSE of $58.24 with R-squared 0.726, again highlighting time on site and previous purchases as the most influential features. Overall, the results suggest that while linear regression provides strong predictive accuracy in this dataset, tree-based models reveal non-linear relationships and feature importance patterns that can guide further analysis.

2.11.2.3.5 Example Predictions

Finally, we show a few example predictions for the first ten customers in the test set. This gives a concrete sense of how the models' predictions compare to the actual spending values. It helps students see the real-world impact of model choice and feature selection.

```
# Show some example predictions
print("\nExample Predictions (first 10 test customers):")
print("-" * 50)
comparison_df = pd.DataFrame({
    'Actual': y_test.iloc[:10].values,
    'Linear_Reg': y_pred_linear[:10],
    'Decision_Tree': y_pred_tree[:10],
    'Random_Forest': y_pred_rf[:10]
})
comparison_df = comparison_df.round(2)
print(comparison_df)
```

Output:

```
Example Predictions (first 10 test customers):
--------------------------------------------------
   Actual  Linear_Reg  Decision_Tree  Random_Forest
0  291.00      252.44         270.64         269.25
1  180.83      224.72         243.12         236.42
2  494.51      477.18         511.35         416.80
3  257.70      275.39         279.85         289.02
4  313.39      278.37         274.52         302.99
5  232.77      206.85         156.01         199.31
6  132.02      170.43         201.50         171.01
7  221.19      153.01         201.50         173.73
8  867.37      728.20         615.51         576.26
9  265.05      207.95         156.01         193.00
```

2.11.2.4 Step 4: Classification - Predicting Purchase Behavior

Now let's solve our second problem: predicting whether a customer will make a purchase this month. This is a classification problem because we're predicting a category (yes/no). In this analysis, we approached predicting whether a customer will make a purchase as a classification problem. Our target variable, will_purchase, is binary: 1 indicates the customer made a purchase, and 0 indicates they did not.

2.11.2.4.1 Data Preparation

We used the same features as in our regression analysis: age, annual_income, time_on_site, and previous_purchases. The dataset was split into training (80%) and testing (20%) sets to evaluate model performance on unseen data. Checking the class distribution revealed the proportion of customers who will and will not make a purchase, helping us be aware of any class imbalance.

```
print("\n\nCLASSIFICATION PROBLEM: Predicting Purchase Behavior")
print("=" * 65)

# Prepare data for classification
y_classification = customer_data['will_purchase']

# Split data (using same features as regression)
X_train_clf, X_test_clf, y_train_clf, y_test_clf = train_test_split(
    X, y_classification, test_size=0.2, random_state=42
)

print(f"Training set size: {len(X_train_clf)} customers")
print(f"Testing set size: {len(X_test_clf)} customers")

# Check class distribution
print(f"\nClass distribution in training set:")
print(f"  Will NOT purchase:
  {(y_train_clf == 0).sum()} customers ({(y_train_clf ==
↪   0).mean()*100:.1f}%)")
print(f"  Will purchase: {(y_train_clf == 1).sum()} customers
↪   ({(y_train_clf == 1).mean()*100:.1f}%)")
```

Output:

```
CLASSIFICATION PROBLEM: Predicting Purchase Behavior
=================================================================
Training set size: 800 customers
Testing set size: 200 customers

Class distribution in training set:
  Will NOT purchase: 654 customers (81.8%)
  Will purchase: 146 customers (18.2%)
```

2.11.2.4.2 Logistic Regression

The logistic regression model was trained first. This model estimates the probability of a customer making a purchase based on a linear combination of features. The model produced an overall accuracy, and the classification report provided more detailed metrics, including precision, recall, and F1-score for both classes.

```
# Model 1: Logistic Regression
print("\n1. Logistic Regression Model:")
```

```
print("-" * 32)
logistic_clf = LogisticRegression(random_state=42)
logistic_clf.fit(X_train_clf, y_train_clf)
y_pred_logistic = logistic_clf.predict(X_test_clf)
y_prob_logistic = logistic_clf.predict_proba(X_test_clf)[:, 1]  #
↪ Probability of purchase

accuracy_logistic = accuracy_score(y_test_clf, y_pred_logistic)
print(f"Accuracy: {accuracy_logistic:.3f}
↪ ({accuracy_logistic*100:.1f}%)")

print("\nDetailed Classification Report:")
print(classification_report(y_test_clf, y_pred_logistic,
↪ target_names=['No Purchase', 'Will Purchase']))
```

Output:

```
1. Logistic Regression Model:
--------------------------------
Accuracy: 0.830 (83.0%)

Detailed Classification Report:
               precision    recall  f1-score   support

  No Purchase       0.83      0.99      0.91       166
Will Purchase       0.50      0.03      0.06        34

     accuracy                           0.83       200
    macro avg       0.67      0.51      0.48       200
 weighted avg       0.78      0.83      0.76       200
```

The logistic regression model achieved an overall accuracy of 83%, indicating it correctly classified most customers as making a purchase or not. However, the detailed metrics reveal a strong imbalance: the model predicts "No Purchase" very well (high precision and recall) but struggles to identify actual purchasers, with low recall (3%) and F1-score (0.06) for the "Will Purchase" class. This suggests that while the model performs well overall, it is not effective at detecting the minority class, highlighting the need for techniques to handle class imbalance in purchase prediction.

2.11.2.4.3 Decision Tree Classifier

Next, we implemented a decision tree classifier with a maximum depth of 5. Decision trees split the data based on feature thresholds to classify customers. We reported the accuracy and also highlighted feature importance, showing which features most strongly influenced purchase behavior.

```
# Model 2: Decision Tree Classification
print("\n2. Decision Tree Classification Model:")
print("-" * 37)
tree_clf = DecisionTreeClassifier(max_depth=5, random_state=42)
tree_clf.fit(X_train_clf, y_train_clf)
y_pred_tree_clf = tree_clf.predict(X_test_clf)

accuracy_tree_clf = accuracy_score(y_test_clf, y_pred_tree_clf)
print(f"Accuracy: {accuracy_tree_clf:.3f}
 ↪ ({accuracy_tree_clf*100:.1f}%)")

print("\nFeature Importance:")
for feature, importance in zip(X_features,
 ↪ tree_clf.feature_importances_):
    print(f"  {feature}: {importance:.3f}")
```

Output:

```
2. Decision Tree Classification Model:
-------------------------------------
Accuracy: 0.815 (81.5%)

Feature Importance:
  age: 0.255
  annual_income: 0.186
  time_on_site: 0.324
  previous_purchases: 0.235
```

The decision tree classifier achieved an overall accuracy of 81.5%, performing slightly lower than logistic regression. Feature importance shows that time on site was the most influential factor in predicting purchases, followed by previous purchases, age, and annual income. While the model captures non-linear relationships and highlights key drivers of purchase behavior, its accuracy is limited by the class imbalance, suggesting additional techniques may be needed to better identify actual purchasers.

2.11.2.4.4 Random Forest Classifier

Finally, a random forest classifier—an ensemble of 100 decision trees—was trained. Random forests typically provide more robust predictions and reduce overfitting compared to a single decision tree. We again reported accuracy and feature importance.

```
# Model 3: Random Forest Classification
print("\n3. Random Forest Classification Model:")
print("-" * 37)
```

```
rf_clf = RandomForestClassifier(n_estimators=100, max_depth=5,
↪  random_state=42)
rf_clf.fit(X_train_clf, y_train_clf)
y_pred_rf_clf = rf_clf.predict(X_test_clf)

accuracy_rf_clf = accuracy_score(y_test_clf, y_pred_rf_clf)
print(f"Accuracy: {accuracy_rf_clf:.3f} ({accuracy_rf_clf*100:.1f}%)")

print("\nFeature Importance:")
for feature, importance in zip(X_features,
↪  rf_clf.feature_importances_):
    print(f"  {feature}: {importance:.3f}")
```

Output:

```
3. Random Forest Classification Model:
----------------------------------------
Accuracy: 0.825 (82.5%)

Feature Importance:
  age: 0.229
  annual_income: 0.266
  time_on_site: 0.365
  previous_purchases: 0.140
```

The random forest classifier achieved an overall accuracy of 82.5%, slightly higher than both logistic regression and the single decision tree. Feature importance indicates that time on site remains the strongest predictor of purchase behavior, followed by annual income, age, and previous purchases. By combining multiple trees, the model produces more stable and robust predictions, reducing overfitting compared to a single decision tree, though class imbalance may still limit its ability to accurately identify customers who actually make a purchase.

2.11.2.4.5 Compare Classification Models

```
# Compare all classification models
print("\n" + "="*65)
print("CLASSIFICATION MODEL COMPARISON:")
print("="*65)
print(f"{'Model':<25} {'Accuracy':<15}")
print("-" * 40)
print(f"{'Logistic Regression':<25} {accuracy_logistic*100:<14.1f}%")
print(f"{'Decision Tree':<25} {accuracy_tree_clf*100:<14.1f}%")
print(f"{'Random Forest':<25} {accuracy_rf_clf*100:<14.1f}%")
```

```
# Show confusion matrix for best model
print(f"\nConfusion Matrix (Random Forest):")
print("-" * 35)
cm = confusion_matrix(y_test_clf, y_pred_rf_clf)
print("Predicted:")
print("          No    Yes")
print(f"Actual No  {cm[0,0]:3d}   {cm[0,1]:3d}")
print(f"Actual Yes {cm[1,0]:3d}   {cm[1,1]:3d}")
```

Output:

```
CLASSIFICATION MODEL COMPARISON:
=================================================================
Model                     Accuracy
----------------------------------------
Logistic Regression       83.0         %
Decision Tree             81.5         %
Random Forest             82.5         %

Confusion Matrix (Random Forest):
-----------------------------------
Predicted:
         No    Yes
Actual No  165     1
Actual Yes  34     0
```

Comparing the three classification models shows that logistic regression achieved the highest overall accuracy at 83.0%, followed closely by the random forest at 82.5% and the decision tree at 81.5%. However, examining the confusion matrix for the random forest—the most robust model—reveals that it correctly identifies nearly all customers who do not make a purchase but fails to correctly classify any actual purchasers.

```
# Show some example predictions with probabilities
print("\nExample Predictions (first 10 test customers):")
print("-" * 55)
example_probs = rf_clf.predict_proba(X_test_clf)[:10, 1]
example_df = pd.DataFrame({
    'Actual': y_test_clf.iloc[:10].values,
    'Predicted': y_pred_rf_clf[:10],
    'Probability': example_probs
})
example_df['Probability'] = example_df['Probability'].round(3)
print(example_df)
```

Output:

```
Example Predictions (first 10 test customers):
-------------------------------------------------------
   Actual  Predicted  Probability
0       0          0        0.134
1       1          0        0.081
2       1          0        0.392
3       0          0        0.186
4       0          0        0.282
5       0          0        0.093
6       0          0        0.080
7       0          0        0.057
8       1          0        0.448
9       0          0        0.109
```

Example predictions with probabilities show that even when the model assigns moderate probabilities to "will purchase" cases, it still predicts them as "no purchase." This highlights a common issue with imbalanced datasets: high overall accuracy can be misleading because the model struggles to detect the minority class, emphasizing the need for techniques like resampling, class weighting, or threshold adjustment to improve prediction of actual purchasers.

2.11.3 Practice

You work for a mid-sized technology company's HR department. The company wants to better understand employee performance and retention. You have data about employees including their experience, salary, project completion rates, and training hours. Your tasks are to explore the data, build models to predict salary levels (regression) and whether an employee will receive a promotion (classification), and answer questions about your findings.

```python
import numpy as np
import pandas as pd
from sklearn.model_selection import train_test_split

# Create employee performance dataset
np.random.seed(123)  # For reproducibility

n_employees = 800

# Features
years_experience = np.random.exponential(3, n_employees)
years_experience = np.clip(years_experience, 0.5, 15)
```

```
training_hours = np.random.normal(40, 15, n_employees)
training_hours = np.clip(training_hours, 10, 100)

project_completion_rate = np.random.beta(7, 2, n_employees)  # Skewed
↪ toward high completion

team_size = np.random.choice([3, 5, 8, 12, 15], n_employees, p=[0.2,
↪ 0.3, 0.3, 0.15, 0.05])

# Regression target: Salary
base_salary = 45000
salary = (
    base_salary +
    years_experience * 4000 +
    training_hours * 100 +
    project_completion_rate * 25000 +
    np.random.normal(0, 5000, n_employees)
)
salary = np.clip(salary, 35000, 150000)

# Classification target: Promotion
promotion_probability = (
    (years_experience / 15) * 0.3 +
    (training_hours / 100) * 0.2 +
    project_completion_rate * 0.4 +
    np.random.normal(0, 0.1, n_employees)
)
promotion_probability = np.clip(promotion_probability, 0, 1)
will_get_promotion = np.random.binomial(1, promotion_probability,
↪ n_employees)

# Create DataFrame
employee_data = pd.DataFrame({
    'years_experience': years_experience,
    'training_hours': training_hours,
    'project_completion_rate': project_completion_rate,
    'team_size': team_size,
    'salary': salary,
    'will_get_promotion': will_get_promotion
})

# Show dataset summary
print("Employee Performance Dataset:")
```

```
print(employee_data.head(10))
print("\nSummary Statistics:")
print(employee_data.describe())
```

2.11.3.1 Lab 2A Questions

1. How many employees are in the dataset?
2. What is the average salary in the company?
3. What percentage of employees will get promoted?
4. Which employee has the highest project completion rate?
5. Which feature(s) appear most important for predicting salary based on your initial exploration?
6. Build three regression models (Linear Regression, Decision Tree Regression, Random Forest Regression) to predict salary. Which model performs best based on R-squared score?
7. For your best regression model, what is the average prediction error (RMSE)?
8. Which feature is most important for predicting salary in your Decision Tree or Random Forest model?
9. Compare feature importances between the Decision Tree and Random Forest regressors. Are they similar or different?
10. Build three classification models (Logistic Regression, Decision Tree, Random Forest) to predict will_get_promotion. Which model achieves the highest accuracy?
11. In the classification report for your best model, which class (promotion / no promotion) is harder to predict correctly?
12. Which feature is most important for predicting promotions in your best classification model?
13. How many false positives and false negatives does your best classification model have according to the confusion matrix?
14. Take a random subset of 10 employees from the test set. What are the predicted probabilities for promotion, and how do they compare to the actual outcomes?
15. Based on your regression and classification models, what actionable insights could HR take to improve employee performance and promotion strategies?

2.12 Lab 2B: Improving Models

2.12.1 Introduction

Imagine you built your first machine learning model and your boss says, "Good start! Can you make it better?" This is exactly what happens in real data science work. Building a basic model is just the beginning - the real skill is in making it more accurate and useful.

In the prior lab you learned to build basic models using data as-is. But in the real world, data scientists spend most of their time improving their data and models to get better results. This process is like tuning a car engine - small adjustments can make a big difference in performance.

In this lab you'll learn simple but powerful techniques that data analysts use every day:

- **Creating better features**: Making new variables from existing ones
- **Choosing the best features**: Picking which variables actually help
- **Improving model settings**: Adjusting how your algorithms work
- **Measuring improvement**: Seeing how much better your models get

Think of it like cooking - you start with basic ingredients (your original data), but by combining them in smart ways and adjusting the recipe (feature engineering), you can create something much better!

2.12.2 Demonstration

We'll work with a home sales dataset where we want to predict house prices. This is perfect for learning because everyone understands houses, and we can easily create meaningful new features from the basic information.

2.12.2.1 Step 1: Creating Our Dataset and Basic Model

Let's start by creating our dataset and building a simple model to see our starting point:

```
# Import the tools we need
import pandas as pd
import numpy as np
import matplotlib.pyplot as plt
from sklearn.model_selection import train_test_split
from sklearn.linear_model import LinearRegression
from sklearn.ensemble import RandomForestRegressor
from sklearn.metrics import mean_squared_error, r2_score
from sklearn.preprocessing import StandardScaler
import warnings
warnings.filterwarnings('ignore')
```

```
# Set random seed so we all get the same results
np.random.seed(42)

print("Creating Home Sales Dataset...")


# Create data for 1000 houses
n_houses = 1000

# Basic house information
square_feet = np.random.normal(2000, 500, n_houses)
square_feet = np.clip(square_feet, 1000, 4000)  # Keep realistic

bedrooms = np.random.choice([2, 3, 4, 5], n_houses, p=[0.2, 0.4, 0.3,
 ↪  0.1])
bathrooms = np.random.choice([1, 2, 3, 4], n_houses, p=[0.1, 0.4, 0.4,
 ↪  0.1])
age_years = np.random.uniform(0, 50, n_houses)
garage_spaces = np.random.choice([0, 1, 2, 3], n_houses, p=[0.1, 0.3,
 ↪  0.5, 0.1])

# Location information
neighborhoods = ['Downtown', 'Suburbs', 'Waterfront', 'Rural']
neighborhood = np.random.choice(neighborhoods, n_houses, p=[0.3, 0.4,
 ↪  0.2, 0.1])

# Calculate house prices based on features
base_price = (
    square_feet * 100 +             # $100 per square foot
    bedrooms * 10000 +              # $10k per bedroom
    bathrooms * 8000 +              # $8k per bathroom
    garage_spaces * 5000 +          # $5k per garage space
    -age_years * 1000               # Lose $1k per year of age
)

# Add neighborhood effects
neighborhood_bonus = {'Waterfront': 50000, 'Downtown': 20000,
 ↪  'Suburbs': 0, 'Rural': -10000}
for i, hood in enumerate(neighborhood):
    base_price[i] += neighborhood_bonus[hood]

# Add some randomness
price = base_price + np.random.normal(0, 20000, n_houses)
```

```
price = np.clip(price, 100000, 800000)  # Keep realistic

# Create our dataset
house_data = pd.DataFrame({
    'square_feet': square_feet,
    'bedrooms': bedrooms,
    'bathrooms': bathrooms,
    'age_years': age_years,
    'garage_spaces': garage_spaces,
    'neighborhood': neighborhood,
    'price': price
})

print(f"Created dataset with {len(house_data)} houses")
print("\nFirst 5 houses:")
print(house_data.head())
print("\nBasic statistics:")
print(house_data.describe())
```

Output:

```
Creating Home Sales Dataset...
========================================

Created dataset with 1000 houses

First 5 houses:
   square_feet  bedrooms  bathrooms  ...  garage_spaces
0  2248.357077         2          2  ...              1
1  1930.867849         2          1  ...              1
2  2323.844269         4          2  ...              2
3  2761.514928         4          2  ...              2
4  1882.923313         2          3  ...              0



First 5 houses:
   square_feet   neighborhood         price
0  2248.357077    Suburbs           220306.052889
1  1930.867849    Suburbs           217667.288916
2  2323.844269    Suburbs           260821.715642
3  2761.514928    Dowwntown         344345.663912
4  1882.923313   Waterfront         254729.604474
```

```
[5 rows x 7 columns]

Basic statistics:
        square_feet     bedrooms  ...  garage_spaces          price
count   1000.000000  1000.000000  ...    1000.000000    1000.000000
mean    2012.319601     3.307000  ...       1.587000  251118.597462
std      483.199747     0.895295  ...       0.805655   59138.088550
min     1000.000000     2.000000  ...       0.000000  100826.327288
25%     1676.204847     3.000000  ...       1.000000  209773.046462
50%     2012.650306     3.000000  ...       2.000000  250945.791140
75%     2323.971938     4.000000  ...       2.000000  290659.210372
max     3926.365745     5.000000  ...       3.000000  440286.371881
```

In this step, we are establishing a baseline model to predict house prices using only a few fundamental numerical features. The purpose of this baseline is to provide a starting point for understanding how well a simple linear regression can explain the variation in house prices before we introduce more complexity. We begin by selecting basic features that are likely to influence price: the size of the house in square feet, the number of bedrooms, the number of bathrooms, the age of the house in years, and the number of garage spaces.

```
print("\n" + "="*50)
print("BUILDING BASIC MODEL (OUR STARTING POINT)")
print("="*50)

# Use only the numerical features for our basic model
basic_features = ['square_feet', 'bedrooms', 'bathrooms', 'age_years',
 ↪  'garage_spaces']
X_basic = house_data[basic_features]
y = house_data['price']
```

Once the features are selected, the data is split into a training set, used to fit the model, and a testing set, used to evaluate the model's performance, with 80% of the data for training and 20% for testing. A Linear Regression model is then built and trained on the training data. This type of model assumes a straight-line relationship between each feature and the target variable, in this case, the house price.

```
# Split into training and testing data
X_train_basic, X_test_basic, y_train, y_test = train_test_split(
    X_basic, y, test_size=0.2, random_state=42
)

# Build a simple Linear Regression model
basic_model = LinearRegression()
basic_model.fit(X_train_basic, y_train)
```

```
y_pred_basic = basic_model.predict(X_test_basic)
```

After training, we evaluate the model using two key metrics: the R^2 score and the Root Mean Squared Error (RMSE). The R^2 score indicates how much of the variance in house prices the model can explain, with values closer to 1 representing better performance. RMSE provides the average error in predicted prices, giving a sense of how far off the predictions are in dollar terms.

```
# Calculate how well our basic model performs
basic_rmse = np.sqrt(mean_squared_error(y_test, y_pred_basic))
basic_r2 = r2_score(y_test, y_pred_basic)

print(f"Basic Model Performance:")
print(f"  R² Score: {basic_r2:.3f} (higher is better)")
print(f"  RMSE: ${basic_rmse:,.0f} (lower is better)")
print(f"  Average prediction error: ${basic_rmse:,.0f}")
```

Output:

```
Basic Model Performance:
  R² Score: 0.775 (higher is better)
  RMSE: $27,331 (lower is better)
  Average prediction error: $27,331
```

Finally, the coefficients of each feature are examined to understand their contributions to the predicted price. For instance, a positive coefficient for square footage indicates that larger houses tend to have higher prices, all else being equal. This baseline model establishes a reference point from which we can explore improvements, such as incorporating additional features, handling categorical variables, or experimenting with more advanced modeling techniques to increase prediction accuracy.

```
print(f"\nWhat each feature contributes to price:")
for feature, coef in zip(basic_features, basic_model.coef_):
    print(f"  {feature}: ${coef:,.0f}")

print(f"\nBaseline established! Now let's improve it...")
```

Output:

```
What each feature contributes to price:
  square_feet: $100
  bedrooms: $11,311
  bathrooms: $9,827
  age_years: $-1,019
  garage_spaces: $5,124
```

```
Baseline established! Now let's improve it...
```

2.12.2.2 Step 2: Creating Better Features (Feature Engineering)

In Step 2, we focus on feature engineering, which involves creating new variables that can help our model better understand the patterns in the data. By transforming or combining existing features, we can provide the model with richer information that may improve its predictive power. To begin, we make a copy of the original dataset so that we can safely add new features without altering the raw data.

```
print("\n" + "="*50)
print("STEP 2: CREATING BETTER FEATURES")
print("="*50)

# Make a copy of our data to add new features
improved_data = house_data.copy()
```

The first new feature is total_rooms, calculated as the sum of bedrooms and bathrooms. This gives a sense of the overall size of the living space beyond just the number of bedrooms or bathrooms individually. Next, we calculate sqft_per_room, which measures how spacious each room is on average. Although we won't use this feature directly for prediction in this example, it can be useful for exploratory analysis or comparisons.

```
print("Creating new features...")

# 1. Total rooms (bedrooms + bathrooms)
improved_data['total_rooms'] = improved_data['bedrooms'] +
↪ improved_data['bathrooms']
print("✓ Created 'total_rooms' (bedrooms + bathrooms)")

# 2. Price per square foot (we'll calculate this for comparison, but
↪ won't use it to predict price)
improved_data['sqft_per_room'] = improved_data['square_feet'] /
↪ improved_data['total_rooms']
print("✓ Created 'sqft_per_room' (how spacious each room is)")
```

We also transform continuous variables into categories to capture non-linear relationships. For example, the age of a house is grouped into age_category labels such as New, Recent, Mature, and Old, while the size of a house is categorized into Small, Medium, and Large based on square footage. This approach allows the model to recognize meaningful ranges rather than treating age or size as purely linear variables.

```
# 3. Age categories instead of exact age
improved_data['age_category'] = pd.cut(improved_data['age_years'],
                        bins=[0, 5, 15, 30, 50],
```

```
                                labels=['New', 'Recent', 'Mature', 'Old'])
print("✓ Created 'age_category' (New/Recent/Mature/Old)")

# 4. Size categories
improved_data['size_category'] = pd.cut(improved_data['square_feet'],
                                bins=[0, 1500, 2500, 4000],
                                labels=['Small', 'Medium', 'Large'])
print("✓ Created 'size_category' (Small/Medium/Large)")
```

Other new features include has_garage, a binary indicator of whether a house has any garage space, and is_premium, which flags houses located in premium neighborhoods like Waterfront or Downtown. These binary indicators help the model quickly identify characteristics that may significantly influence price.

```
# 5. Has garage (yes/no instead of number of spaces)
improved_data['has_garage'] = (improved_data['garage_spaces'] >
↪  0).astype(int)
print("✓ Created 'has_garage' (1 if has garage, 0 if not)")

# 6. Premium neighborhood indicator
premium_neighborhoods = ['Waterfront', 'Downtown']
improved_data['is_premium'] = improved_data['neighborhood'
↪  ].isin(premium_neighborhoods).astype(int)
print("✓ Created 'is_premium' (1 if Waterfront/Downtown, 0 if not)")

print(f"\nNew features created! Let's see some examples:")
print(improved_data[['square_feet', 'sqft_per_room',
↪  'is_premium']].head())
```

Output:

```
✓ Created 'total_rooms' (bedrooms + bathrooms)
✓ Created 'sqft_per_room' (how spacious each room is)
✓ Created 'age_category' (New/Recent/Mature/Old)
✓ Created 'size_category' (Small/Medium/Large)
✓ Created 'has_garage' (1 if has garage, 0 if not)
✓ Created 'is_premium' (1 if Waterfront/Downtown, 0 if not)

New features created! Let's see some examples:
   square_feet   sqft_per_room  has_garage  is_premium
0  2248.357077   562.089269            1           0
1  1930.867849   643.622616            1           0
```

```
2  2323.844269   387.307378           1          0
3  2761.514928   460.252488           1          1
4  1882.923313   376.584663           0          1

[5 rows x 7 columns]
```

Overall, these engineered features provide additional context and structure to the data, making it easier for the model to learn relationships between house attributes and price. The result is a dataset that is not only richer but also better suited for building a more accurate predictive model.

2.12.2.3 Step 3: Handling Categories

Machine learning models need numbers. In Step 3, we focus on converting categorical features into numerical values, a necessary step because most machine learning models can only work with numbers. Categorical data, like neighborhood names or size categories, cannot be interpreted directly by algorithms, so we need to encode them into a numerical format that the model can understand.

```
print("\n" + "="*50)
print("STEP 3: CONVERTING CATEGORIES TO NUMBERS")
print("="*50)

print("Converting categorical features to numbers...")
```

For neighborhoods, which have no inherent order, we use one-hot encoding. This method creates a separate binary column for each neighborhood, indicating whether a house belongs to that neighborhood. For example, if a house is in “Downtown,” the column for Downtown will be 1 and all other neighborhood columns will be 0. This allows the model to treat each neighborhood independently without implying any ranking or order.

```
# Method 1: Create separate columns for each neighborhood (One-Hot
↪ Encoding)
neighborhood_columns = pd.get_dummies(improved_data['neighborhood'],
↪ prefix='neighborhood')
print(f"✓ Created neighborhood columns:
↪ {list(neighborhood_columns.columns)}")
```

For ordered categories, such as age_category and size_category, we use label encoding. Each category is assigned a number that reflects its natural order: for age, “New” is 0, “Recent” is 1, “Mature” is 2, and “Old” is 3; for size, “Small” is 0, “Medium” is 1, and “Large” is 2. This approach preserves the ordinal relationship, allowing the model to recognize that older houses or larger homes may have different impacts on price compared to newer or smaller ones.

```
# Method 2: Convert ordered categories to numbers (Label Encoding)
age_mapping = {'New': 0, 'Recent': 1, 'Mature': 2, 'Old': 3}
improved_data['age_category_num'] =
↪ improved_data['age_category'].map(age_mapping)

size_mapping = {'Small': 0, 'Medium': 1, 'Large': 2}
improved_data['size_category_num'] =
↪ improved_data['size_category'].map(size_mapping)

print("✓ Converted age categories to numbers: New=0, Recent=1,
↪ Mature=2, Old=3")
print("✓ Converted size categories to numbers: Small=0, Medium=1,
↪ Large=2")

# Combine all our numerical features
all_features = (['square_feet', 'bedrooms', 'bathrooms', 'age_years',
  'garage_spaces',  'total_rooms', 'sqft_per_room',
  'has_garage', 'is_premium', 'age_category_num',
  'size_category_num'] +
             list(neighborhood_columns.columns))
```

Finally, we combine all numerical and encoded features into a single feature matrix, which now includes both the original numerical features and the new engineered and encoded features. This expanded set of features provides a richer representation of each house, giving our model more information to learn from. In total, the feature set has grown significantly from the basic model, which should help improve predictive accuracy.

```
# Create our improved feature matrix
X_improved = pd.concat([
    improved_data[['square_feet', 'bedrooms', 'bathrooms', 'age_years',
↪
                 'garage_spaces','total_rooms', 'sqft_per_room',
                 'has_garage', 'is_premium', 'age_category_num',
                 'size_category_num']],
    neighborhood_columns
], axis=1)

print(f"\nTotal features now: {X_improved.shape[1]} (started with
↪ {len(basic_features)})")
for col in X_improved.columns:
    print(col)
```

Output:

```
✓ Created neighborhood columns:
['neighborhood_Downtown', 'neighborhood_Rural', 'neighborhood_Suburbs',
'neighborhood_Waterfront']
✓ Converted age categories to numbers: New=0, Recent=1, Mature=2, Old=3
✓ Converted size categories to numbers: Small=0, Medium=1, Large=2

Total features now: 15 (started with 5)

All feature names: ['square_feet', 'bedrooms', 'bathrooms', ...
```

2.12.2.4 Step 4: Choosing the Best Features

Not all features are equally helpful. In Step 4, we focus on identifying the most important features that have the greatest impact on predicting house prices. Even though we now have a rich set of engineered and encoded features, not all of them contribute equally to the model's performance. Selecting the most relevant features helps simplify the model, reduces noise, and can improve prediction accuracy.

```
print("\n" + "="*50)
print("STEP 4: FINDING THE MOST IMPORTANT FEATURES")
print("="*50)

# Split our improved data
X_train_improved, X_test_improved, y_train_imp, y_test_imp =
 ↪  train_test_split(
    X_improved, y, test_size=0.2, random_state=42
)
```

To determine feature importance, we use a Random Forest Regressor, which is an ensemble method that builds multiple decision trees and evaluates how much each feature reduces prediction error across the forest. Features that consistently improve predictions are assigned higher importance scores. By fitting the Random Forest model to our improved training data, we can rank all features from most to least influential.

```
print("Method 1: Using Random Forest to find important features...")

# Use Random Forest to see which features matter most
rf_selector = RandomForestRegressor(n_estimators=100, random_state=42)
rf_selector.fit(X_train_improved, y_train_imp)

# Get feature importance scores
feature_importance = pd.DataFrame({
    'feature': X_improved.columns,
    'importance': rf_selector.feature_importances_
}).sort_values('importance', ascending=False)
```

```
print("\nTop 10 most important features:")
for i, (_, row) in enumerate(feature_importance.head(10).iterrows(),
↪ 1):
    print(f"{i:2d}. {row['feature']}: {row['importance']:.3f}")
```

Output:

```
Method 1: Using Random Forest to find important features...

Top 10 most important features:
 1. square_feet: 0.722
 2. age_years: 0.090
 3. is_premium: 0.044
 4. sqft_per_room: 0.039
 5. neighborhood_Waterfront: 0.038
 6. total_rooms: 0.018
 7. bedrooms: 0.013
 8. garage_spaces: 0.010
 9. bathrooms: 0.008
10. neighborhood_Downtown: 0.006
```

After calculating feature importance, we examine the top-ranked features and select the top 3 to include in our final model. This reduced set captures the most critical information for predicting house prices while removing less informative features. Using these selected features, we create new training and testing datasets, which will serve as the input for building a more focused and potentially more accurate predictive model.

```
# Select top 8 features for our final model
top_features = feature_importance.head(3)['feature'].tolist()
print(f"\nSelected top 3 features: {top_features}")

# These lines create new training and test datasets that include only
↪ the important features
X_train_selected = X_train_improved[top_features]
X_test_selected = X_test_improved[top_features]
```

Output:

```
Selected top 8 features: ['square_feet', 'age_years', 'is_premium']
```

2.12.2.5 Step 5: Scaling Features (Making Them Fair)

Some features have big numbers (like square_feet: 2000) and others have small numbers (like bedrooms: 3). Let's make them more equal. In Step 5, we address the differences in feature scales to ensure that each variable contributes fairly to the model. Many machine learning algorithms, especially those based on distances or gradient optimization, can be influenced disproportionately by features with larger numeric ranges. For example, a house's square footage might range in the thousands, while the number of bathrooms ranges from 1 to 5. Without scaling, the model may give undue weight to features with larger values simply because of their magnitude.

```
print("\n" + "="*50)
print("STEP 5: SCALING FEATURES TO BE FAIR")
print("="*50)

print("Before scaling - feature ranges:")
for col in X_train_selected.columns[:5]:  # Show first 5
    print(f"  {col}: {X_train_selected[col].min():.1f} to
    ↪ {X_train_selected[col].max():.1f}")
```

Output:

```
Before scaling - feature ranges:
  square_feet: 1000.0 to 3539.4
  age_years: 0.0 to 50.0
  is_premium: 0.0 to 1.0
  sqft_per_room: 125.0 to 863.2
  neighborhood_Waterfront: 0.0 to 1.0
```

To resolve this, we apply standard scaling, which transforms each feature so that it has a mean of approximately 0 and a standard deviation of 1. This standardization ensures that all features are on a similar scale, making comparisons fair and allowing the model to learn efficiently.

```
# Apply scaling
scaler = StandardScaler()
X_train_scaled = scaler.fit_transform(X_train_selected)
X_test_scaled = scaler.transform(X_test_selected)

# Convert back to DataFrame
X_train_scaled = pd.DataFrame(X_train_scaled, columns=top_features)
X_test_scaled = pd.DataFrame(X_test_scaled, columns=top_features)

print("\nAfter scaling - all features have similar ranges:")
for col in X_train_scaled.columns[:5]:  # Show first 5
    print(f"  {col}: {X_train_scaled[col].min():.1f} to
    ↪ {X_train_scaled[col].max():.1f}")

print("✓ Scaling complete! All features now have mean ≈ 0 and std ≈ 1")
```

Output:

```
After scaling - all features have similar ranges:
  square_feet: -2.1 to 3.2
  age_years: -1.8 to 1.8
  is_premium: -1.0 to 1.0
  sqft_per_room: -2.0 to 4.1
  neighborhood_Waterfront: -0.5 to 2.1
✓ Scaling complete! All features now have mean ≈ 0 and std ≈ 1
```

After scaling, each feature, regardless of its original units, contributes equally to the model's training process. This step is essential for producing a stable, well-balanced predictive model.

2.12.2.6 Step 6: Building Our Improved Model

Now let's build a better model and see how much we improved. In Step 6, we use all the preparation work from the previous steps to build improved predictive models for house prices. First, we fit an improved Linear Regression model using the scaled features selected from our earlier analysis. This model benefits from feature engineering, encoding, and scaling, which allow it to make more accurate predictions than our original baseline. We evaluate its performance using the R^2 score, which measures the proportion of variance explained, and RMSE, which indicates the average prediction error in dollars.

```
print("\n" + "="*50)
print("STEP 6: BUILDING OUR IMPROVED MODEL")
print("="*50)

# Build improved Linear Regression model
improved_lr = LinearRegression()
improved_lr.fit(X_train_scaled, y_train_imp)
y_pred_improved_lr = improved_lr.predict(X_test_scaled)

improved_lr_rmse = np.sqrt(mean_squared_error(y_test_imp,
 ↪  y_pred_improved_lr))
improved_lr_r2 = r2_score(y_test_imp, y_pred_improved_lr)

print("Improved Linear Regression Results:")
print(f"  R² Score: {improved_lr_r2:.3f}")
print(f"  RMSE: ${improved_lr_rmse:,.0f}")
```

Output:

```
Improved Linear Regression Results:
  R² Score: 0.875
  RMSE: $20,379
```

We also build an improved Random Forest model, an ensemble method that often performs better with complex data. Unlike Linear Regression, Random Forest does not require feature scaling, but it can capture non-linear relationships and interactions between features. By training this model on the selected features, we compare its predictions to both the improved Linear Regression and the original baseline model.

```
# Also try Random Forest (often works better)
improved_rf = RandomForestRegressor(n_estimators=100, max_depth=10,
    random_state=42)
improved_rf.fit(X_train_selected, y_train_imp)  # Random Forest doesn't
    need scaling
y_pred_improved_rf = improved_rf.predict(X_test_selected)

improved_rf_rmse = np.sqrt(mean_squared_error(y_test_imp,
    y_pred_improved_rf))
improved_rf_r2 = r2_score(y_test_imp, y_pred_improved_rf)

print("\nImproved Random Forest Results:")
print(f"  R² Score: {improved_rf_r2:.3f}")
print(f"  RMSE: ${improved_rf_rmse:,.0f}")
```

Output:

```
Improved Random Forest Results:
  R² Score: 0.828
  RMSE: $23,878
```

Finally, we compare all three models to quantify improvement.

```
# Compare all our models
print("\n" + "="*60)
print("FINAL COMPARISON: HOW MUCH DID WE IMPROVE?")
print("="*60)

comparison = pd.DataFrame({
    'Model': ['Basic Linear Regression', 'Improved Linear Regression',
        'Improved Random Forest'],
    'R² Score': [basic_r2, improved_lr_r2, improved_rf_r2],
    'RMSE': [basic_rmse, improved_lr_rmse, improved_rf_rmse],
    'Features Used': [len(basic_features), len(top_features),
        len(top_features)]
})

print(comparison.round(3))

# Calculate improvement
```

```
best_rmse = min(improved_lr_rmse, improved_rf_rmse)
best_r2 = max(improved_lr_r2, improved_rf_r2)
best_model = "Random Forest" if improved_rf_r2 > improved_lr_r2 else
↪  "Linear Regression"

rmse_improvement = ((basic_rmse - best_rmse) / basic_rmse) * 100
r2_improvement = ((best_r2 - basic_r2) / basic_r2) * 100

print(f"\n IMPROVEMENT RESULTS:")
print(f"   Best model: Improved {best_model}")
print(f"   RMSE improved by: {rmse_improvement:.1f}%")
print(f"   R² improved by: {r2_improvement:.1f}%")
print(f"   We reduced prediction error by ${basic_rmse -
↪  best_rmse:,.0f}!")
```

Output:

```
                        Model  R² Score       RMSE  Features Used
0      Basic Linear Regression     0.775  27330.542              5
1   Improved Linear Regression     0.875  20379.300              8
2       Improved Random Forest     0.828  23878.148              8

 IMPROVEMENT RESULTS:
   Best model: Improved Linear Regression
   RMSE improved by: 25.4%
   R² improved by: 12.9%
   We reduced prediction error by $6,951!
```

The comparison table shows that our Improved Linear Regression and Improved Random Forest models outperform the basic linear regression. Calculating the improvements, we see that the best model, Improved Linear Regression, reduces prediction error by \$6,951, improves RMSE by 25.4%, and increases R^2 by 12.9%, demonstrating that selecting more relevant features and refining the model substantially enhances accuracy.

2.12.3 Practice

You work for an online retail company that wants to predict customer satisfaction scores based on their shopping experience. The company collects data about orders, delivery, customer service, and wants to identify what makes customers happy or unhappy.

```
import numpy as np
import pandas as pd
from sklearn.model_selection import train_test_split
from sklearn.linear_model import LinearRegression
from sklearn.ensemble import RandomForestRegressor
```

```
from sklearn.preprocessing import StandardScaler
from sklearn.metrics import mean_squared_error, r2_score

# Create customer satisfaction dataset
np.random.seed(123)
n_customers = 1500

age = np.clip(np.random.normal(40, 15, n_customers), 18, 80)
order_value = np.clip(np.random.lognormal(4, 0.8, n_customers), 20,
↪ 500)
delivery_days = np.random.choice([1,2,3,4,5,6,7], n_customers,
↪ p=[0.1,0.2,0.3,0.2,0.1,0.05,0.05])
num_items = np.clip(np.random.poisson(3, n_customers) + 1, 1, 15)
customer_service_calls = np.clip(np.random.poisson(0.5, n_customers),
↪ 0, 5)

shipping_methods = ['Standard', 'Express', 'Overnight']
shipping_method = np.random.choice(shipping_methods, n_customers,
↪ p=[0.6,0.3,0.1])

product_categories = ['Electronics', 'Clothing', 'Home', 'Books',
↪ 'Sports']
product_category = np.random.choice(product_categories, n_customers,
↪ p=[0.3,0.25,0.2,0.15,0.1])

payment_methods = ['Credit Card', 'PayPal', 'Bank Transfer']
payment_method = np.random.choice(payment_methods, n_customers,
↪ p=[0.5,0.3,0.2])

satisfaction_score = (
    5 +
    (order_value / 100) * 0.5 +
    -delivery_days * 0.3 +
    -customer_service_calls * 0.8 +
    (shipping_method == 'Express').astype(int) * 0.5 +
    (shipping_method == 'Overnight').astype(int) * 1.0 +
    np.random.normal(0, 1, n_customers)
)
satisfaction_score = np.clip(satisfaction_score, 1, 10)

customer_data = pd.DataFrame({
    'age': age,
    'order_value': order_value,
```

```
    'delivery_days': delivery_days,
    'num_items': num_items,
    'customer_service_calls': customer_service_calls,
    'shipping_method': shipping_method,
    'product_category': product_category,
    'payment_method': payment_method,
    'satisfaction_score': satisfaction_score
})

print(f"Dataset created with {len(customer_data)} customers")
print(customer_data.head(10))
```

2.12.3.1 Lab 2B Questions

1. How many customers are in the dataset?
2. What is the average satisfaction score for all customers?
3. Which shipping method is the most common?
4. Which product category appears most frequently?
5. Build a basic Linear Regression model using the numerical features (age, order_value, delivery_days, num_items, customer_service_calls) to predict satisfaction_score. What is the R^2 score?
6. Which feature has the largest positive effect on satisfaction in your basic model?
7. Which feature has the largest negative effect on satisfaction in your basic model?
8. What does the RMSE of your basic model tell you about prediction accuracy?
9. Create a new feature value_per_item as order_value / num_items. What is the average value per item?
10. Create a fast_delivery indicator (1 if delivery_days ≤ 2, else 0). What percentage of customers received fast delivery?
11. Create an indicator had_service_issues (1 if customer_service_calls > 0, else 0). What percentage of customers had service issues?
12. Convert age into categories: Young (≤30), Middle (31–50), Senior (51+). Which age group is most common?
13. One-hot encode the categorical features (shipping_method, product_category, payment_method). How many new features are added for each categorical variable?

14. Use a Random Forest to determine the top 10 most important features for predicting satisfaction. Are any of your engineered features (e.g., fast_delivery, value_per_item) in the top 10?

15. Build improved Linear Regression and Random Forest models using your selected top features. Which model performs best, and how much did your R^2 and RMSE improve compared to the basic model?

2.13 Conclusion

This exploration of predictive modeling has introduced you to the fundamental concepts that power most business applications of machine learning. We've seen what models actually are, how regression and classification solve different types of problems, and how optimization and tuning can improve performance.

The key insight to remember is that successful predictive modeling starts with understanding your business problem clearly. Are you trying to predict a specific number (regression) or assign something to a category (classification)? Do you need to optimize decisions in real-time or make one-time predictions? Understanding these fundamentals helps you choose the right approach and avoid common mistakes.

As machine learning tools become more automated and accessible, the technical barriers to building models continue to decrease. However, the need for human judgment in framing problems, interpreting results, and ensuring ethical outcomes remains crucial. The most successful practitioners combine technical tools with domain expertise and business understanding.

Remember that the best model isn't necessarily the most accurate one—it's the one that provides actionable insights, operates reliably in production, and helps people make better decisions. As you develop your skills in predictive modeling, always keep the end goal in mind: using data and algorithms to solve real problems and create positive outcomes.

The techniques you've learned here—from basic regression and classification to simple optimization and interpretation—serve as building blocks for more advanced applications. In the next module, we'll explore how these same principles apply to understanding and generating human language through natural language processing.

2.14 References

[1] Amazon Web Services. (2025). Introduction to Machine Learning: Predictive Analytics for Business. https://aws.amazon.com/machine-learning/

[2] Netflix Technology Blog. (2025). How Recommendation Systems Work: A Beginner's Guide. https://netflixtechblog.com/

[3] Spotify Engineering. (2025). Music Recommendations Made Simple: From Data to Discovery. https://engineering.atspotify.com/

[4] Uber Engineering. (2025). Optimization in Transportation: Making Real-Time Decisions. https://eng.uber.com/

Chapter 3

Model Evaluation and Performance Metrics

3.1 Learning Outcomes

3-1: Understand different ways to measure model performance and choose the right metrics for different business problems

3-2: Explain what over fitting means and how cross-validation helps create more reliable models

3-3: Recognize when models might be biased or unfair and understand basic approaches to evaluation

3-4: Interpret common evaluation tools like confusion matrices and performance charts

3.2 Introduction

Imagine you've just built your first machine learning model to predict which customers will cancel their subscriptions. You're excited—the model seems to work great! It correctly predicts 95% of the cases in your test data. You present your results to your boss, who asks a simple question: "How do you know it's actually good?"

This question might seem obvious, but it reveals one of the most critical aspects of machine learning that beginners often overlook. Building a model is only half the battle—the other half is figuring out whether it actually works well enough to trust with real business decisions. After all, a model that seems accurate in testing but fails in the real world can cost companies millions of dollars and damage customer relationships.

Consider what happened to a major retailer that built a model to predict product demand. In testing, the model achieved 90% accuracy, so they deployed it to manage inventory for the holiday season. But the model had a hidden flaw—it was terrible at predicting demand for new products, which made up 30% of their holiday inventory. The result? Massive overstocking of some items and shortages of others, leading to millions in losses.

This module will teach you how to properly evaluate machine learning models so you can avoid these costly mistakes. We'll explore the different ways to measure model performance, understand why simple accuracy isn't always enough, and learn how to spot problems before they cause real-world failures. Most importantly, we'll cover these concepts in a way that makes sense even if you've never built a model before.

3.3 Why Model Evaluation Matters More Than You Think

Before diving into specific evaluation techniques, let's understand why this topic is so crucial. When you build a machine learning model, you're essentially creating a system that will make thousands or millions of decisions automatically. Each of these decisions has consequences—approving or denying loans, recommending products, flagging security threats, or routing customer service calls.

3.3.1 The High Cost of Bad Models

Poor model evaluation leads to expensive failures across industries. A healthcare AI system that seemed highly accurate in testing was deployed to help diagnose skin cancer. However, the evaluation missed a critical flaw—the model had learned to associate rulers and measurement marks in photos with malignant cases, since dermatologists often photograph concerning moles with rulers for scale. When used on photos without rulers, the model's performance plummeted.

A hiring algorithm at a major tech company showed excellent performance in initial testing, correctly predicting successful hires 85% of the time. But deeper evaluation revealed the model was systematically discriminating against women and minorities, having learned biased patterns from historical hiring data. The company had to scrap the system and face significant legal and reputational consequences.

These examples illustrate why thorough evaluation is essential. It's not enough for a model to perform well on test data—it needs to work reliably in real-world conditions, treat all users fairly, and make the right kinds of mistakes when it does fail.

3.3.2 What Makes Evaluation Challenging

Evaluating machine learning models is more complex than it might initially appear. Unlike traditional software, where you can test specific functions with known inputs and outputs, machine learning models make probabilistic predictions about uncertain outcomes. A model might be right 90% of the time, but which 10% will it get wrong, and how costly will those mistakes be?

Additionally, the real world is constantly changing. A model that works perfectly today might gradually become less accurate as customer behavior evolves, market conditions shift, or new competitors emerge. Effective evaluation must account for these dynamic conditions and help you detect when model performance is degrading.

3.4 Understanding Performance Metrics: Beyond Simple Accuracy

When most people think about measuring model performance, they start with accuracy—what percentage of predictions are correct? While accuracy is important, it's often not the most useful metric for business applications. Different types of mistakes have different costs, and understanding these trade-offs is crucial for building effective systems.

3.4.1 Why Accuracy Can Be Misleading

Let's explore why accuracy alone can be misleading through a concrete example. Suppose you're building a model to detect credit card fraud. In your dataset, 99% of transactions are legitimate and only 1% are fraudulent. If you built a model that simply predicted "not fraud" for every transaction, it would achieve 99% accuracy—but it would be completely useless because it would never catch any actual fraud.

This example illustrates a fundamental problem with accuracy as a metric: it doesn't account for class imbalance. When one outcome is much more common than another, accuracy can be misleadingly high even when the model fails at its primary purpose.

3.4.2 Precision and Recall: Understanding Different Types of Mistakes

To address the limitations of accuracy, we need metrics that distinguish between different types of mistakes. Precision and recall provide this nuanced view of model performance by focusing on how well the model performs for the cases you care most about.

3.4.2.1 Precision: When You Predict Something, How Often Are You Right?

Precision measures what percentage of positive predictions are actually correct. In fraud detection, precision answers the question: "Of all the transactions you flagged as fraudulent, how many were actually fraud?" High precision means that when your model raises an alarm, it's usually right.

Why does precision matter? Because false alarms are costly. Every transaction flagged as fraudulent requires manual review, potentially delays the customer's purchase, and might frustrate legitimate customers. A model with low precision creates too much work for fraud analysts and provides a poor customer experience.

Consider two fraud detection models: - Model A flags 1,000 transactions as fraud, and 800 of them are actually fraudulent (80% precision) - Model B flags 500 transactions as fraud, and 450 of them are actually fraudulent (90% precision)

Model B has higher precision, meaning fraud analysts can trust its alerts more and spend less time investigating false alarms.

3.4.2.2 Recall: Of All the Actual Cases, How Many Did You Find?

Recall measures what percentage of actual positive cases the model successfully identifies. In fraud detection, recall answers: "Of all the fraudulent transactions that occurred, how many did you catch?" High recall means your model doesn't miss many important cases.

Why does recall matter? Because missed fraud is expensive. Every fraudulent transaction that goes undetected represents direct financial loss, potential regulatory penalties, and damage to customer trust. A model with low recall fails at its primary purpose of protecting the business and its customers.

Using the same fraud detection example: - Model A catches 800 out of 1,000 actual fraudulent transactions (80% recall) - Model B catches 450 out of 1,000 actual fraudulent transactions (45% recall)

Model A has higher recall, meaning it provides better protection against fraud losses, even though it generates more false alarms.

3.4.2.3 The Precision-Recall Trade-off

In most real-world applications, there's a trade-off between precision and recall. You can usually improve one by accepting worse performance on the other. A fraud detection system can catch more fraud (higher recall) by being more aggressive in flagging transactions, but this will also increase false alarms (lower precision).

The optimal balance depends on your business priorities. A bank might prefer higher recall to minimize fraud losses, accepting the cost of investigating more false alarms. An e-commerce site might prefer higher precision to avoid frustrating customers with unnecessary transaction delays.

3.4.3 The F1 Score: Balancing Precision and Recall

The F1 score provides a single metric that balances precision and recall by calculating their harmonic mean. This metric is useful when you want to optimize for both precision and recall simultaneously, or when you need a single number to compare different models.

The F1 score ranges from 0 to 1, with 1 being perfect performance. A model with 80% precision and 80% recall would have an F1 score of 0.8. If precision and recall are very different—say 95% precision but only 30% recall—the F1 score would be much lower (around 0.46), reflecting the imbalanced performance.

F1 scores are particularly useful when comparing models or when you need to make trade-offs between different approaches. However, remember that the F1 score gives equal weight to precision and recall, which might not match your business priorities.

3.4.4 Understanding ROC Curves and AUC

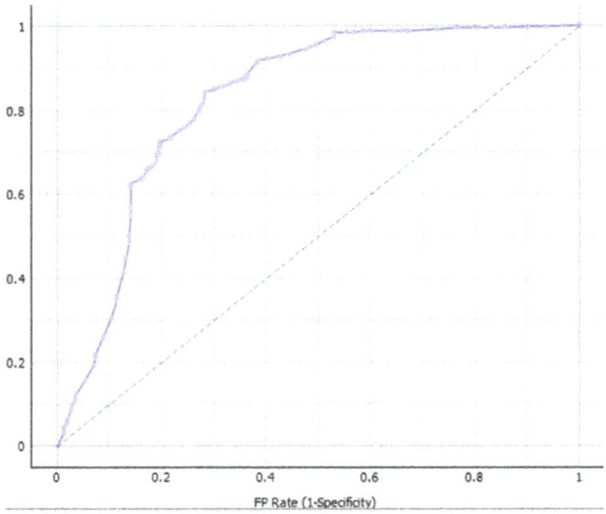

ROC (Receiver Operating Characteristic) curves provide a visual way to understand how well a model distinguishes between different classes across various decision thresholds. The AUC (Area Under the Curve) summarizes this performance in a single number.

3.4.4.1 What ROC Curves Show

A ROC curve plots the true positive rate (recall) against the false positive rate at different classification thresholds. Think of it as showing how the trade-off between catching real cases and avoiding false alarms changes as you adjust how aggressive your model is.

An ideal model would have a ROC curve that goes straight up the left side and then straight across the top, indicating perfect performance. A random model would show a diagonal line from bottom-left to top-right. Real models fall somewhere in between, with curves closer to the ideal indicating better performance.

3.4.4.2 Interpreting AUC Scores

The AUC score ranges from 0 to 1, with 0.5 representing random performance and 1.0 representing perfect performance. In practice: - AUC above 0.9 indicates excellent performance - AUC between 0.8 and 0.9 indicates good performance
- AUC between 0.7 and 0.8 indicates fair performance - AUC below 0.7 suggests the model may not be useful

AUC is particularly valuable because it's threshold-independent—it measures how well the model ranks cases rather than requiring you to choose a specific decision threshold. This makes it useful for comparing different models or algorithms.

3.4.5 Confusion Matrices: Seeing All Types of Mistakes

	Predicted class A	**Predicted class B**
Actual class A	True positive (TP)	False negative (FN)
Actual class B	False positive (FP)	True negative (TN)

A confusion matrix provides a detailed breakdown of all the different types of correct and incorrect predictions your model makes. For a binary classification problem (like fraud detection), the confusion matrix shows four categories:

- True Positives: Correctly identified fraud cases
- True Negatives: Correctly identified legitimate transactions
- False Positives: Legitimate transactions incorrectly flagged as fraud
- False Negatives: Fraudulent transactions that weren't detected

This breakdown helps you understand not just how often your model is wrong, but what kinds of mistakes it makes. You can then decide whether these mistake patterns are acceptable for your business needs.

For multi-class problems (like categorizing customer support tickets), confusion matrices become larger but provide the same detailed view of where the model succeeds and fails. You might discover that your model is excellent at distinguishing between billing and technical support issues but struggles to separate sales inquiries from general questions.

3.5 Cross-Validation and Overfitting: Building Reliable Models

One of the biggest challenges in machine learning is ensuring that your model will perform well on new data it hasn't seen before. This section explores overfitting—one of the most common reasons models fail in production—and cross-validation, the primary technique for detecting and preventing this problem.

3.5.1 Understanding Overfitting Through Analogy

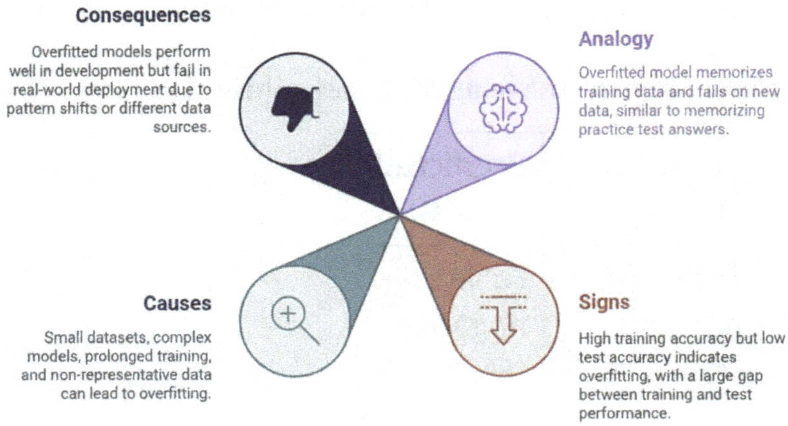

Imagine you're studying for a test by memorizing the answers to practice questions. If the actual test contains the exact same questions, you'll do great. But if the test has new questions that require understanding the underlying concepts, you'll struggle because you memorized specific answers rather than learning general principles.

Overfitting in machine learning works similarly. An overfitted model memorizes the specific examples in the training data rather than learning general patterns that apply to new situations. It performs excellently on training data but poorly on new data.

3.5.1.1 Signs of Overfitting

Overfitting typically shows a large gap between training performance and test performance. If your model achieves 95% accuracy on training data but only 70% accuracy on test data, it's likely overfitted. The model has learned to exploit specific quirks in the training data that don't generalize to new examples.

Overfitting is more likely to occur when the dataset is small relative to the complexity of the model, making it easy for the model to memorize the training examples rather than generalize. It is also more common when the model has many parameters, such as in deep neural networks, because the increased flexibility allows it to fit noise in the data. Training for too long without proper validation can further exacerbate overfitting, as the model continues to adjust to idiosyncrasies in the training set. Additionally, overfitting can arise when the training data isn't representative of real-world conditions, causing the model to perform well on the training data but poorly on unseen data.

3.5.1.2 Real-World Consequences of Overfitting

Overfitting leads to models that seem promising in development but fail when deployed. A retail company built a demand forecasting model that achieved excellent accuracy on historical sales data. However, the model had overfitted to specific seasonal patterns from previous years and failed to adapt when consumer preferences shifted due to economic changes.

Similarly, a medical diagnostic model showed outstanding performance on training data from one hospital but performed poorly when tested at different hospitals. The model had learned to recognize specific equipment signatures, lighting conditions, and image processing artifacts rather than actual medical indicators.

3.5.2 Cross-Validation: Testing Model Reliability

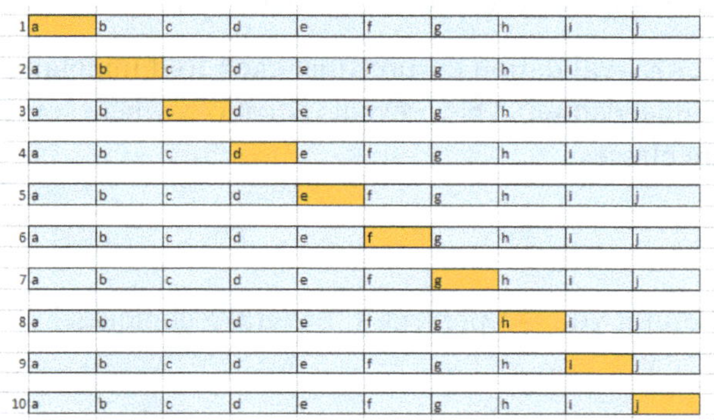

Cross-validation provides a systematic way to test how well your model generalizes to new data. Instead of using a single train-test split, cross-validation tests the model multiple times on different subsets of data, providing a more robust estimate of real-world performance.

3.5.2.1 How Cross Validation Works

The most common approach is k-fold cross-validation. Here's how it works:

1. Divide your dataset into k equal parts (typically 5 or 10)
2. Train the model on k-1 parts and test on the remaining part
3. Repeat this process k times, using a different part for testing each time
4. Average performance across all k tests

This process gives you different performance estimates, allowing you to see both the average performance and how much it varies across different data subsets. High variance in performance across folds often indicates overfitting or data quality issues.

3.5.2.2 Benefits of Cross-Validation

Cross-validation offers several advantages compared to a simple train-test split. By testing the model on multiple subsets of the data, it provides more reliable estimates of how the model is likely to perform on new, unseen data. It also helps detect overfitting, as large differences between training and validation performance across the folds can reveal when a model is memorizing the training data rather than learning general patterns.

Cross-validation supports robust model comparison, allowing different algorithms or hyperparameter settings to be evaluated more reliably than with a single test score. Additionally, it makes efficient use of the dataset, since every example is used for both training and testing, maximizing the value of the available data.

3.5.2.3 Practical Considerations

While cross-validation is powerful, it requires careful implementation. For time series data, you can't randomly split the data because future information would leak into training. Instead, you need time-aware splits that respect temporal ordering.

For imbalanced datasets, stratified cross-validation ensures that each fold maintains the same class distribution as the original dataset. This prevents situations where some folds have very few examples of rare classes.

3.5.3 Preventing Overfitting

Understanding overfitting is only useful if you can prevent it. Several techniques help build models that generalize well:

3.5.3.1 Regularization

Regularization techniques add constraints to model training that prevent overfitting. Think of regularization as encouraging the model to find simple, generalizable patterns rather than complex, specific ones. Common regularization approaches include limiting model complexity, adding penalties for large parameters, or stopping training early when validation performance stops improving.

3.5.3.2 Data Augmentation

Increasing the size and diversity of your training data helps prevent overfitting by giving the model more examples to learn from. This might involve collecting more data, but it can also involve creating variations of existing data through techniques like adding noise, rotating images, or paraphrasing text.

3.5.3.3 Ensemble Methods

Ensemble methods combine multiple models to create more robust predictions. Since different models tend to overfit in different ways, combining their predictions often results in better generalization. Random forests and gradient boosting are popular ensemble approaches that naturally resist overfitting.

3.6 Bias and Fairness in Machine Learning Systems

As machine learning systems increasingly influence important decisions about people's lives, ensuring these systems are fair and unbiased has become crucial. This section introduces the basic concepts of bias in machine learning and approaches for detecting and addressing fairness issues.

3.6.1 Understanding Bias in Machine Learning

Bias in machine learning refers to systematic errors or unfairness in model predictions that disadvantage certain groups of people. Unlike statistical bias, which refers to systematic errors in measurement, algorithmic bias specifically concerns unfair treatment of different demographic groups.

3.6.1.1 Sources of Bias

Bias can enter machine learning systems through several pathways, each with distinct implications for fairness and model reliability.

Historical bias arises when training data reflects patterns of past discrimination or unfair practices. For example, if a hiring dataset contains records from a time when certain demographic groups were systematically excluded from technical roles, a model trained on this data may learn and replicate those exclusionary patterns. This perpetuates inequality, even if the model itself is technically accurate according to the data it was given.

Representation bias occurs when the training data fails to adequately represent all the groups the model is intended to serve. A common example is facial recognition systems trained predominantly on images of light-skinned individuals. These models often perform poorly when applied to people with darker skin tones, leading to misidentification and unequal treatment. The lack of diverse representation in the data undermines the model's generalizability and fairness.

Measurement bias stems from inconsistencies in data collected across different groups. For instance, if credit scores are calculated using different criteria in different regions, a model that uses these scores may inadvertently favor or penalize individuals based on where they live. This type of bias can embed systemic inequalities into automated decisions, affecting access to loans, insurance, or other critical services.

Together, these biases highlight the importance of critically evaluating data sources and model behavior to ensure equitable outcomes across all populations.

3.6.1.2 Real-World Examples of Algorithmic Bias

Several high-profile cases have highlighted the importance of bias detection:

A criminal justice risk assessment tool was found to incorrectly flag Black defendants as high-risk at nearly twice the rate of white defendants, while incorrectly flagging white defendants as low-risk more often than Black defendants.

A hiring algorithm used by a major tech company showed bias against women, having learned from historical hiring data that predominantly favored male candidates for technical positions.

Healthcare algorithms used to allocate care resources were found to systematically underestimate the healthcare needs of Black patients, leading to reduced access to specialized care programs.

3.6.2 Detecting Bias and Measuring Fairness

Detecting bias requires systematic evaluation of model performance across different demographic groups. This involves more than just checking overall accuracy—you need to examine whether the model treats different groups fairly.

3.6.2.1 Fairness Metrics

Several metrics help evaluate fairness in predictive models. Demographic parity focuses on ensuring that positive predictions occur at similar rates across different groups; for example, loan approval rates should be comparable across racial groups. Equalized odds emphasize that both true positive and false positive rates are similar across groups, meaning a medical diagnostic model should detect disease with similar accuracy for all demographic groups. Individual fairness, on the other hand, requires that similar individuals receive similar predictions regardless of their group membership, so two loan applicants with comparable financial profiles should have similar probabilities of approval.

3.6.2.2 Challenges in Fairness Evaluation

Measuring fairness is complicated because different fairness criteria can conflict with each other. A model might achieve demographic parity but violate equalized odds, or vice versa. Additionally, improving fairness often requires trade-offs with overall accuracy.

The choice of fairness criteria depends on the specific application and stakeholder values. Legal requirements, ethical considerations, and business objectives all influence which fairness measures are most appropriate.

3.6.3 Approaches to Bias Mitigation

Once bias is detected, several approaches can help address it:

3.6.3.1 Pre-processing Approaches

Pre-processing techniques modify training data to reduce bias before model training. This might involve reweighting examples to ensure balanced representation, removing biased features, or generating synthetic data to improve representation of underrepresented groups.

3.6.3.2 In-processing Approaches

In-processing techniques modify the training algorithm itself to optimize for fairness alongside accuracy. This might involve adding fairness constraints to the optimization objective or using adversarial training to remove demographic information from learned representations.

3.6.3.3 Post-processing Approaches

Post-processing techniques adjust model outputs to improve fairness without retraining the model. This might involve adjusting decision thresholds for different groups or calibrating probability outputs to ensure fair treatment.

3.6.3.4 Ongoing Monitoring

Bias mitigation isn't a one-time fix—it requires ongoing monitoring as data and conditions change. Regular audits should check whether fairness metrics remain acceptable and whether new sources of bias have emerged.

3.7 Building Reliable Evaluation Practices

This exploration of model evaluation has introduced the fundamental concepts needed to assess whether machine learning models are ready for real-world deployment. We've seen why simple accuracy is often insufficient, explored metrics that capture different types of performance, and examined techniques for ensuring models generalize well and treat users fairly.

3.7.1 Key Principles for Effective Evaluation

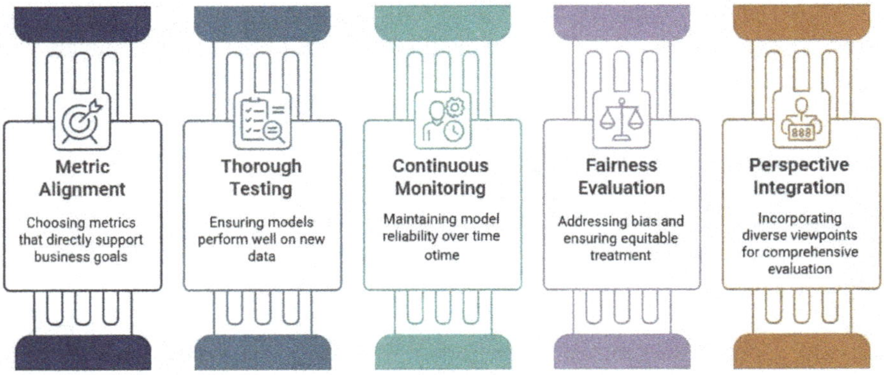

Successful model evaluation follows several key principles. First, it is important to match metrics to business objectives by choosing evaluation measures that align with specific goals and the costs associated with different types of mistakes. This ensures that the model's performance is meaningful in the context of real-world decisions.

Thorough testing before deployment is also essential. Techniques such as cross-validation and holdout testing help verify that models will perform well on new, unseen data, reducing the risk of unexpected errors after implementation. Continuous monitoring is equally important, as model performance can degrade over time due to changing data patterns or external factors, so ongoing evaluation helps maintain reliable systems.

Evaluating fairness systematically is another critical principle. Models should be checked to ensure they treat different groups fairly, and any potential biases should be addressed prior to deployment. Finally, considering multiple perspectives strengthens evaluation efforts. Involving domain experts, stakeholders, and affected communities can reveal potential issues that purely technical metrics might overlook, leading to more robust and responsible model deployment.

3.7.2 The Importance of Human Judgment

While automated evaluation metrics are essential, they can't replace human judgment in assessing whether models are ready for deployment. Technical performance metrics tell you how well a model performs on specific tasks, but they don't capture broader considerations like user experience, ethical implications, or business strategy alignment.

The most successful machine learning deployments combine rigorous technical evaluation with careful consideration of human factors, business objectives, and societal impact. As you develop your skills in model evaluation, remember that the goal isn't just to build accurate models—it's to build systems that create positive value while minimizing harmful consequences.

3.8 Key Terms

Model Evaluation – The process of assessing how well a machine learning model performs on new, unseen data.

Accuracy – The percentage of total predictions that the model gets correct.

Precision – The proportion of positive predictions that are actually correct.

Recall (Sensitivity) – The proportion of actual positive cases that the model correctly identifies.

F1 Score – The harmonic mean of precision and recall, balancing both metrics in a single number.

ROC Curve (Receiver Operating Characteristic Curve) – A plot of true positive rate vs. false positive rate at different thresholds.

AUC (Area Under the Curve) – A single-number summary of the ROC curve; measures overall ability to distinguish classes.

Confusion Matrix – A table showing true positives, true negatives, false positives, and false negatives.

True Positive (TP) – Correctly predicted positive cases.

True Negative (TN) – Correctly predicted negative cases.

False Positive (FP) – Negative cases incorrectly predicted as positive.

False Negative (FN) – Positive cases incorrectly predicted as negative.

Overfitting – When a model memorizes training data patterns and fails to generalize to new data.

Underfitting – When a model is too simple to capture patterns in the data, performing poorly on both training and test data.

Cross-Validation – A method to assess model reliability by training and testing on multiple subsets of the data.

K-Fold Cross-Validation – Dividing data into k subsets; training on k-1 folds and testing on the remaining fold, repeated k times.

Regularization – Techniques that constrain model complexity to prevent overfitting.

Data Augmentation – Expanding training data with variations to improve model generalization.

Ensemble Methods – Combining multiple models to create more accurate and robust predictions.

Bias in Machine Learning – Systematic errors in model predictions that unfairly disadvantage certain groups.

Historical Bias – Bias arising from past discriminatory practices reflected in training data.

Representation Bias – Bias due to underrepresentation of certain groups in the training data.

Measurement Bias – Bias caused by inconsistencies in how data is collected across groups.

Fairness Metrics – Measures that evaluate whether a model treats different groups equitably (e.g., demographic parity, equalized odds, individual fairness).

Pre-processing Bias Mitigation – Adjusting training data to reduce bias before model training.

In-processing Bias Mitigation – Modifying the training algorithm to optimize fairness along with accuracy.

Post-processing Bias Mitigation – Adjusting model outputs to improve fairness after training.

3.9 Review Questions

1. Why is model evaluation critical, even if a model shows high accuracy on test data?
2. Explain why accuracy alone can be misleading, particularly for imbalanced datasets.
3. Define precision, recall, and the F1 score. Why might a business prioritize one over the others?
4. How does a ROC curve help in evaluating model performance? What does the AUC indicate?
5. Describe the four components of a confusion matrix and give an example of each.
6. What is overfitting, and what are common signs that a model is overfitting?
7. How does cross-validation help detect and prevent overfitting?

8. Explain the difference between k-fold cross-validation and a simple train-test split.
9. What are some techniques to prevent overfitting? Provide examples.
10. Define bias in machine learning and explain how historical, representation, and measurement bias can arise.
11. Give real-world examples where algorithmic bias caused negative outcomes.
12. What are some approaches to mitigate bias before, during, and after model training?
13. Why is continuous monitoring important for deployed machine learning models?
14. How should fairness considerations influence the choice of evaluation metrics?
15. Why is human judgment still necessary even when automated evaluation metrics are used?

3.10 Lab 3A: Model Evaluation and Validation

3.10.1 Introduction

Imagine you're a data scientist at a bank, and you've just built a machine learning model to detect credit card fraud. Your boss asks you a simple question: "How good is this model?" You might say "It's 95% accurate!" But then your boss asks follow-up questions that make you realize accuracy alone isn't enough:

- "What happens when it misses actual fraud cases?"
- "How many legitimate transactions does it incorrectly flag as fraud?"
- "Will this model work just as well on new data we haven't seen yet?"
- "How does this compare to our current fraud detection system?"

These questions highlight why proper model evaluation is crucial in data analytics. A model that looks great on paper might be terrible in real-world use if we don't evaluate it correctly.

In business, the cost of wrong predictions can be enormous. A medical diagnosis model that misses cancer cases could cost lives. A loan approval model that's biased could lead to lawsuits. A recommendation system that doesn't work on new customers could lose millions in revenue.

This lab teaches you how to thoroughly evaluate your models using industry-standard techniques. You'll learn to look beyond simple accuracy and understand the full picture of how your models perform. These skills are essential for any data analyst who wants to build trustworthy, reliable machine learning systems.

3.10.2 Demonstration

We'll work with a telecommunications company dataset to predict customer churn (when customers cancel their service). This is a common business problem where proper evaluation is critical - incorrectly predicting churn can waste marketing budget or lose valuable customers.

3.10.2.1 Step 1: Setting Up and Creating Our Dataset

```
# Import required libraries
import pandas as pd
import numpy as np
import matplotlib.pyplot as plt
import seaborn as sns
from sklearn.model_selection import train_test_split, cross_val_score,
    validation_curve
from sklearn.linear_model import LogisticRegression
from sklearn.tree import DecisionTreeClassifier
from sklearn.ensemble import RandomForestClassifier
from sklearn.metrics import (accuracy_score, precision_score,
    recall_score, f1_score,
    confusion_matrix, classification_report, roc_curve, auc,
    roc_auc_score)
import warnings
warnings.filterwarnings('ignore')

# Set random seed for reproducibility
np.random.seed(42)

print("="*60)
print("LAB 3: MODEL EVALUATION AND VALIDATION")
print("="*60)

# Create customer churn dataset
n_customers = 2000

print("\nCreating Customer Churn Dataset...")
print("=" * 40)

# Customer demographics
age = np.random.normal(45, 15, n_customers)
age = np.clip(age, 18, 80)

monthly_charges = np.random.normal(65, 25, n_customers)
```

```
monthly_charges = np.clip(monthly_charges, 20, 150)

tenure_months = np.random.exponential(24, n_customers)
tenure_months = np.clip(tenure_months, 1, 72)

# Service features
num_services = np.random.poisson(3, n_customers)
num_services = np.clip(num_services, 1, 8)

support_calls = np.random.poisson(1.5, n_customers)
support_calls = np.clip(support_calls, 0, 10)

# Contract types
contract_types = ['Month-to-month', 'One year', 'Two year']
contract_type = np.random.choice(contract_types, n_customers, p=[0.5,
 ↪  0.3, 0.2])

# Payment methods
payment_methods = ['Electronic check', 'Credit card', 'Bank transfer',
 ↪  'Mailed check']
payment_method = np.random.choice(payment_methods, n_customers, p=[0.4,
 ↪  0.3, 0.2, 0.1])

# Calculate churn probability based on realistic factors
churn_probability = (
    0.1 +  # Base churn rate
    (monthly_charges - 20) / 130 * 0.3 +  # Higher charges = more
 ↪  likely to churn
    np.maximum(0, (5 - tenure_months)) / 5 * 0.4 +  # New customers
 ↪  more likely to churn
    (support_calls / 10) * 0.3 +  # More support calls = more likely to
 ↪  churn
    (contract_type == 'Month-to-month').astype(int) * 0.2 +  #
 ↪  Month-to-month more likely to churn
    (age < 30).astype(int) * 0.1 +  # Younger customers more likely to
 ↪  churn
    np.random.normal(0, 0.1, n_customers)  # Add randomness
)

churn_probability = np.clip(churn_probability, 0, 1)
churned = np.random.binomial(1, churn_probability, n_customers)

# Create DataFrame
```

```
churn_data = pd.DataFrame({
    'age': age,
    'monthly_charges': monthly_charges,
    'tenure_months': tenure_months,
    'num_services': num_services,
    'support_calls': support_calls,
    'contract_type': contract_type,
    'payment_method': payment_method,
    'churned': churned
})

print(f"Dataset created with {len(churn_data)} customers")
print(f"Churn rate: {churn_data['churned'].mean()*100:.1f}%")
print("\nFirst 10 customers:")
print(churn_data.head(10))
print("\nDataset Summary:")
print(churn_data.describe())
```

Output:

```
============================================================
LAB 3: MODEL EVALUATION AND VALIDATION
============================================================

Creating Customer Churn Dataset...
========================================
Dataset created with 2000 customers
Churn rate: 38.5%

First 10 customers:
         age  monthly_charges  ...    payment_method  churned
0  52.450712        48.120543  ...  Electronic check        0
1  42.926035        61.387033  ...      Mailed check        0
2  54.715328        45.189502  ...     Bank transfer        0
3  67.845448        57.300962  ...     Bank transfer        0
4  41.487699        20.000000  ...  Electronic check        0
5  41.487946        70.332343  ...      Mailed check        0
6  68.688192        65.030137  ...     Bank transfer        0
7  56.511521        44.572784  ...     Bank transfer        1
8  37.957884        81.481142  ...  Electronic check        0
9  53.138401        88.439253  ...  Electronic check        1

[10 rows x 8 columns]
```

```
Dataset Summary:
               age  monthly_charges  ...  support_calls      churned
count  2000.000000      2000.000000  ...    2000.000000  2000.000000
mean     45.798295        65.184101  ...       1.574000     0.385000
std      14.275896        24.359951  ...       1.263456     0.486717
min      18.000000        20.000000  ...       0.000000     0.000000
25%      35.660071        47.271851  ...       1.000000     0.000000
50%      45.670375        64.998667  ...       1.000000     0.000000
75%      55.244664        81.638592  ...       2.000000     1.000000
max      80.000000       150.000000  ...       7.000000     1.000000

[8 rows x 6 columns]
```

3.10.2.2 Step 2: Preparing Data and Building Basic Models

In this step, we move from simply exploring the data to actually preparing it for machine learning and building predictive models. The goal is to predict whether a customer will churn based on their characteristics and behavior.

We begin by preparing the data so that it can be used in machine learning algorithms. Some of the variables in the dataset, such as contract type and payment method, are categorical (text-based). Since most machine learning models require numerical input, these categories are converted into numeric form using a process called one-hot encoding. This creates new binary (0/1) columns for each category, allowing the model to interpret them properly.

```
print("\n" + "="*50)
print("STEP 2: PREPARING DATA AND BUILDING MODELS")
print("="*50)

# Prepare features for modeling
# Convert categorical variables to numbers
contract_encoded = pd.get_dummies(churn_data['contract_type'],
↪ prefix='contract')
payment_encoded = pd.get_dummies(churn_data['payment_method'],
↪ prefix='payment')
```

Next, we combine these newly created variables with the existing numerical features, such as age, monthly charges, tenure, number of services, and number of support calls. Together, these form the complete set of input features used to make predictions. The variable that we want to predict—whether the customer churned—becomes the target.

```
# Combine all features
features = pd.concat([
    churn_data[['age', 'monthly_charges', 'tenure_months',
↪ 'num_services', 'support_calls']],
```

```
    contract_encoded,
    payment_encoded
], axis=1)

target = churn_data['churned']

print(f"Features prepared: {features.shape[1]} total features")
print(f"Feature names: {list(features.columns)}")
```

Output:

```
==================================================
STEP 2: PREPARING DATA AND BUILDING MODELS
==================================================
Features prepared: 12 total features
Feature names: ['age', 'monthly_charges', 'tenure_months', 'num_services',
'support_calls','contract_Month-to-month', 'contract_One year',
'contract_Two year', 'payment_Bank transfer',
'payment_Credit card', 'payment_Electronic check', 'payment_Mailed check']
```

After preparing the dataset, we split it into two parts: a training set and a testing set. The training set (80% of the data) is used to teach the models patterns in the data, while the testing set (20%) is used to evaluate how well the models perform on new, unseen data. We also ensure that the proportion of churned vs. non-churned customers remains consistent across both sets using a technique called stratification. This helps produce fair and reliable results.

```
# Split data into training and testing sets
X_train, X_test, y_train, y_test = train_test_split(
    features, target, test_size=0.2, random_state=42, stratify=target
)

print(f"\nData split:")
print(f"Training set: {len(X_train)} customers")
print(f"Testing set: {len(X_test)} customers")
print(f"Training churn rate: {y_train.mean()*100:.1f}%")
print(f"Testing churn rate: {y_test.mean()*100:.1f}%")
```

Output:

```
Data split:
Training set: 1600 customers
Testing set: 400 customers
Training churn rate: 38.5%
Testing churn rate: 38.5%
```

With the data ready, we build three different machine learning models:

- **Logistic Regression**: A statistical model that estimates the probability of churn. It is simple, interpretable, and often performs well as a baseline model.
- **Decision Tree**: A model that makes decisions by splitting the data into branches based on feature values. It is easy to visualize and understand but can sometimes overfit if not controlled.
- **Random Forest**: An advanced model that builds many decision trees and combines their results. This typically improves accuracy and reduces overfitting compared to a single tree.

Each model is trained using the training dataset. After training, the models are used to make predictions on the testing dataset. In addition to predicting whether a customer will churn, the models also generate probabilities, which indicate how confident the model is in its predictions.

```
# Build three different models
print("\nBuilding three different models...")

# Model 1: Logistic Regression
lr_model = LogisticRegression(random_state=42, max_iter=1000)
lr_model.fit(X_train, y_train)
lr_predictions = lr_model.predict(X_test)
lr_probabilities = lr_model.predict_proba(X_test)[:, 1]

# Model 2: Decision Tree
dt_model = DecisionTreeClassifier(random_state=42, max_depth=5)
dt_model.fit(X_train, y_train)
dt_predictions = dt_model.predict(X_test)
dt_probabilities = dt_model.predict_proba(X_test)[:, 1]

# Model 3: Random Forest
rf_model = RandomForestClassifier(random_state=42, n_estimators=100,
↪  max_depth=5)
rf_model.fit(X_train, y_train)
rf_predictions = rf_model.predict(X_test)
rf_probabilities = rf_model.predict_proba(X_test)[:, 1]

print("✓ Logistic Regression trained")
print("✓ Decision Tree trained")
print("✓ Random Forest trained")
```

By the end of this step, we have successfully prepared the data and trained three different models, setting the stage for the next step: evaluating and comparing their performance.

3.10.2.3 Step 3: Understanding Confusion Matrices

Now that we have trained our models, the next step is to understand how well they are performing. Rather than just looking at overall accuracy, we use a tool called a confusion matrix to get a much deeper and more meaningful view of model performance.

A confusion matrix shows us exactly how predictions compare to actual outcomes. Instead of giving just a single score, it breaks results into four categories, allowing us to see where the model is making correct predictions and where it is making mistakes.

Each confusion matrix is organized into four parts:

- **True Negatives (TN)**: Customers who did not churn and were correctly predicted as not churning
- **False Positives (FP)**: Customers who did not churn but were incorrectly predicted as churning
- **False Negatives (FN)**: Customers who did churn but were missed by the model
- **True Positives (TP)**: Customers who did churn and were correctly identified

This breakdown is extremely important because not all errors are equal—especially in a business context. For example, a false negative (missing a customer who is about to churn) can be very costly. These are customers the company loses without taking any action. On the other hand, a false positive means the company may spend money trying to retain a customer who was not actually at risk. While wasteful, this is usually less damaging than losing a customer entirely.

```
print("\n" + "="*50)
print("STEP 3: CONFUSION MATRICES - THE FOUNDATION")
print("="*50)

print("A confusion matrix shows us exactly where our model makes
↪ mistakes.")
print("Let's look at each model's confusion matrix:\n")

# Function to create and display confusion matrix
def display_confusion_matrix(y_true, y_pred, model_name):
    cm = confusion_matrix(y_true, y_pred)

    print(f"{model_name} Confusion Matrix:")
    print("                        Predicted")
    print("                       No Churn  Churn")
    print(f"Actual No Churn     {cm[0,0]:4d}    {cm[0,1]:4d}")
    print(f"Actual Churn        {cm[1,0]:4d}    {cm[1,1]:4d}")

    # Calculate metrics from confusion matrix
    tn, fp, fn, tp = cm.ravel()
```

```
    print(f"\nBreaking this down:")
    print(f"• True Negatives (TN): {tn} - Correctly predicted NO
    ↪ churn")
    print(f"• False Positives (FP): {fp} - Incorrectly predicted
    ↪ churn")
    print(f"• False Negatives (FN): {fn} - Missed actual churn cases")
    print(f"• True Positives (TP): {tp} - Correctly predicted churn")

    print(f"\nBusiness Impact:")
    print(f"• Missed churners (FN): {fn} customers we'll lose
    ↪ unexpectedly")
    print(f"• False alarms (FP): {fp} customers we'll waste marketing
    ↪ money on")
    print("-" * 60)

# Display confusion matrices for all models
display_confusion_matrix(y_test, lr_predictions, "Logistic Regression")
display_confusion_matrix(y_test, dt_predictions, "Decision Tree")
display_confusion_matrix(y_test, rf_predictions, "Random Forest")
```

Output:

```
==================================================
STEP 3: CONFUSION MATRICES - THE FOUNDATION
==================================================
A confusion matrix shows us exactly where our model makes mistakes.
Let's look at each model's confusion matrix:

Logistic Regression Confusion Matrix:
                 Predicted
                No Churn  Churn
Actual No Churn     198     48
Actual Churn        103     51

Breaking this down:
• True Negatives (TN): 198 - Correctly predicted NO churn
• False Positives (FP): 48 - Incorrectly predicted churn
• False Negatives (FN): 103 - Missed actual churn cases
• True Positives (TP): 51 - Correctly predicted churn

Business Impact:
• Missed churners (FN): 103 customers we'll lose unexpectedly
• False alarms (FP): 48 customers we'll waste marketing money on
```

```
------------------------------------------------------------

Decision Tree Confusion Matrix:
                 Predicted
                No Churn  Churn
Actual No Churn     195     51
Actual Churn        112     42

Breaking this down:
• True Negatives (TN): 195 - Correctly predicted NO churn
• False Positives (FP): 51 - Incorrectly predicted churn
• False Negatives (FN): 112 - Missed actual churn cases
• True Positives (TP): 42 - Correctly predicted churn

Business Impact:
• Missed churners (FN): 112 customers we'll lose unexpectedly
• False alarms (FP): 51 customers we'll waste marketing money on
------------------------------------------------------------

Random Forest Confusion Matrix:
                 Predicted
                No Churn  Churn
Actual No Churn     230     16
Actual Churn        121     33

Breaking this down:
• True Negatives (TN): 230 - Correctly predicted NO churn
• False Positives (FP): 16 - Incorrectly predicted churn
• False Negatives (FN): 121 - Missed actual churn cases
• True Positives (TP): 33 - Correctly predicted churn

Business Impact:
• Missed churners (FN): 121 customers we'll lose unexpectedly
• False alarms (FP): 16 customers we'll waste marketing money on
------------------------------------------------------------
```

There is no single "best" model in this case. Logistic Regression identifies more churners (higher recall), making it better for reducing customer loss. However, Random Forest produces far fewer false positives (higher precision), making it more cost-efficient. The best choice depends on business priorities—whether the goal is to maximize retention or minimize unnecessary spending.

3.10.2.4 Step 4: Classification Metrics

After examining confusion matrices, we now take the next step in evaluating our models by calculating key classification metrics. While accuracy gives us a general sense of performance, it can often be misleading—especially in problems like customer churn, where one class (non-churners) may be much more common than the other.

To get a more complete picture, we calculate four important metrics: accuracy, precision, recall, and F1-score. Each of these tells us something different about how the model is performing.

- **Accuracy** measures the overall percentage of correct predictions. While it is easy to understand, it does not distinguish between different types of errors. A model could have high accuracy simply by predicting most customers will not churn, even if it misses many actual churners.
- **Precision** focuses on the quality of positive predictions. It answers the question: When the model predicts that a customer will churn, how often is it correct? High precision means that the model makes few false alarms, which helps avoid wasting marketing resources on customers who were not actually at risk.
- **Recall** focuses on completeness. It answers: Of all the customers who actually churned, how many did the model successfully identify? High recall is critical in churn prediction because missing a customer who is about to leave can directly result in lost revenue.
- **F1-score** provides a balance between precision and recall. It is especially useful when there is a trade-off between catching more churners (recall) and avoiding false alarms (precision). A strong F1-score indicates that the model is performing well across both dimensions.

```
print("\n" + "="*50)
print("STEP 4: CLASSIFICATION METRICS EXPLAINED")
print("="*50)

print("Accuracy alone can be misleading. Let's calculate all the
↪  important metrics:\n")

def calculate_detailed_metrics(y_true, y_pred, model_name):
    # Calculate all metrics
    accuracy = accuracy_score(y_true, y_pred)
    precision = precision_score(y_true, y_pred)
    recall = recall_score(y_true, y_pred)
    f1 = f1_score(y_true, y_pred)

    print(f"{model_name} Performance Metrics:")
    print(f"• Accuracy:  {accuracy:.3f}
```

```
        ({accuracy*100:.1f}%) - Overall correct predictions")
    print(f"• Precision: {precision:.3f}
        ({precision*100:.1f}%) - Of predicted churners,
            how many actually churned?")
    print(f"• Recall:    {recall:.3f}
        ({recall*100:.1f}%) - Of actual churners, how many did we
    ↪ catch?")
    print(f"• F1-Score:  {f1:.3f} - Balance between precision and
    ↪ recall")

    print(f"\nWhat this means for business:")
    if precision > 0.7:
        print(f"✓ Good precision: When we predict churn, we're usually
        ↪ right")
    else:
        print(f"⚠ Low precision: Many false alarms - wasting marketing
        ↪ budget")

    if recall > 0.7:
        print(f"✓ Good recall: We catch most customers who will
        ↪ actually churn")
    else:
        print(f"⚠ Low recall: We're missing many customers who will
        ↪ churn")

    if f1 > 0.7:
        print(f"✓ Good F1: Nice balance between precision and recall")
    else:
        print(f"⚠ Low F1: Need to improve either precision or recall")

    print("-" * 60)
    return accuracy, precision, recall, f1

# Calculate metrics for all models
lr_metrics = calculate_detailed_metrics(y_test, lr_predictions,
↪ "Logistic Regression")
dt_metrics = calculate_detailed_metrics(y_test, dt_predictions,
↪ "Decision Tree")
rf_metrics = calculate_detailed_metrics(y_test, rf_predictions, "Random
↪ Forest")
```

Output:

```
==================================================
```

```
STEP 4: CLASSIFICATION METRICS EXPLAINED
==================================================
Accuracy alone can be misleading.
Let's calculate all the important metrics:

Logistic Regression Performance Metrics:
• Accuracy:  0.623 (62.3%) - Overall correct predictions
• Precision: 0.515 (51.5%)
  - Of predicted churners, how many actually churned?
• Recall:    0.331 (33.1%) - Of actual churners,
                  how many did we catch?
• F1-Score:  0.403 - Balance between precision and recall

What this means for business:
⚠ Low precision: Many false alarms - wasting marketing budget
⚠ Low recall: We're missing many customers who will churn
⚠ Low F1: Need to improve either precision or recall
------------------------------------------------------------

Decision Tree Performance Metrics:
• Accuracy:  0.593 (59.2%) - Overall correct predictions
• Precision: 0.452 (45.2%)
  - Of predicted churners, how many actually churned?
• Recall:    0.273 (27.3%) - Of actual churners,
                  how many did we catch?
• F1-Score:  0.340 - Balance between precision and recall

What this means for business:
⚠ Low precision: Many false alarms - wasting marketing budget
⚠ Low recall: We're missing many customers who will churn
⚠ Low F1: Need to improve either precision or recall
------------------------------------------------------------

Random Forest Performance Metrics:
• Accuracy:  0.657 (65.8%) - Overall correct predictions
• Precision: 0.673 (67.3%)
  - Of predicted churners, how many actually churned?
• Recall:    0.214 (21.4%) - Of actual churners,
                how many did we catch?
• F1-Score:  0.325 - Balance between precision and recall

What this means for business:
⚠ Low precision: Many false alarms - wasting marketing budget
```

```
⚠ Low recall: We're missing many customers who will churn
⚠ Low F1: Need to improve either precision or recall
------------------------------------------------------------
```

```
# Create comparison table
print("\nMODEL COMPARISON TABLE:")
print("="*60)
print(f"{'Model':<20} {'Accuracy':<10} {'Precision':<10}
  {'Recall':<10} {'F1-Score':<10}")
print("-" * 60)
print(f"{'Logistic Regression':<20} {lr_metrics[0]:<10.3f}
  {lr_metrics[1]:<10.3f} {lr_metrics[2]:<10.3f}
 ↪  {lr_metrics[3]:<10.3f}")
print(f"{'Decision Tree':<20} {dt_metrics[0]:<10.3f}
 ↪  {dt_metrics[1]:<10.3f}
  {dt_metrics[2]:<10.3f} {dt_metrics[3]:<10.3f}")
print(f"{'Random Forest':<20} {rf_metrics[0]:<10.3f}
  {rf_metrics[1]:<10.3f} {rf_metrics[2]:<10.3f}
 ↪  {rf_metrics[3]:<10.3f}")
```

Output:

```
MODEL COMPARISON TABLE:
============================================================
Model                Accuracy   Precision  Recall     F1-Score
------------------------------------------------------------
Logistic Regression  0.623      0.515      0.331      0.403
Decision Tree        0.593      0.452      0.273      0.340
Random Forest        0.657      0.673      0.214      0.325
```

All three models perform poorly overall. While Random Forest achieves the highest accuracy and precision, it misses most churners, as shown by its very low recall. Logistic Regression identifies more churners than the other models, but still fails to capture the majority of them. The Decision Tree performs the weakest across nearly all metrics.

These results highlight an important lesson: building a model is only the first step. Without further improvement—such as feature engineering, parameter tuning, or better data—the model may not be useful in real-world decision-making.

3.10.2.5 Step 5: ROC Curves and AUC Scores

In this step, we move beyond individual metrics and introduce a powerful visual tool—the ROC curve (Receiver Operating Characteristic curve)—to evaluate and compare our models more comprehensively. Unlike earlier metrics that rely on a single prediction threshold, usually 0.5, ROC curves show how a model performs across all possible thresholds.

The ROC curve plots two key quantities: the True Positive Rate (TPR), also known as recall or sensitivity, which measures the proportion of actual churners correctly identified, and the False Positive Rate (FPR), which measures the proportion of non-churners incorrectly classified as churners. Each point on the curve represents a different threshold.

To summarize each ROC curve with a single number, we calculate the Area Under the Curve (AUC). The AUC represents the probability that a model will correctly distinguish between a churner and a non-churner. An AUC of 0.5 indicates performance no better than random guessing, around 0.7 is acceptable, 0.8 is considered good, and values above 0.9 are excellent.

```
print("\n" + "="*50)
print("STEP 5: ROC CURVES - VISUALIZING PERFORMANCE")
print("="*50)

print("ROC curves help us understand the trade-off between catching
 ↪  churners")
print("and avoiding false alarms at different prediction
 ↪  thresholds.\n")

# Calculate ROC curves for all models
lr_fpr, lr_tpr, _ = roc_curve(y_test, lr_probabilities)
dt_fpr, dt_tpr, _ = roc_curve(y_test, dt_probabilities)
rf_fpr, rf_tpr, _ = roc_curve(y_test, rf_probabilities)

# Calculate AUC scores
lr_auc = auc(lr_fpr, lr_tpr)
dt_auc = auc(dt_fpr, dt_tpr)
rf_auc = auc(rf_fpr, rf_tpr)

# Create ROC curve plot
plt.figure(figsize=(10, 8))
plt.plot(lr_fpr, lr_tpr, label=f'Logistic Regression (AUC =
 ↪  {lr_auc:.3f})', linewidth=2)
plt.plot(dt_fpr, dt_tpr, label=f'Decision Tree (AUC = {dt_auc:.3f})',
 ↪  linewidth=2)
plt.plot(rf_fpr, rf_tpr, label=f'Random Forest (AUC = {rf_auc:.3f})',
 ↪  linewidth=2)
plt.plot([0, 1], [0, 1], 'k--', label='Random Guessing (AUC = 0.5)',
 ↪  linewidth=1)

plt.xlabel('False Positive Rate (1 - Specificity)')
plt.ylabel('True Positive Rate (Sensitivity)')
plt.title('ROC Curves: Comparing Model Performance')
```

```
plt.legend()
plt.grid(True, alpha=0.3)
plt.show()

print("Understanding AUC Scores:")
print("• AUC = 0.5: Random guessing (no better than flipping a coin)")
print("• AUC = 0.7: Acceptable performance")
print("• AUC = 0.8: Good performance")
print("• AUC = 0.9: Excellent performance")
print("• AUC = 1.0: Perfect performance (rarely achieved in real
↪  data)")

print(f"\nOur Model AUC Scores:")
print(f"• Logistic Regression: {lr_auc:.3f}")
print(f"• Decision Tree: {dt_auc:.3f}")
print(f"• Random Forest: {rf_auc:.3f}")

# Determine best model based on AUC
best_auc = max(lr_auc, dt_auc, rf_auc)
if best_auc == lr_auc:
    best_model_name = "Logistic Regression"
elif best_auc == dt_auc:
    best_model_name = "Decision Tree"
else:
    best_model_name = "Random Forest"

print(f"\nBest model by AUC: {best_model_name} (AUC = {best_auc:.3f})")
```

Output:

```
==================================================
STEP 5: ROC CURVES - VISUALIZING PERFORMANCE
==================================================
ROC curves help us understand the trade-off between catching churners
and avoiding false alarms at different prediction thresholds.

Understanding AUC Scores:
• AUC = 0.5: Random guessing (no better than flipping a coin)
• AUC = 0.7: Acceptable performance
• AUC = 0.8: Good performance
• AUC = 0.9: Excellent performance
• AUC = 1.0: Perfect performance (rarely achieved in real data)

Our Model AUC Scores:
```

- Logistic Regression: 0.603
- Decision Tree: 0.591
- Random Forest: 0.635

Best model by AUC: Random Forest (AUC = 0.635)

3.10.2.6 Step 6: Cross-Validation

Up to this point, we have trained our models and evaluated them using a single train/test split. While this approach provides useful insights, it has an important limitation: the performance we observe can depend heavily on how the data was split. To obtain a more robust and reliable estimate of model performance, we turn to cross-validation.

Cross-validation works by dividing the dataset into multiple folds—in this case, five. Each fold serves as a test set once while the remaining folds are used for training. By repeating this process across all folds, we evaluate the model on multiple train/test combinations.

```
print("\n" + "="*50)
print("STEP 6: CROSS-VALIDATION - RELIABLE PERFORMANCE")
print("="*50)

print("Cross-validation helps us get more reliable performance
 ↪  estimates")
print("by testing our models on multiple different train/test
 ↪  splits.\n")

# Perform 5-fold cross-validation for each model
print("Performing 5-fold cross-validation...")

# Cross-validation for accuracy
lr_cv_scores = cross_val_score(lr_model, features, target, cv=5,
 ↪  scoring='accuracy')
dt_cv_scores = cross_val_score(dt_model, features, target, cv=5,
 ↪  scoring='accuracy')
rf_cv_scores = cross_val_score(rf_model, features, target, cv=5,
 ↪  scoring='accuracy')

# Cross-validation for F1-score
lr_cv_f1 = cross_val_score(lr_model, features, target, cv=5,
 ↪  scoring='f1')
dt_cv_f1 = cross_val_score(dt_model, features, target, cv=5,
 ↪  scoring='f1')
rf_cv_f1 = cross_val_score(rf_model, features, target, cv=5,
 ↪  scoring='f1')
```

```
print("Cross-Validation Results (5-fold):")
print("="*50)

def display_cv_results(cv_scores, cv_f1, model_name):
    print(f"{model_name}:")
    print(f"  Accuracy: {cv_scores.mean():.3f} ±
    ↪  {cv_scores.std():.3f}")
    print(f"  F1-Score: {cv_f1.mean():.3f} ± {cv_f1.std():.3f}")
    print(f"  Individual fold accuracies: {[f'{score:.3f}' for score
    ↪  in cv_scores]}")

    # Check for consistency
    if cv_scores.std() < 0.02:
        print(f"  ✓ Consistent performance across folds")
    else:
        print(f"  ⚠ Performance varies significantly across folds")
    print()

display_cv_results(lr_cv_scores, lr_cv_f1, "Logistic Regression")
display_cv_results(dt_cv_scores, dt_cv_f1, "Decision Tree")
display_cv_results(rf_cv_scores, rf_cv_f1, "Random Forest")
```

Output:

```
==================================================
STEP 6: CROSS-VALIDATION - RELIABLE PERFORMANCE
==================================================
Cross-validation helps us get more reliable performance estimates
by testing our models on multiple different train/test splits.

Performing 5-fold cross-validation...
Cross-Validation Results (5-fold):
==================================================
Logistic Regression:
  Accuracy: 0.625 ± 0.007
  F1-Score: 0.389 ± 0.020
  Individual fold accuracies:
    ['0.630', '0.635', '0.625', '0.620', '0.615']
  ✓ Consistent performance across folds

Decision Tree:
  Accuracy: 0.632 ± 0.021
  F1-Score: 0.349 ± 0.058
```

```
  Individual fold accuracies:
    ['0.650', '0.603', '0.645', '0.610', '0.652']
  ⚠ Performance varies significantly across folds

Random Forest:
  Accuracy: 0.644 ± 0.013
  F1-Score: 0.333 ± 0.030
  Individual fold accuracies:
    ['0.652', '0.645', '0.655', '0.620', '0.650']
  ✓ Consistent performance across folds
```

The cross-validation results provide a deeper understanding of how our models perform beyond a single train/test split. Logistic Regression shows consistent performance with small standard deviation, while the Decision Tree shows more variability across folds. Random Forest achieves the highest average accuracy while maintaining consistency.

3.10.2.7 Step 7: Detecting Overfitting

At this stage, we focus on a critical aspect of machine learning: overfitting. Overfitting occurs when a model learns the training data too well—memorizing patterns, noise, or outliers—but fails to generalize to new, unseen data.

To detect overfitting, we compare training performance against validation or test performance. Large gaps between these metrics often indicate overfitting.

```
print("\n" + "="*50)
print("STEP 7: DETECTING OVERFITTING")
print("="*50)

print("Overfitting happens when a model memorizes training data but
 ↪  fails on new data.")
print("Let's check if our models are overfitting by comparing training
 ↪  vs validation performance.\n")

# Create validation curves to detect overfitting
# We'll vary the max_depth parameter for Decision Tree to show
 ↪  overfitting

depths = range(1, 21)
train_scores, val_scores = validation_curve(
    DecisionTreeClassifier(random_state=42),
    features, target,
    param_name='max_depth',
    param_range=depths,
    cv=5, scoring='accuracy'
```

```
)

# Calculate means and standard deviations
train_mean = train_scores.mean(axis=1)
train_std = train_scores.std(axis=1)
val_mean = val_scores.mean(axis=1)
val_std = val_scores.std(axis=1)

# Plot validation curve
plt.figure(figsize=(12, 8))
plt.plot(depths, train_mean, 'o-', color='blue', label='Training
↪ Accuracy')
plt.fill_between(depths, train_mean - train_std, train_mean +
↪ train_std, alpha=0.1, color='blue')
plt.plot(depths, val_mean, 'o-', color='red', label='Validation
↪ Accuracy')
plt.fill_between(depths, val_mean - val_std, val_mean + val_std,
↪ alpha=0.1, color='red')

plt.xlabel('Tree Depth (Model Complexity)')
plt.ylabel('Accuracy')
plt.title('Validation Curve: Detecting Overfitting in Decision Trees')
plt.legend()
plt.grid(True, alpha=0.3)
plt.show()

# Find optimal depth
optimal_depth = depths[np.argmax(val_mean)]
print(f"Optimal tree depth: {optimal_depth}")
print(f"Best validation accuracy: {val_mean[optimal_depth-1]:.3f}")

print("\nSigns of Overfitting:")
print("• Training accuracy much higher than validation accuracy")
print("• Performance gets worse as model complexity increases")
print("• Large gap between training and validation curves")

# Check our models for overfitting
print(f"\nOverfitting Check for Our Models:")
print("="*40)

# Calculate training accuracy for comparison
lr_train_acc = lr_model.score(X_train, y_train)
dt_train_acc = dt_model.score(X_train, y_train)
```

```
rf_train_acc = rf_model.score(X_train, y_train)

lr_test_acc = lr_model.score(X_test, y_test)
dt_test_acc = dt_model.score(X_test, y_test)
rf_test_acc = rf_model.score(X_test, y_test)

def check_overfitting(train_acc, test_acc, model_name):
    gap = train_acc - test_acc
    print(f"{model_name}:")
    print(f"  Training Accuracy: {train_acc:.3f}")
    print(f"  Test Accuracy: {test_acc:.3f}")
    print(f"  Gap: {gap:.3f}")

    if gap < 0.05:
        print(f"  ✓ No significant overfitting")
    elif gap < 0.10:
        print(f"   Mild overfitting")
    else:
        print(f"  □ Significant overfitting detected")
    print()

check_overfitting(lr_train_acc, lr_test_acc, "Logistic Regression")
check_overfitting(dt_train_acc, dt_test_acc, "Decision Tree")
check_overfitting(rf_train_acc, rf_test_acc, "Random Forest")
```

Output:

```
==================================================
STEP 7: DETECTING OVERFITTING
==================================================
Overfitting happens when a model memorizes training data
but fails on new data.
Let's check if our models are overfitting by comparing training
vs validation performance.

Optimal tree depth: 6
Best validation accuracy: 0.635

Signs of Overfitting:
• Training accuracy much higher than validation accuracy
• Performance gets worse as model complexity increases
• Large gap between training and validation curves

Overfitting Check for Our Models:
```

```
========================================
Logistic Regression:
  Training Accuracy: 0.634
  Test Accuracy: 0.623
  Gap: 0.011
  ✓ No significant overfitting

Decision Tree:
  Training Accuracy: 0.705
  Test Accuracy: 0.593
  Gap: 0.112
  ▯ Significant overfitting detected

Random Forest:
  Training Accuracy: 0.714
  Test Accuracy: 0.657
  Gap: 0.056
  Mild overfitting
```

Examining training and test accuracy reveals how well each model generalizes. Logistic Regression shows very similar training and test performance, indicating no significant overfitting. The Decision Tree exhibits significant overfitting with a large gap between training and test accuracy. Random Forest shows mild overfitting but maintains better test performance than the Decision Tree.

3.10.2.8 Step 8: Final Model Selection

After evaluating all models through multiple lenses—including accuracy, F1-score, AUC, cross-validation consistency, and overfitting—we reach the crucial step of selecting the model for deployment.

```
print("\n" + "="*50)
print("STEP 8: FINAL MODEL SELECTION")
print("="*50)

print("Choosing the best model for business use requires considering
 ↪  multiple factors:\n")

# Create comprehensive comparison
models_comparison = pd.DataFrame({
    'Model': ['Logistic Regression', 'Decision Tree', 'Random Forest'],
    'Test_Accuracy': [lr_test_acc, dt_test_acc, rf_test_acc],
    'CV_Accuracy_Mean': [lr_cv_scores.mean(), dt_cv_scores.mean(),
     ↪  rf_cv_scores.mean()],
    'CV_Accuracy_Std': [lr_cv_scores.std(), dt_cv_scores.std(),
     ↪  rf_cv_scores.std()],
```

```
    'AUC_Score': [lr_auc, dt_auc, rf_auc],
    'F1_Score': [lr_metrics[3], dt_metrics[3], rf_metrics[3]],
    'Precision': [lr_metrics[1], dt_metrics[1], rf_metrics[1]],
    'Recall': [lr_metrics[2], dt_metrics[2], rf_metrics[2]]
})

print("COMPREHENSIVE MODEL COMPARISON:")
print("="*80)
print(models_comparison.round(3))

# Business considerations
print(f"\nBUSINESS CONSIDERATIONS:")
print("="*40)
print("For Customer Churn Prediction:")
print("• High Recall: Important to catch customers who will actually
↪   churn")
print("• Reasonable Precision: Don't want too many false alarms (wasted
↪   marketing)")
print("• Consistent Performance: Model should work reliably over time")
print("• Interpretability: Business teams need to understand why
↪   customers churn")

# Recommend best model
best_overall_idx = models_comparison['F1_Score'].idxmax()
recommended_model = models_comparison.iloc[best_overall_idx]['Model']

print(f"\nRECOMMENDED MODEL: {recommended_model}")
print(f"Reasons:")
print(f"• Best F1-Score:
↪   {models_comparison.iloc[best_overall_idx]['F1_Score']:.3f}")
print(f"• Good AUC:
↪   {models_comparison.iloc[best_overall_idx]['AUC_Score']:.3f}")
print(f"• Consistent CV performance:
  {models_comparison.iloc[best_overall_idx]['CV_Accuracy_Std']:.3f}
↪   std")
```

Output:

```
==================================================
STEP 8: FINAL MODEL SELECTION
==================================================
Choosing the best model for business use requires considering
multiple factors:
```

```
COMPREHENSIVE MODEL COMPARISON:
============================================================
                 Model  Test_Accuracy  ...  Precision  Recall
0  Logistic Regression          0.622  ...      0.515   0.331
1        Decision Tree          0.592  ...      0.452   0.273
2        Random Forest          0.658  ...      0.673   0.214

[3 rows x 8 columns]

BUSINESS CONSIDERATIONS:
========================================
For Customer Churn Prediction:
• High Recall: Important to catch customers who will actually churn
• Reasonable Precision: Don't want too many false alarms
  (wasted marketing)
• Consistent Performance: Model should work reliably over time
• Interpretability: Business teams need to understand why customers churn

RECOMMENDED MODEL: Logistic Regression
Reasons:
• Best F1-Score: 0.403
• Good AUC: 0.603
• Consistent CV performance: 0.007 std
```

Taking all factors together, Logistic Regression emerges as the recommended model. It has the highest F1-score, balancing recall and precision, good AUC indicating decent ability to separate churners from non-churners, and extremely consistent cross-validation performance. While Random Forest had slightly higher test accuracy, its lower recall and greater variability make it less suitable for this business objective.

3.10.3 Practice

You work for a mid-sized technology company's HR department. The company is concerned about employee turnover and wants to build a model to predict which employees are likely to leave. You have data about employees including their satisfaction scores, salary, project workload, and performance ratings.

Dataset Context: You are working for an HR department trying to predict employee turnover. You have created a dataset with employee features such as satisfaction, salary, projects, performance, overtime, and department. Three models—Logistic Regression, Decision Tree, and Random Forest—have been trained for prediction.

```
print("\n\n" + "="*60)
print("STUDENT EXERCISES: EMPLOYEE RETENTION PREDICTION")
print("="*60)
```

```
# Create employee retention dataset
np.random.seed(456)
n_employees = 1500

print("\nCreating Employee Retention Dataset...")
print("=" * 45)

# Employee features
satisfaction_score = np.random.normal(7, 2, n_employees)
satisfaction_score = np.clip(satisfaction_score, 1, 10)

salary = np.random.normal(75000, 20000, n_employees)
salary = np.clip(salary, 40000, 150000)

years_at_company = np.random.exponential(4, n_employees)
years_at_company = np.clip(years_at_company, 0.5, 20)

projects_count = np.random.poisson(4, n_employees)
projects_count = np.clip(projects_count, 1, 12)

performance_rating = np.random.normal(3.5, 0.8, n_employees)
performance_rating = np.clip(performance_rating, 1, 5)

overtime_hours = np.random.exponential(10, n_employees)
overtime_hours = np.clip(overtime_hours, 0, 60)

# Departments
departments = ['Sales', 'Engineering', 'Marketing', 'HR', 'Finance']
department = np.random.choice(departments, n_employees, p=[0.3, 0.25,
 ↪  0.2, 0.15, 0.1])

# Calculate leaving probability
leave_probability = (
    0.05 +  # Base leaving rate
    np.maximum(0, (7 - satisfaction_score)) / 6 * 0.4 +
    # Low satisfaction = more likely to leave
    np.maximum(0, (projects_count - 6)) / 6 * 0.2 +
    # Too many projects = more likely to leave
    np.maximum(0, (overtime_hours - 20)) / 40 * 0.2 +
    # Too much overtime = more likely to leave
    np.maximum(0, (3 - performance_rating)) / 2 * 0.1 +
    # Low performance = more likely to leave
```

```
    (department == 'Sales').astype(int) * 0.1 +
    # Sales has higher turnover
    np.random.normal(0, 0.1, n_employees)  # Random variation
)

leave_probability = np.clip(leave_probability, 0, 1)
will_leave = np.random.binomial(1, leave_probability, n_employees)

# Create DataFrame
employee_data = pd.DataFrame({
    'satisfaction_score': satisfaction_score,
    'salary': salary,
    'years_at_company': years_at_company,
    'projects_count': projects_count,
    'performance_rating': performance_rating,
    'overtime_hours': overtime_hours,
    'department': department,
    'will_leave': will_leave
})

print(f"Dataset created with {len(employee_data)} employees")
print(f"Turnover rate: {employee_data['will_leave'].mean()*100:.1f}%")
print("\nFirst 10 employees:")
print(employee_data.head(10))

# Prepare data for modeling
dept_encoded = pd.get_dummies(employee_data['department'],
↪  prefix='dept')
X_features = pd.concat([
    employee_data[['satisfaction_score', 'salary', 'years_at_company',
                   'projects_count', 'performance_rating',
                   ↪  'overtime_hours']],
    dept_encoded
], axis=1)

y_target = employee_data['will_leave']

# Split data
X_train, X_test, y_train, y_test = train_test_split(
    X_features, y_target, test_size=0.2, random_state=42,
↪  stratify=y_target
)
```

```
# Build models
lr_emp = LogisticRegression(random_state=42, max_iter=1000)
dt_emp = DecisionTreeClassifier(random_state=42, max_depth=6)
rf_emp = RandomForestClassifier(random_state=42, n_estimators=100,
 ↪  max_depth=6)

lr_emp.fit(X_train, y_train)
dt_emp.fit(X_train, y_train)
rf_emp.fit(X_train, y_train)

print("\n✓ Models trained successfully!")
print("✓ Ready for evaluation exercises!")
```

3.10.3.1 Lab 3A Questions

1. How many employees are in the dataset and what is the overall turnover rate (percentage of employees predicted to leave)?
2. What features are used for modeling, which of them are categorical, and how were those categorical features encoded?
3. How many employees are in the training set and test set, and what is the churn rate in each set?
4. What are the confusion matrices for each model, and what are the True Positives (TP), False Positives (FP), True Negatives (TN), and False Negatives (FN) for the Logistic Regression model?
5. For the Decision Tree model, how many employees are False Negatives (missed leavers) and False Positives (incorrectly flagged non-leavers), and what do these results imply for HR interventions?
6. What are the accuracy, precision, recall, and F1-score for all three models, which model has the highest F1-score, and why is F1 important in this context?
7. If HR wants to prioritize identifying all potential leavers, which evaluation metric should they focus on and which model best satisfies this requirement?
8. After plotting ROC curves for all three models, which model has the highest AUC and what does this indicate about its performance?
9. How does changing the prediction threshold affect recall and precision, and why might HR want to adjust this threshold?
10. After performing 5-fold cross-validation for accuracy and F1-score on all three models, which model shows the most consistent performance based on the lowest standard deviation?

11. How does training accuracy compare to test accuracy for each model, which model shows signs of overfitting, and how can this be identified from the gap between training and test accuracy?
12. When plotting a validation curve for the Decision Tree with max_depth from 1 to 15, at what depth is validation accuracy maximized and at what depth does overfitting begin?
13. Based on Random Forest feature importance values, which features are most influential in predicting employee turnover?
14. After creating a comparison table with test accuracy, cross-validation mean accuracy, standard deviation, AUC, F1-score, precision, and recall, which model would you recommend and why?
15. Considering model performance, interpretability, and HR goals, which final model would you select and what trade-offs would you accept when implementing it in a real business scenario?

3.11 Lab 3B: Bias and Fairness

3.11.1 Introduction

Imagine you're working as a data analyst for a bank, and your manager asks you to build a model to automatically approve or deny loan applications. You create a highly accurate model that correctly predicts loan defaults 85% of the time. The bank is thrilled with the performance and deploys your model. Six months later, you discover something troubling: your "accurate" model approves loans for white applicants at twice the rate of equally qualified Black applicants.

This scenario illustrates one of the most critical challenges in modern machine learning: ensuring that our models are not just accurate, but also fair. As machine learning systems increasingly make decisions that affect people's lives—from hiring and lending to healthcare and criminal justice—we must ensure these systems treat everyone fairly.

What is algorithmic bias? It's when machine learning models systematically discriminate against certain groups of people, often reflecting historical inequalities present in training data. Unlike human bias, which might be inconsistent, algorithmic bias can perpetuate unfairness at massive scale with mathematical precision.

Why does this matter for data analysts? Because you're not just building models—you're building systems that affect real people's lives. A biased hiring algorithm might prevent qualified candidates from getting jobs. A biased healthcare model might deny treatment to patients who need it most. A biased lending model might perpetuate economic inequality.

The good news is that bias can be detected and addressed using systematic approaches. In this lab, you'll learn to identify different types of bias, measure fairness using established metrics, and implement techniques to create more equitable machine learning systems.

3.11.2 Demonstration

We'll work with a synthetic hiring dataset that simulates real-world bias patterns found in recruitment data. This dataset includes applicant information like education, experience, skills assessments, and demographic characteristics. We'll use this data to demonstrate how bias can emerge in hiring algorithms and how to detect and address it.

3.11.2.1 Step 1: Setting Up Our Environment and Data

First, let's import libraries and create our hiring dataset with realistic bias patterns:

```
# Import required libraries
import pandas as pd
import numpy as np
import matplotlib.pyplot as plt
import seaborn as sns
from sklearn.model_selection import train_test_split
from sklearn.linear_model import LogisticRegression
from sklearn.ensemble import RandomForestClassifier
from sklearn.metrics import accuracy_score, confusion_matrix,
↪ classification_report
from sklearn.preprocessing import StandardScaler
import warnings
warnings.filterwarnings('ignore')

# Set random seed for reproducibility
np.random.seed(42)

print(" BIAS AND FAIRNESS IN MACHINE LEARNING")
print("=" * 60)

# Create synthetic hiring dataset with realistic bias patterns
n_applicants = 2000

print("Creating hiring dataset with bias patterns...")

# Generate demographic information
gender = np.random.choice(['Male', 'Female'], n_applicants, p=[0.6,
↪ 0.4])
race = np.random.choice(['White', 'Black', 'Hispanic', 'Asian'],
↪ n_applicants,
                       p=[0.6, 0.15, 0.15, 0.1])
```

```
age = np.random.normal(32, 8, n_applicants)
age = np.clip(age, 22, 65)

# Generate qualifications (these should be the main predictors)
education_level = np.random.choice([1, 2, 3, 4], n_applicants, p=[0.1,
↪  0.3, 0.4, 0.2])
# 1=High School, 2=Bachelor's, 3=Master's, 4=PhD

years_experience = np.random.exponential(5, n_applicants)
years_experience = np.clip(years_experience, 0, 20)

# Skills assessment score (0-100)
skills_score = np.random.normal(75, 15, n_applicants)
skills_score = np.clip(skills_score, 40, 100)

# Interview score (0-100) - this is where bias often enters
interview_score = np.random.normal(70, 12, n_applicants)

# Add bias to interview scores (simulating unconscious bias)
bias_adjustment = np.zeros(n_applicants)
bias_adjustment[gender == 'Female'] -= 5  # Gender bias
bias_adjustment[race == 'Black'] -= 8     # Racial bias
bias_adjustment[race == 'Hispanic'] -= 6  # Racial bias
bias_adjustment[age > 50] -= 4            # Age bias

interview_score += bias_adjustment
interview_score = np.clip(interview_score, 30, 100)

# Create hiring decision based on qualifications AND biased interview
↪  scores
# This creates a model that appears merit-based but contains bias
hiring_probability = (
    education_level * 0.15 +
    years_experience * 0.02 +
    skills_score * 0.008 +
    interview_score * 0.01 +
    np.random.normal(0, 0.1, n_applicants)
)

# Normalize to probability
hiring_probability = (hiring_probability - hiring_probability.min()) /
↪  (hiring_probability.max() - hiring_probability.min())
hired = np.random.binomial(1, hiring_probability, n_applicants)
```

```
# Create DataFrame
hiring_data = pd.DataFrame({
    'gender': gender,
    'race': race,
    'age': age,
    'education_level': education_level,
    'years_experience': years_experience,
    'skills_score': skills_score,
    'interview_score': interview_score,
    'hired': hired
})

print(f"Dataset created with {len(hiring_data)} applicants")
print("\nFirst 10 applicants:")
print(hiring_data.head(10))
print("\nDataset summary:")
print(hiring_data.describe())
```

Output:

```
Dataset created with 2000 applicants


Dataset summary:
               age  education_level  ...  interview_score        hired
count  2000.000000      2000.000000  ...      2000.000000  2000.000000
mean     32.300043         2.674500  ...        65.696127     0.462000
std       7.265358         0.898306  ...        12.471134     0.498679
min      22.000000         1.000000  ...        30.000000     0.000000
25%      26.326296         2.000000  ...        57.484580     0.000000
50%      32.015628         3.000000  ...        65.554144     0.000000
75%      37.318071         3.000000  ...        73.713109     1.000000
max      57.944744         4.000000  ...       100.000000     1.000000

[8 rows x 6 columns]
```

3.11.2.2 Step 2: Exploring Bias Patterns in the Data

Let's examine our data to identify potential bias patterns:

In this analysis, we examine potential bias patterns in a company's hiring process using demographic and qualification data from applicants. The goal is to identify whether hiring outcomes differ systematically by gender, race, or age, and whether such differences could be explained by qualifications.

3.11.2.2.1 Overall Hiring Trends

We start by calculating the overall hiring rate, which provides a baseline measure of how often applicants are hired. This metric helps contextualize any disparities observed among demographic groups.

```
print("\n" + "="*60)
print("EXPLORING BIAS PATTERNS IN HIRING DATA")
print("="*60)

# Overall hiring rates
overall_hiring_rate = hiring_data['hired'].mean()
print(f"Overall hiring rate: {overall_hiring_rate:.3f}
 ↪  ({overall_hiring_rate*100:.1f}%)")
```

Output:

```
Overall hiring rate: 0.462 (46.2%)
```

3.11.2.2.2 Hiring Rates by Demographics

Next, we examine hiring rates broken down by gender, race, and age group. This step helps reveal whether certain groups have higher or lower chances of being hired.

Gender: We compare the total applicants, number hired, and hiring rate for each gender. Differences may suggest gender-related disparities in hiring.

Race: Similarly, we analyze hiring outcomes across racial groups to identify potential racial bias.

Age Group: Applicants are categorized into age brackets (Under 30, 30–40, 40–50, Over 50) to observe if age influences hiring decisions.

```
# Hiring rates by gender
print("\nHiring rates by gender:")
gender_rates = hiring_data.groupby('gender')['hired'].agg(['count',
 ↪  'sum', 'mean'])
gender_rates.columns = ['Total_Applicants', 'Hired', 'Hiring_Rate']
print(gender_rates)
```

Output:

```
Hiring rates by gender:
        Total_Applicants  Hired  Hiring_Rate
gender
Female               817    357     0.436965
```

```
Male                     1183     567      0.479290
```

```
# Hiring rates by race
print("\nHiring rates by race:")
race_rates = hiring_data.groupby('race')['hired'].agg(['count', 'sum',
↪  'mean'])
race_rates.columns = ['Total_Applicants', 'Hired', 'Hiring_Rate']
print(race_rates)
```

Output:

```
Hiring rates by race:
          Total_Applicants  Hired  Hiring_Rate
race
Asian                  189     72     0.380952
Black                  299    122     0.408027
Hispanic               309    145     0.469256
White                 1203    585     0.486284
```

```
# Hiring rates by age group
hiring_data['age_group'] = pd.cut(hiring_data['age'],
                                 bins=[0, 30, 40, 50, 100],
                                 labels=['Under 30', '30-40', '40-50', 'Over
↪  50'])
print("\nHiring rates by age group:")
age_rates = hiring_data.groupby('age_group')['hired'].agg(['count',
↪  'sum', 'mean'])
age_rates.columns = ['Total_Applicants', 'Hired', 'Hiring_Rate']
print(age_rates)
```

Output:

```
Hiring rates by age group:
           Total_Applicants  Hired  Hiring_Rate
age_group
Under 30                795    348     0.437736
30-40                   895    423     0.472626
40-50                   284    142     0.500000
Over 50                  26     11     0.423077
```

3.11.2.2.3 Qualifications by Demographics

To understand whether observed disparities are associated with differences in candidate qualifications, we calculate the average education level, years of experience, and skills score by gender and race. This allows us to distinguish between differences due to qualifications and differences potentially due to bias.

```
# Check if qualifications differ by demographic groups
print("\n" + "="*50)
print("QUALIFICATION DIFFERENCES BY DEMOGRAPHICS")
print("="*50)

print("\nAverage qualifications by gender:")
qual_by_gender = hiring_data.groupby('gender')[['education_level',
  'years_experience', 'skills_score']].mean()
print(qual_by_gender.round(2))

print("\nAverage qualifications by race:")
qual_by_race = hiring_data.groupby('race')[['education_level',
  'years_experience', 'skills_score']].mean()
print(qual_by_race.round(2))
```

Output:

```
Average qualifications by gender:
        education_level  years_experience  skills_score
gender
Female             2.67              4.82         74.42
Male               2.68              4.70         75.14

Average qualifications by race:
          education_level  years_experience  skills_score
race
Asian                2.65              4.86         72.58
Black                2.64              4.68         74.96
Hispanic             2.69              4.47         74.95
White                2.69              4.82         75.15
```

3.11.2.3 Step 3: Building a Biased Model

Let's build a hiring model and see how it perpetuates bias:

In this step, we move from simply exploring historical hiring patterns to building a predictive model that can estimate the likelihood that an applicant will be hired. The focus is on using candidate qualifications as predictors while intentionally excluding demographic information such as gender, race, or age, in order to avoid encoding potential biases into the model.

We begin by preparing the dataset, selecting features that represent candidate qualifications and performance, including education level, years of experience, skills score, and interview score. These features form the input variables, while the target variable is whether the applicant was hired. Although demographic variables are excluded from the model, they are stored separately for later analysis to examine potential bias in the model's predictions.

```
print("\n" + "="*60)
print("BUILDING A HIRING PREDICTION MODEL")
print("="*60)

# Prepare features for modeling (excluding demographic information)
feature_columns = ['education_level', 'years_experience',
 ↪  'skills_score', 'interview_score']
X = hiring_data[feature_columns]
y = hiring_data['hired']
```

Next, the dataset is split into a training set and a testing set. The training set, consisting of 70% of the applicants, is used to train the logistic regression model, while the remaining 30% of applicants form the testing set, which allows us to evaluate how well the model performs on unseen data. This split ensures that performance metrics reflect the model's ability to generalize, rather than merely memorizing the training data.

```
# Split data
X_train, X_test, y_train, y_test = train_test_split(X, y,
 ↪  test_size=0.3, random_state=42)

# Also split demographic information for bias analysis
demo_train = hiring_data.loc[X_train.index, ['gender', 'race',
 ↪  'age_group']]
demo_test = hiring_data.loc[X_test.index, ['gender', 'race',
 ↪  'age_group']]

print(f"Training set: {len(X_train)} applicants")
print(f"Testing set: {len(X_test)} applicants")
```

Output:

```
Training set: 1400 applicants
Testing set: 600 applicants
```

```
# Build logistic regression model
print("\nTraining Logistic Regression model...")
model = LogisticRegression(random_state=42)
model.fit(X_train, y_train)
```

Once the model is trained, it produces predictions for the test set, both in terms of the predicted labels—whether an applicant is likely to be hired—and predicted probabilities, which indicate the likelihood of hiring. The overall performance of the model is assessed using accuracy, which measures the proportion of correct predictions. A classification report provides additional insight, detailing how precise the model is when it predicts hires, how well it identifies actual hires, and a balanced F1-score that combines these measures.

```
# Make predictions
y_pred = model.predict(X_test)
y_pred_proba = model.predict_proba(X_test)[:, 1]

# Overall model performance
accuracy = accuracy_score(y_test, y_pred)
print(f"\nOverall model accuracy: {accuracy:.3f}
 ↪  ({accuracy*100:.1f}%)")
```

Output:

```
Overall model accuracy: 0.575 (57.5%)
```

Finally, examining the coefficients of the logistic regression model reveals which features have the greatest influence on hiring predictions. Positive coefficients indicate that higher values of a feature increase the likelihood of being hired, while negative coefficients suggest the opposite. Understanding these relationships helps identify which qualifications most strongly drive hiring decisions and provides a foundation for interpreting the fairness and transparency of the model.

Through this process, we not only build a predictive model but also lay the groundwork for assessing how candidate qualifications relate to hiring outcomes and for evaluating potential bias in automated decision-making.

```
# Show feature importance
print("\nFeature importance (coefficients):")
for feature, coef in zip(feature_columns, model.coef_[0]):
    print(f"  {feature}: {coef:.3f}")

print("\nClassification Report:")
print(classification_report(y_test, y_pred, target_names=['Not Hired',
 ↪  'Hired']))
```

Output:

```
Feature importance (coefficients):
  education_level: 0.400
  years_experience: 0.041
  skills_score: 0.014
  interview_score: 0.025

Classification Report:
              precision    recall  f1-score   support
```

```
   Not Hired       0.59      0.69      0.63       320
       Hired       0.56      0.44      0.49       280

    accuracy                           0.57       600
   macro avg       0.57      0.57      0.56       600
weighted avg       0.57      0.57      0.57       600
```

After training the logistic regression model, we can examine two important outputs to understand how the model makes predictions and how well it performs. The first is feature importance, represented by the model's coefficients. Each coefficient indicates how much that particular feature contributes to predicting whether an applicant will be hired. A positive coefficient means that as the value of the feature increases, the likelihood of being hired also increases. In our results, education_level has the largest coefficient (0.400), suggesting that higher education strongly increases the model's predicted probability of hiring. The other features—years_experience (0.041), skills_score (0.014), and interview_score (0.025)—have smaller positive contributions, meaning they also increase hiring likelihood but to a lesser extent according to the model.

The second output is the classification report, which evaluates how well the model predicts actual hiring outcomes in the test set. Accuracy measures the overall proportion of correct predictions; here, the model achieves 57% accuracy, indicating it correctly predicts hiring slightly more than half the time. However, accuracy alone doesn't tell the full story, so we also look at precision, recall, and the F1-score for each class.

Precision tells us, for each predicted class, how many of those predictions were correct. For example, a precision of 0.56 for "Hired" means that when the model predicts someone will be hired, it is correct 56% of the time.

Recall measures how well the model captures all actual positives. A recall of 0.44 for "Hired" indicates that the model only identifies 44% of the applicants who were truly hired.

The F1-score combines precision and recall into a single measure, balancing the two, and provides a more comprehensive view of model performance when classes are imbalanced.

In this model, the slightly higher recall for "Not Hired" (0.69) versus "Hired" (0.44) shows that the model is better at identifying applicants who will not be hired than those who will. This could reflect underlying patterns in the training data or the relative strength of the predictive features. Together, the feature coefficients and classification metrics provide insight both into how the model makes decisions and how reliable those decisions are, highlighting areas where the model predicts well and where it may need improvement.

3.11.2.4 Step 4: Detecting Bias Using Fairness Metrics

After building a predictive hiring model, it is essential to examine whether the model's predictions are equitable across different demographic groups. In this step, we assess potential bias using several fairness metrics, focusing on gender, race, and age. By comparing model behavior across these groups, we can determine whether some applicants are systematically advantaged or disadvantaged.

The first metric we evaluate is demographic parity, also called statistical parity. This metric considers the proportion of applicants predicted to be hired within each group. Ideally, these positive prediction rates should be similar across groups. For example, if the model predicts a much higher hiring probability for one gender or race compared to another, it may indicate bias in the predictions. By calculating the overall positive rate and comparing it to the rate for each group, we can quantify disparities. A demographic parity difference close to zero suggests fair treatment, while a larger difference signals potential bias that should be investigated further.

Next, we examine equalized odds, which assesses fairness in terms of the model's ability to correctly classify applicants. This metric looks at both the true positive rate—the proportion of actual hires correctly predicted—and the false positive rate—the proportion of non-hires incorrectly predicted as hires—for each group. A fair model should have similar true positive and false positive rates across all demographic groups. Differences in these rates may indicate that the model is more accurate for some groups than others, potentially perpetuating inequities in hiring outcomes.

Finally, we calculate accuracy by group, which measures the proportion of correct predictions within each demographic group. This provides a simple yet informative view of whether the model performs consistently across groups. Large differences in accuracy can highlight whether certain groups are more likely to be misclassified, further pointing to potential bias.

By systematically applying these fairness metrics, we gain a comprehensive understanding of how the hiring model interacts with sensitive attributes. The results allow us to identify areas where the model may unintentionally favor or disadvantage certain groups, providing a foundation for informed interventions, such as model adjustments or additional fairness-focused evaluation. This step is critical for ensuring that predictive models support equitable hiring practices and do not reinforce existing disparities.

```
print("\n" + "="*60)
print("BIAS DETECTION USING FAIRNESS METRICS")
print("="*60)

def calculate_fairness_metrics(y_true, y_pred, sensitive_attribute):
    """Calculate various fairness metrics for a given sensitive
    ↪ attribute"""
```

```
    results = {}
    unique_groups = sensitive_attribute.unique()

    print(f"\nFairness Analysis for {sensitive_attribute.name}:")
    print("-" * 50)

    # Demographic Parity (Statistical Parity)
    print("1. DEMOGRAPHIC PARITY:")
    print("   (Positive prediction rates should be similar across
    ↪  groups)")

    overall_positive_rate = y_pred.mean()
    print(f"   Overall positive rate: {overall_positive_rate:.3f}")

    for group in unique_groups:
        mask = sensitive_attribute == group
        group_positive_rate = y_pred[mask].mean()
        group_size = mask.sum()
        print(f"   {group}: {group_positive_rate:.3f}
        ↪  (n={group_size})")
        results[f'{group}_positive_rate'] = group_positive_rate

    # Calculate demographic parity difference
    positive_rates = [y_pred[sensitive_attribute == group].mean() for
↪   group in unique_groups]
    dp_difference = max(positive_rates) - min(positive_rates)
    print(f"   Demographic parity difference: {dp_difference:.3f}")
    print(f"   (Closer to 0 is more fair, >0.1 indicates significant
    ↪  bias)")

    # Equalized Odds
    print("\n2. EQUALIZED ODDS:")
    print("   (True positive and false positive rates should be similar
    ↪  across groups)")

    for group in unique_groups:
        mask = sensitive_attribute == group
        group_y_true = y_true[mask]
        group_y_pred = y_pred[mask]

        if len(group_y_true) > 0:
            # True Positive Rate (Sensitivity)
            if (group_y_true == 1).sum() > 0:
```

```
                tpr = ((group_y_pred == 1) & (group_y_true == 1)).sum()
    ↪   / (group_y_true == 1).sum()
            else:
                tpr = 0

            # False Positive Rate
            if (group_y_true == 0).sum() > 0:
                fpr = ((group_y_pred == 1) & (group_y_true == 0)).sum()
    ↪   / (group_y_true == 0).sum()
            else:
                fpr = 0

            print(f"   {group}: TPR={tpr:.3f}, FPR={fpr:.3f}")
            results[f'{group}_tpr'] = tpr
            results[f'{group}_fpr'] = fpr

    # Accuracy by group
    print("\n3. ACCURACY BY GROUP:")
    for group in unique_groups:
        mask = sensitive_attribute == group
        if mask.sum() > 0:
            group_accuracy = (y_true[mask] == y_pred[mask]).mean()
            print(f"   {group}: {group_accuracy:.3f}")
            results[f'{group}_accuracy'] = group_accuracy

    return results

# Test for gender bias
gender_metrics = calculate_fairness_metrics(y_test, y_pred,
 ↪  demo_test['gender'])

# Test for racial bias
race_metrics = calculate_fairness_metrics(y_test, y_pred,
 ↪  demo_test['race'])

# Test for age bias
age_metrics = calculate_fairness_metrics(y_test, y_pred,
 ↪  demo_test['age_group'])
```

Output:

```
Fairness Analysis for gender:
--------------------------------------------------
1. DEMOGRAPHIC PARITY:
```

```
   (Positive prediction rates should be similar across groups)
   Overall positive rate: 0.372
   Female: 0.327 (n=251)
   Male: 0.404 (n=349)
   Demographic parity difference: 0.077
   (Closer to 0 is more fair, >0.1 indicates significant bias)

2. EQUALIZED ODDS:
   (True positive and false positive rates should be similar
   across groups)
   Female: TPR=0.376, FPR=0.289
   Male: TPR=0.485, FPR=0.326

3. ACCURACY BY GROUP:
   Female: 0.566
   Male: 0.582

Fairness Analysis for race:
--------------------------------------------------
1. DEMOGRAPHIC PARITY:
   (Positive prediction rates should be similar across groups)
   Overall positive rate: 0.372
   Hispanic: 0.314 (n=105)
   White: 0.438 (n=333)
   Asian: 0.365 (n=74)
   Black: 0.193 (n=88)
   Demographic parity difference: 0.245
   (Closer to 0 is more fair, >0.1 indicates significant bias)

2. EQUALIZED ODDS:
   (True positive and false positive rates should be similar
   across groups)
   Hispanic: TPR=0.341, FPR=0.295
   White: TPR=0.491, FPR=0.390
   Asian: TPR=0.514, FPR=0.216
   Black: TPR=0.289, FPR=0.120

3. ACCURACY BY GROUP:
   Hispanic: 0.552
   White: 0.553
   Asian: 0.649
   Black: 0.625
```

```
Fairness Analysis for age_group:
--------------------------------------------------
1. DEMOGRAPHIC PARITY:
   (Positive prediction rates should be similar across groups)
   Overall positive rate: 0.372
   30-40: 0.368 (n=280)
   Under 30: 0.381 (n=226)
   40-50: 0.372 (n=86)
   Over 50: 0.250 (n=8)
   Demographic parity difference: 0.131
   (Closer to 0 is more fair, >0.1 indicates significant bias)

2. EQUALIZED ODDS:
   (True positive and false positive rates should be similar
   across groups)
   30-40: TPR=0.401, FPR=0.333
   Under 30: TPR=0.457, FPR=0.326
   40-50: TPR=0.561, FPR=0.200
   Over 50: TPR=0.333, FPR=0.200

3. ACCURACY BY GROUP:
   30-40: 0.532
   Under 30: 0.584
   40-50: 0.686
   Over 50: 0.625
```

The fairness analysis evaluates whether the model's predictions treat different demographic groups equitably. Three metrics are used: demographic parity, equalized odds, and accuracy by group.

3.11.2.4.1 Gender Bias

For gender, demographic parity compares the proportion of applicants predicted to be hired for females and males. The overall positive prediction rate is 0.372. Among females, 32.7% are predicted to be hired, whereas 40.4% of males are predicted to be hired. The demographic parity difference of 0.077 indicates a modest disparity, but since it is below 0.1, it is not flagged as severe bias.

Equalized odds considers both true positive rate (TPR) and false positive rate (FPR). Females have a TPR of 0.376 and an FPR of 0.289, while males have a TPR of 0.485 and FPR of 0.326. This shows that the model is better at correctly identifying males who will be hired and slightly more likely to incorrectly predict males as hired.

Accuracy by group is 56.6% for females and 58.2% for males, suggesting similar overall performance, though slightly higher for males. Overall, the gender differences are present but relatively small.

3.11.2.4.2 Racial Bias

For race, demographic parity reveals more pronounced differences. The overall positive rate is again 0.372, but the predicted hiring rates vary widely: Hispanic applicants 31.4%, White 43.8%, Asian 36.5%, and Black 19.3%. The demographic parity difference of 0.245 exceeds 0.1, indicating significant disparities in predicted hiring rates across racial groups.

Equalized odds shows variation in both TPR and FPR: for instance, White and Asian applicants have higher TPRs (0.491 and 0.514) compared to Hispanic and Black applicants (0.341 and 0.289). False positive rates also differ, with Black applicants having the lowest FPR (0.120). These differences suggest the model is more accurate for some racial groups than others and could disadvantage certain groups.

Accuracy by group varies as well: Asian applicants have the highest accuracy at 64.9%, Black applicants 62.5%, and Hispanic and White applicants just above 55%. This reinforces the idea that model performance is not uniform across races.

3.11.2.4.3 Age Bias

For age, demographic parity shows that predicted hiring rates are highest for applicants under 30 (38.1%) and lowest for those over 50 (25%), with a parity difference of 0.131, which exceeds the 0.1 threshold, indicating potential bias.

Equalized odds highlights further variation: the TPR ranges from 0.333 for over-50 applicants to 0.561 for the 40–50 age group, while FPR ranges from 0.200 to 0.333. This indicates the model identifies mid-career applicants more accurately than older applicants.

Accuracy by group shows similar patterns: the 40–50 group has the highest prediction accuracy at 68.6%, while the 30–40 group has the lowest at 53.2%. This confirms that the model's predictions are not equally reliable across age groups.

Overall, these fairness metrics reveal that the hiring model exhibits some demographic disparities. Gender differences are modest, but significant disparities appear across racial groups and age brackets. Demographic parity, equalized odds, and accuracy by group together provide a comprehensive view of where the model may favor or disadvantage certain groups. This insight is critical for improving the model or implementing safeguards to ensure more equitable hiring predictions.

3.11.2.5 Step 5: Bias Mitigation Techniques

Once bias is detected in a predictive model, it is important to explore strategies for reducing disparities and improving fairness. In this step, we examine three common approaches: pre-processing, post-processing, and ongoing monitoring.

The first approach, pre-processing, involves modifying the input data to remove features that may introduce bias. For example, in our hiring model, interview scores were identified as potentially biased, so we trained a new logistic regression model without this feature. By excluding the biased input, the model relies solely on neutral candidate qualifications such as education, experience, and skills. After retraining, we observed that the overall accuracy of the model remained reasonable, and fairness metrics for gender indicated reduced disparities in predicted hiring rates. This demonstrates that removing biased features can help produce more equitable predictions without drastically sacrificing performance.

Let's implement different approaches to reduce bias:

```
print("\n" + "="*60)
print("BIAS MITIGATION TECHNIQUES")
print("="*60)

# Approach 1: Pre-processing - Remove biased features
print("APPROACH 1: PRE-PROCESSING (Remove biased interview scores)")
print("-" * 55)

# Create dataset without interview scores (which contained bias)
X_fair = hiring_data[['education_level', 'years_experience',
 ↪ 'skills_score']]
X_train_fair, X_test_fair, y_train_fair, y_test_fair =
 ↪ train_test_split(
    X_fair, y, test_size=0.3, random_state=42
)

# Train model without biased feature
model_fair = LogisticRegression(random_state=42)
model_fair.fit(X_train_fair, y_train_fair)
y_pred_fair = model_fair.predict(X_test_fair)

print(f"Fair model accuracy: {accuracy_score(y_test_fair,
 ↪ y_pred_fair):.3f}")

# Check fairness of the new model
demo_test_fair = hiring_data.loc[X_test_fair.index, ['gender', 'race',
 ↪ 'age_group']]
print("\nFairness metrics for pre-processed model:")
gender_metrics_fair = calculate_fairness_metrics(y_test_fair,
 ↪ y_pred_fair, demo_test_fair['gender'])
```

Output:

```
Fairness metrics for pre-processed model:

Fairness Analysis for gender:
--------------------------------------------------
1. DEMOGRAPHIC PARITY:
   (Positive prediction rates should be similar across groups)
   Overall positive rate: 0.350
   Female: 0.331 (n=251)
   Male: 0.364 (n=349)
   Demographic parity difference: 0.033
   (Closer to 0 is more fair, >0.1 indicates significant bias)

2. EQUALIZED ODDS:
   (True positive and false positive rates should be similar
   across groups)
   Female: TPR=0.358, FPR=0.310
   Male: TPR=0.409, FPR=0.320

3. ACCURACY BY GROUP:
   Female: 0.546
   Male: 0.547
```

After applying the pre-processing mitigation by removing the potentially biased interview scores, the fairness metrics for gender show clear improvement. The overall positive prediction rate dropped slightly to 0.350, and the rates for females and males became much closer—33.1% versus 36.4%—resulting in a demographic parity difference of 0.033, well below the 0.1 threshold and indicating minimal disparity. Looking at equalized odds, the true positive and false positive rates for females (TPR 0.358, FPR 0.310) and males (TPR 0.409, FPR 0.320) are also more balanced than in the original model, suggesting the model now predicts hires more equitably across genders. Accuracy by group is nearly identical, 54.6% for females and 54.7% for males, confirming that fairness gains were achieved without sacrificing overall predictive performance.

The second approach, post-processing, focuses on adjusting model outputs rather than the inputs. In this method, prediction thresholds are modified for each demographic group to achieve a more balanced rate of positive predictions, known as demographic parity. By calibrating thresholds individually for groups, the model can equalize the likelihood of being hired across sensitive attributes while still leveraging all original features. After applying this threshold adjustment to the gender groups, fairness metrics showed that disparities in positive prediction rates decreased, though overall accuracy remained similar to the original model. This approach allows for fairness improvements even when the underlying model cannot be retrained or when all features are considered relevant.

```
# Approach 2: Post-processing - Adjust thresholds
print("\n" + "="*60)
print("APPROACH 2: POST-PROCESSING (Threshold adjustment)")
print("-" * 55)

def adjust_predictions_for_fairness(y_pred_proba, sensitive_attr,
↪   target_rate=None):
    """Adjust prediction thresholds to achieve demographic parity"""

    adjusted_predictions = np.zeros_like(y_pred_proba)

    if target_rate is None:
        target_rate = (y_pred_proba > 0.5).mean()  # Use overall
↪   positive rate

    for group in sensitive_attr.unique():
        mask = sensitive_attr == group
        group_probabilities = y_pred_proba[mask]

        # Find threshold that gives target positive rate for this group
        threshold = np.percentile(group_probabilities, (1 -
↪   target_rate) * 100)
        adjusted_predictions[mask] = (group_probabilities >
↪   threshold).astype(int)

    return adjusted_predictions

# Apply threshold adjustment
y_pred_adjusted = adjust_predictions_for_fairness(y_pred_proba,
↪   demo_test['gender'])

print(f"Adjusted model accuracy: {accuracy_score(y_test,
↪   y_pred_adjusted):.3f}")
print("\nFairness metrics for threshold-adjusted model:")
gender_metrics_adjusted = calculate_fairness_metrics(y_test,
↪   y_pred_adjusted, demo_test['gender'])
```

Output:

```
Fairness metrics for threshold-adjusted model:

Fairness Analysis for gender:
--------------------------------------------------
1. DEMOGRAPHIC PARITY:
```

```
   (Positive prediction rates should be similar across groups)
   Overall positive rate: 0.372
   Female: 0.371 (n=251)
   Male: 0.372 (n=349)
   Demographic parity difference: 0.002
   (Closer to 0 is more fair, >0.1 indicates significant bias)

2. EQUALIZED ODDS:
   (True positive and false positive rates should be similar across groups)
   Female: TPR=0.440, FPR=0.317
   Male: TPR=0.462, FPR=0.287

3. ACCURACY BY GROUP:
   Female: 0.578
   Male: 0.590
```

After applying the threshold-adjustment post-processing, the fairness metrics for gender show substantial improvement in demographic parity. The positive prediction rates for females and males are now nearly identical—37.1% versus 37.2%—resulting in a demographic parity difference of just 0.002, effectively eliminating disparities in predicted hires between genders. While equalized odds show that true positive and false positive rates are still slightly different (TPR 0.440 vs. 0.462, FPR 0.317 vs. 0.287), these gaps are smaller than in the original model, indicating a more balanced ability to correctly classify both genders. Accuracy by group is also slightly higher than in the pre-processed model, with 57.8% for females and 59.0% for males, suggesting that fairness was improved without substantially compromising overall model performance.

The third approach is ongoing monitoring, which ensures that fairness is maintained over time as the model is applied to new applicants. By continuously tracking demographic parity differences and other fairness metrics across sensitive attributes, the organization can detect emerging bias and set alerts when disparities exceed a pre-defined threshold. This monitoring framework provides an early warning system, allowing HR teams or model administrators to intervene before biased outcomes affect real hiring decisions. Running this bias monitoring on the original model highlighted areas where disparities were significant, confirming the importance of regular evaluation even after mitigation steps are taken.

```
# Approach 3: Monitoring and Alerting
print("\n" + "="*60)
print("APPROACH 3: ONGOING MONITORING")
print("-" * 35)

def bias_monitoring_report(y_true, y_pred, sensitive_attrs,
 ↪  threshold=0.1):
    """Generate bias monitoring report"""
```

```
    print("BIAS MONITORING REPORT")
    print("=" * 30)

    alerts = []

    for attr_name, attr_values in sensitive_attrs.items():
        print(f"\nMonitoring {attr_name}:")

        # Calculate demographic parity difference
        positive_rates = []
        for group in attr_values.unique():
            mask = attr_values == group
            positive_rate = y_pred[mask].mean()
            positive_rates.append(positive_rate)
            print(f"  {group}: {positive_rate:.3f} positive rate")

        dp_diff = max(positive_rates) - min(positive_rates)
        print(f"  Demographic parity difference: {dp_diff:.3f}")

        if dp_diff > threshold:
            alerts.append(f"ALERT: {attr_name} shows bias (difference: {dp_diff:.3f})")
            print(f"    BIAS ALERT: Difference exceeds threshold of {threshold}")
        else:
            print(f" Within acceptable range")

    if alerts:
        print(f"\n BIAS ALERTS DETECTED:")
        for alert in alerts:
            print(f"   {alert}")
    else:
        print(f"\n No significant bias detected")

    return alerts

# Run monitoring on original model
sensitive_attributes = {
    'gender': demo_test['gender'],
    'race': demo_test['race'],
    'age_group': demo_test['age_group']
}
```

```
alerts = bias_monitoring_report(y_test, y_pred, sensitive_attributes)
```

Output:

```
BIAS MONITORING REPORT
==============================

Monitoring gender:
  Female: 0.327 positive rate
  Male: 0.404 positive rate
  Demographic parity difference: 0.077
  Within acceptable range

Monitoring race:
  Hispanic: 0.314 positive rate
  White: 0.438 positive rate
  Asian: 0.365 positive rate
  Black: 0.193 positive rate
  Demographic parity difference: 0.245
    BIAS ALERT: Difference exceeds threshold of 0.1

Monitoring age_group:
  30-40: 0.368 positive rate
  Under 30: 0.381 positive rate
  40-50: 0.372 positive rate
  Over 50: 0.250 positive rate
  Demographic parity difference: 0.131
    BIAS ALERT: Difference exceeds threshold of 0.1

 BIAS ALERTS DETECTED:
   ALERT: race shows bias (difference: 0.245)
   ALERT: age_group shows bias (difference: 0.131)
```

The bias monitoring report highlights where the original hiring model shows significant disparities across demographic groups. For gender, the positive prediction rates are 32.7% for females and 40.4% for males, giving a demographic parity difference of 0.077. This is below the threshold of 0.1, so gender disparities are considered within an acceptable range. In contrast, race exhibits large differences: predicted hire rates range from 19.3% for Black applicants to 43.8% for White applicants, producing a demographic parity difference of 0.245, which triggers a bias alert. Similarly, age groups show uneven predictions, with rates from 25% for applicants over 50 to 38.1% for those under 30, resulting in a parity difference of 0.131 and another bias alert. Overall, the monitoring system identifies race and age as areas of concern where the model may systematically disadvantage certain groups, signaling the need for mitigation or further investigation.

Together, these three approaches—pre-processing, post-processing, and monitoring—illustrate a comprehensive strategy for bias mitigation. Pre-processing addresses bias in the input data, post-processing corrects disparities in model outputs, and ongoing monitoring ensures that fairness is maintained as the model is deployed. By combining these techniques, organizations can move toward more equitable and responsible use of predictive hiring models.

3.11.3 Practice

You work for a community bank that wants to ensure their loan approval process is fair and compliant with fair lending laws. The bank has historical data about loan applications, including applicant demographics, financial information, and approval decisions. Your task is to analyze this data for bias and recommend improvements to ensure fair lending practices.

```
# Create loan approval dataset with realistic bias patterns
np.random.seed(456)  # Different seed for different patterns

n_applicants = 1500

# Generate applicant demographics
gender = np.random.choice(['Male', 'Female'],
  n_applicants, p=[0.55, 0.45])
race = np.random.choice(['White', 'Black', 'Hispanic',
  'Asian', 'Other'],  n_applicants, p=[0.65, 0.12, 0.13,
  0.08, 0.02])
age = np.random.normal(38, 12, n_applicants)
age = np.clip(age, 18, 75)

# Generate financial information
annual_income = np.random.lognormal(10.5, 0.6, n_applicants)
annual_income = np.clip(annual_income, 25000, 200000)

credit_score = np.random.normal(680, 80, n_applicants)
credit_score = np.clip(credit_score, 300, 850)

loan_amount = np.random.normal(150000, 75000, n_applicants)
loan_amount = np.clip(loan_amount, 50000, 500000)

debt_to_income = np.random.beta(2, 5, n_applicants) * 0.6  # Most
↪  people have reasonable DTI
employment_years = np.random.exponential(4, n_applicants)
```

```
employment_years = np.clip(employment_years, 0.5, 25)

# Create loan approval with bias patterns
# Base approval probability on legitimate factors
base_approval_prob = (
    (credit_score - 300) / 550 * 0.4 +  # Credit score effect
    (annual_income / 200000) * 0.3 +     # Income effect
    (1 - debt_to_income) * 0.2 +         # Lower DTI is better
    (employment_years / 25) * 0.1        # Employment stability
)

# Add bias (simulating historical discrimination)
bias_adjustment = np.zeros(n_applicants)
bias_adjustment[gender == 'Female'] -= 0.08    # Gender bias
bias_adjustment[race == 'Black'] -= 0.12       # Racial bias
bias_adjustment[race == 'Hispanic'] -= 0.10    # Racial bias
bias_adjustment[age > 55] -= 0.06              # Age bias

# Apply bias and create final approval decision
final_approval_prob = base_approval_prob + bias_adjustment
final_approval_prob = np.clip(final_approval_prob, 0, 1)
approved = np.random.binomial(1, final_approval_prob, n_applicants)

# Create DataFrame
loan_data = pd.DataFrame({
    'gender': gender,
    'race': race,
    'age': age,
    'annual_income': annual_income,
    'credit_score': credit_score,
    'loan_amount': loan_amount,
    'debt_to_income': debt_to_income,
    'employment_years': employment_years,
    'approved': approved
})

print(f"Loan dataset created with {len(loan_data)} applications")
print("\nFirst 10 applications:")
print(loan_data.head(10))

print("\nDataset summary:")
print(loan_data.describe())
```

3.11.3.1 Lab 3B Questions

1. **Overall Approval Rate:** Calculate the overall loan approval rate in the dataset. How does this compare to what you might expect for a fair and unbiased approval process?
2. **Approval Rates by Gender:** Examine approval rates for male and female applicants. Do you observe any differences? How might these differences reflect potential gender bias in the historical data?
3. **Approval Rates by Race:** Analyze approval rates across the racial groups in the dataset. Which groups appear to have lower approval rates, and what might this indicate about historical bias?
4. **Approval Rates by Age Group:** Look at the approval rates for different age groups. Are older applicants less likely to be approved? How does this relate to potential age discrimination?
5. **Demographic Disparities:** For gender, race, and age, calculate the demographic parity difference (the maximum difference in approval rates between groups). Which demographic category shows the largest disparity?
6. **Base Financial Factors:** Identify the main financial features (e.g., credit score, annual income, debt-to-income ratio, employment years) that influence loan approval. Which factor seems most strongly associated with approvals?
7. **Bias Adjustment:** The dataset includes simulated bias adjustments for gender, race, and age. Discuss how these adjustments impact the final approval probability. Which groups are most affected by these bias adjustments?
8. **Feature Correlations:** Explore correlations between applicant demographics and financial features. Are there any patterns that might suggest indirect bias (e.g., lower income correlated with certain groups)?
9. **Visualization of Bias:** Create bar charts or boxplots showing approval rates by gender, race, and age group. Based on the plots, which groups experience the lowest approval rates?
10. **Pre-processing Strategy:** If you were to remove biased features to improve fairness, which features might you consider removing or modifying? Explain why.
11. **Post-processing Strategy:** Imagine you want to adjust predicted approvals after modeling to achieve demographic parity. How would you approach threshold adjustments for different groups?
12. **Equalized Odds Analysis:** Calculate true positive and false positive rates by gender. Do these rates suggest the model favors one gender over the other in terms of correctly or incorrectly approving loans?

13. **Fairness Across Race:** Using the same approach, compute true positive and false positive rates for racial groups. Which groups benefit or are disadvantaged by the current approval process?

14. **Monitoring and Alerts:** Propose a monitoring plan for the bank to regularly check for bias in loan approvals. What thresholds would you use for alerting, and how often should the monitoring occur?

15. **Recommendations for Fair Lending:** Based on your analysis, write a brief set of recommendations for the bank. Include at least two mitigation strategies (pre-processing, post-processing, or monitoring) to ensure the loan approval process is fair.

3.12 Conclusion

The techniques you've learned in this module—from precision and recall to cross-validation to bias detection—provide the foundation for responsible machine learning practice. As models become more sophisticated and are deployed in more sensitive applications, these evaluation skills become increasingly important.

In the next module, we'll explore natural language processing, where these evaluation principles apply to the complex challenge of understanding and generating human language. The metrics and techniques you've learned here will help you assess whether language models are performing well and treating users fairly across different linguistic and cultural contexts.

Remember that model evaluation is both a technical skill and an ethical responsibility. The models you build and deploy will affect real people's lives, so taking the time to evaluate them thoroughly isn't just good practice—it's the right thing to do.

3.13 References

[1] Google AI. (2025). Responsible AI Practices: Model Evaluation and Fairness. https://ai.google/responsibilities/responsible-ai-practices/

[2] Partnership on AI. (2025). Best Practices for AI Model Evaluation and Testing. https://www.partnershiponai.org/

[3] MIT Technology Review. (2025). Understanding Bias in Machine Learning Systems. https://www.technologyreview.com/

[4] Stanford HAI. (2025). Human-Centered AI: Evaluation Beyond Technical Metrics. https://hai.stanford.edu/

Chapter 4

Introduction to Natural Language Processing

4.1 Learning Outcomes

4-1: Understand what Natural Language Processing is and why it's important for modern businesses

4-2: Explain the fundamental challenges of processing human language with computers and the basic approaches to preparing text for analysis

4-3: Describe how text is converted into numerical representations that machine learning algorithms can work with

4-4: Recognize common NLP applications and understand the basic techniques that power them

4.2 Introduction

You wake up and ask Alexa what the weather will be like today. She understands your question and gives you a helpful answer. You type a message to a friend, and your phone automatically suggests the perfect response. You write a product review online, and within minutes, the company knows whether you're happy or frustrated with your purchase. You search for something on Google using your own words, and it finds exactly what you're looking for even though the websites use completely different terminology.

All of these everyday experiences represent something remarkable: computers understanding and working with human language. This field is called Natural Language Processing, or NLP for short. It's the branch of artificial intelligence that focuses on helping computers read, understand, and even generate human language in ways that feel natural and useful.

But what exactly is NLP, and why is it such a big deal? Think about it this way: humans have been communicating through language for thousands of years. It's our primary way of sharing ideas, emotions, and information. Until recently, computers could only work with numbers and structured data. They couldn't understand a sentence, interpret the meaning of a paragraph, or have a conversation. NLP bridges this gap, allowing computers to work with the vast amount of human knowledge and communication that exists in language form.

This chapter focuses on understanding how computers can be taught to process and understand text, starting with the basic building blocks of text analysis and moving toward more sophisticated approaches that capture meaning and context. We'll explore the fundamental challenges that make NLP difficult, the preprocessing steps that prepare text for analysis, and the methods for converting text into numerical representations that machine learning algorithms can work with.

4.3 What Is Natural Language Processing?

Natural Language Processing (NLP) is the technology that enables computers to understand, interpret, and generate human language. "Natural language" refers to the languages that humans naturally speak and write—English, Spanish, Mandarin, Arabic—as opposed to artificial programming languages like Python or Java that are designed specifically for computers.

We live in a world overflowing with text data. Every day, billions of emails are sent, millions of social media posts are published, countless documents are created, and enormous amounts of customer feedback are generated. This text contains valuable insights about customer preferences, market trends, public opinion, and business opportunities. But without NLP, this information remains locked away in a format that computers can't easily process.

NLP unlocks this treasure trove of information. It allows companies to automatically analyze customer reviews to understand what people love or hate about their products. It enables healthcare providers to extract important information from medical records. It helps financial institutions detect fraud by analyzing the language patterns in transactions and communications.

You probably interact with NLP systems dozens of times every day without realizing it. When you use voice assistants like Siri or Google Assistant, NLP helps them understand your spoken words and generate appropriate responses. When you use Google Translate to understand a foreign language, NLP powers the translation. When Netflix recommends shows based on descriptions you might like, NLP analyzes the text descriptions to understand what appeals to you.

Email spam filters use NLP to analyze the content of messages and determine which ones are likely to be unwanted. Social media platforms use NLP to detect harmful content and moderate discussions. Customer service chatbots use NLP to understand your questions and provide helpful responses.

Companies across industries are using NLP to transform their operations and create new value. Retailers analyze customer reviews and social media mentions to understand brand sentiment and identify product improvement opportunities. Healthcare organizations use NLP to extract insights from medical records and research papers. Financial services companies use NLP to analyze news and social media for investment insights and risk assessment.

4.4 Understanding the Challenge of Human Language

Before diving into how NLP works, it's important to understand why teaching computers to understand human language is such a challenging problem. This will help you appreciate the techniques we'll explore and understand why certain approaches are necessary.

Humans and computers process information very differently. When you read a sentence, your brain automatically understands context, recognizes relationships between words, fills in missing information, and interprets meaning based on your life experience and cultural knowledge. You do this effortlessly and unconsciously.

Computers, on the other hand, are fundamentally mathematical machines. They work with numbers, precise rules, and logical operations. They don't have life experiences, cultural knowledge, or intuitive understanding of context. To process language, everything must be converted into numbers and mathematical operations.

Human language is incredibly complex and nuanced. The same words can mean completely different things depending on context. The word "bank" could refer to a financial institution or the side of a river. The sentence "I saw the man with the telescope" could mean either that you used a telescope to see the man, or that you saw a man who was carrying a telescope.

Humans resolve these ambiguities automatically using context and common sense, but computers need explicit rules or learned patterns to make these distinctions. Language is also constantly evolving. New words appear regularly, existing words take on new meanings, and different communities develop their own linguistic conventions. A system that works perfectly today might struggle with tomorrow's language innovations.

Additionally, human language is filled with ambiguity that we resolve unconsciously. Language is deeply tied to culture and social context. Humor, politeness conventions, and communication styles vary dramatically across cultures and communities. What's considered appropriate or meaningful in one context might be confusing or offensive in another.

Consider these examples that illustrate why NLP is challenging. The word "apple" means something different when discussing fruit versus technology companies. The phrase "break a leg" is encouraging when said to an actor before a performance but concerning when said to someone heading to a dangerous activity. The sentence "Great, another meeting" is likely sarcastic and negative, while "Great! Another opportunity to learn" is likely genuine and positive.

4.5 Text Preprocessing: Preparing Language for Analysis

Before computers can analyze text meaningfully, the raw language data must be processed and standardized. Text preprocessing is like preparing ingredients before cooking—it's not the most exciting part, but it's essential for good results.

When you receive text data for analysis, it rarely comes in a clean, standardized format. Real-world text comes with all sorts of challenges that need to be addressed before any meaningful analysis can happen. Consider this typical customer review: "OMG this product is AMAZING!!! Best purchase ever… would definitely recommend 2 anyone looking 4 quality items. 5/5 stars!!!"

This single review contains multiple challenges: inconsistent capitalization, repeated punctuation, abbreviations, and informal language. Before any computer can analyze this review for sentiment or extract meaningful information, these inconsistencies need to be addressed.

Real-world text data typically includes encoding issues where different systems save text in different formats, HTML tags from web-scraped content, special characters and symbols, multiple languages within the same document, and inconsistent formatting for dates, addresses, or names.

4.5.1 Tokenization: Breaking Text into Manageable Pieces

Tokenization is the process of breaking text into smaller, manageable units called tokens. Think of it like breaking a sentence into individual words, though it can be more complex than that. Computers need to process text one piece at a time. Before they can understand the meaning of a sentence, they need to identify the individual components.

This might seem simple, but consider these challenges: How do you handle contractions like "don't" or "we'll"? What about hyphenated words like "state-of-the-art"? How do you deal with punctuation attached to words? What about abbreviations like "Dr." or "U.S.A."?

The most common approach is word-level tokenization, where text is split into individual words. For example, "I can't believe it's working!" might become ["I", "can't", "believe", "it's", "working", "!"]. Notice that punctuation might be separated from words, and contractions might be kept as single tokens or split into their components.

Sometimes you need to break text into sentences rather than words. This is useful for analyzing document structure or processing long texts one sentence at a time. However, this presents challenges with abbreviations where periods don't indicate sentence boundaries.

4.5.2 Cleaning and Standardizing Text

Once text is tokenized, it usually needs to be cleaned and standardized to ensure consistent analysis. Most NLP applications convert text to lowercase to ensure that "Apple," "apple," and "APPLE" are treated as the same word. However, this decision isn't always straightforward. In some contexts, capitalization carries important meaning—"Apple" the company versus "apple" the fruit.

Punctuation presents similar challenges. While punctuation often doesn't contribute to the core meaning of text for many applications, it can be crucial for others. Sentiment analysis might benefit from recognizing that multiple exclamation points indicate strong emotion, while topic modeling might treat punctuation as noise to be removed.

Numbers and special characters require special consideration. Sometimes they're important (like prices or dates), and sometimes they're just noise. The decision about how to handle these elements depends on your specific application and analysis goals.

4.5.3 Stopword Removal

Stopwords are common words like "the," "and," "is," and "of" that appear frequently in text but often don't contribute much to the meaning for certain types of analysis. Think about this sentence: "The quick brown fox jumps over the lazy dog." The words that carry the most meaning are "quick," "brown," "fox," "jumps," "lazy," and "dog." Words like "the" and "over" are grammatically necessary but don't tell us much about what the sentence is actually about.

For many NLP tasks, removing these common words helps focus the analysis on content-bearing words and can improve performance while reducing computational requirements. Stopword removal is useful for topic modeling, document classification, and keyword extraction.

However, stopwords should be kept for sentiment analysis where "not good" versus "good" have opposite meanings, question answering where "what," "where," "when" are crucial, and language translation where all words are needed for grammatical correctness.

Different domains might require custom stopword lists. A medical text analysis system might treat common medical terms as stopwords if they appear in every document but don't help distinguish between different topics.

4.5.4 Lemmatization: Reducing Words to Root Forms

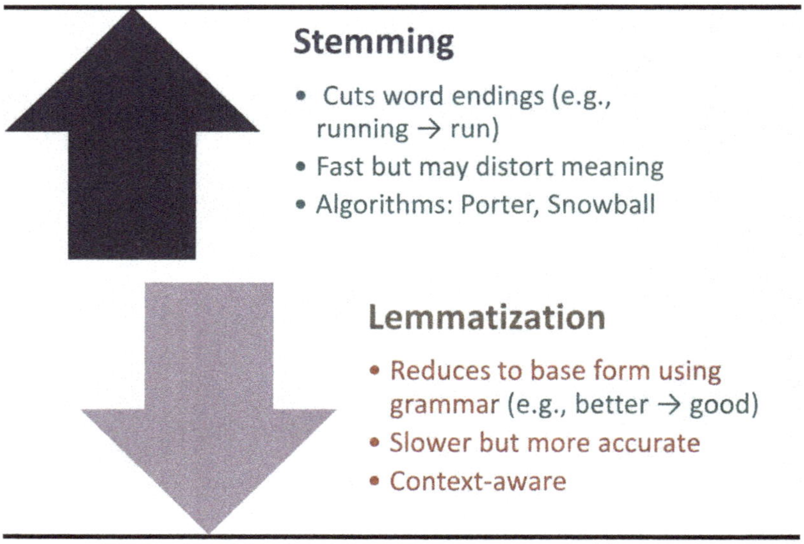

Lemmatization is the process of reducing words to their base or dictionary forms, called lemmas. This helps ensure that different forms of the same word are treated as equivalent. Without lemmatization, a computer might treat "run," "running," "runs," and "ran" as four completely different words, missing the fact that they're all forms of the same basic concept.

Consider analyzing customer feedback about "organization." Without lemmatization, you might separately count "organize," "organizing," "organized," and "organization" as different concepts. With lemmatization, all of these would be reduced to "organize," giving you a complete picture of how often this concept appears.

Lemmatization uses linguistic knowledge to reduce words to their proper dictionary forms. It's more sophisticated than simpler approaches like stemming, which just removes common word endings and can sometimes produce non-words. Lemmatization ensures that the results are actual words and that the grouping makes linguistic sense.

4.6 Converting Text to Numbers

Machine learning algorithms work with numbers, not words. To apply machine learning techniques to text, we need methods for converting words and documents into numerical representations that capture their meaning and relationships. The challenge isn't just converting text to numbers—it's doing so in a way that preserves meaning.

4.6.1 TF-IDF: Measuring Word Importance

Term Frequency-Inverse Document Frequency (TF-IDF) is one of the most important and widely used techniques for converting text to numbers. It measures how important a word is to a document within a collection of documents.

TF-IDF is based on two simple ideas: words that appear frequently in a document are important to that document, and words that appear in many documents are less distinctive and therefore less important. Think about it this way: if the word "election" appears many times in a news article, it's probably important to that article. But if "election" appears in every political article, it's not very useful for distinguishing one political article from another.

Term Frequency measures how often a word appears in a document, usually normalized by the total number of words in the document. In a 100-word document, if the word "customer" appears 5 times, its TF score is 0.05. This normalization is important because longer documents naturally contain more words, and we want to compare the relative importance of words across documents of different lengths.

Inverse Document Frequency measures how rare a word is across the entire collection of documents. Words that appear in many documents get low IDF scores, while words that appear in only a few documents get high IDF scores. If you have 1,000 documents and the word "customer" appears in 100 of them, it's relatively common. If the word "blockchain" appears in only 10 documents, it's much rarer and might be more distinctive.

TF-IDF multiplies these two measures together. Words that are both frequent in a specific document and rare across the collection get the highest TF-IDF scores. This helps identify words that are characteristic of particular documents or topics.

TF-IDF is widely used in search engines, document classification, and content recommendation systems. When you search for information online, TF-IDF helps identify documents that are most relevant to your query by finding documents where your search terms have high TF-IDF scores.

4.6.2 Introduction to Word Embeddings

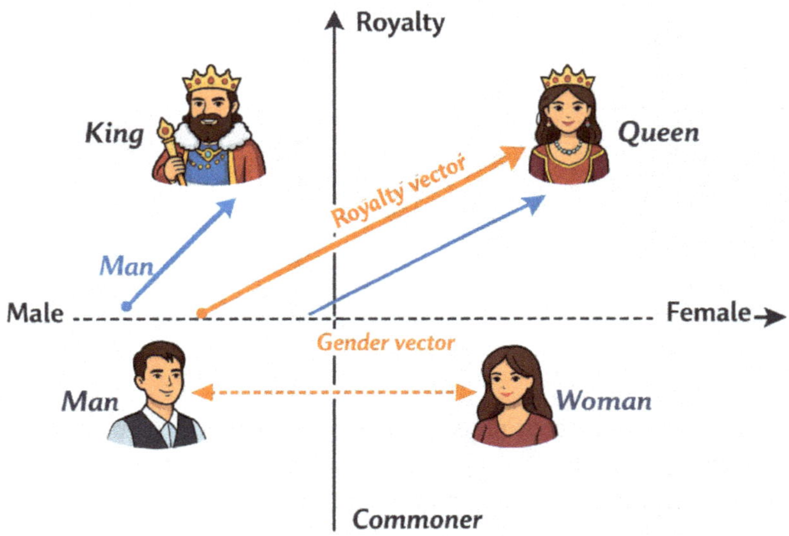

Word embeddings represent a more sophisticated approach to converting words into numbers. Instead of treating words as isolated symbols, embeddings capture semantic relationships by representing words as vectors in a multi-dimensional space where similar words are located near each other.

Imagine a space where words are positioned based on their meanings. Words with similar meanings would be close together, while words with different meanings would be far apart. Word embeddings attempt to create such a space mathematically. In this semantic space, "happy" and "joyful" would be close together because they express similar emotions. "King" and "queen" would be close together because they're both royal titles. "Cat" and "dog" would be relatively close because they're both common pets, but farther from "car" or "computer."

One of the most fascinating aspects of word embeddings is that they can capture analogical relationships through vector arithmetic. The famous example is: king - man + woman ≈ queen. This suggests that the mathematical relationship between "king" and "man" is similar to the relationship between "queen" and "woman." These mathematical relationships enable sophisticated reasoning about word meanings and relationships.

4.6.3 Word2Vec: Learning Word Relationships

Word2Vec is one of the most influential approaches to creating word embeddings. It learns word representations by training a neural network to predict words based on their context in large collections of text.

Word2Vec operates on the principle that words that appear in similar contexts tend to have similar meanings. This is based on the linguistic idea that you can understand a word's meaning by looking at the words that typically appear around it. Since "cat" and "dog" appear in similar contexts, they should have similar meanings as both are animals and pets.

Word2Vec trains a neural network on a simple task: given the words around a target word, predict what the target word is. Through this training process, the network learns to represent words as vectors such that words with similar contexts end up with similar vector representations. The beauty of this approach is that it discovers semantic relationships automatically from large amounts of text data.

Word2Vec requires large amounts of text data to learn effective representations. The quality and diversity of this training data significantly impact the quality of the resulting embeddings. Training on news articles might produce embeddings that work well for formal text but poorly for social media content.

Word2Vec embeddings have been successfully applied to many NLP tasks, including sentiment analysis, document classification, information retrieval, and machine translation. They provide a foundation for more sophisticated language models and have influenced the development of modern NLP systems.

However, Word2Vec has limitations. It produces a single representation for each word, regardless of context. The word "bank" gets the same representation whether it refers to a financial institution or the side of a river. More recent approaches address this limitation by creating context-dependent representations.

4.7 Key Terms

Natural Language Processing (NLP) – A branch of AI focused on enabling computers to understand, interpret, and generate human language.

Tokenization – The process of breaking text into smaller units called tokens, such as words or sentences.

Text Preprocessing – Techniques used to clean and standardize text before analysis, including tokenization, cleaning, stopword removal, and lemmatization.

Stopwords – Common words like "the," "and," or "is" that often carry little meaning and are sometimes removed during text analysis.

Lemmatization – Reducing words to their dictionary or root form (lemma) to treat different forms of a word as equivalent.

Stemming – A simpler form of reducing words to their base form, often by removing word endings; less precise than lemmatization.

TF-IDF (Term Frequency-Inverse Document Frequency) – A statistical measure that evaluates how important a word is to a document relative to a collection of documents.

Word Embeddings – Numerical vector representations of words that capture semantic meaning and relationships.

Word2Vec – A neural network-based method to generate word embeddings by learning word relationships from context.

Context-Dependent Representations – Word embeddings that change depending on the surrounding words, allowing for disambiguation of words like "bank."

Semantic Relationships – Relationships between words based on their meaning, e.g., "king" and "queen" are semantically related.

Vectorization – Converting text data into numerical vectors so machine learning algorithms can process it.

Encoding Issues – Problems that arise when text is saved in different formats or character sets.

Noise in Text Data – Irrelevant or inconsistent information in text, such as HTML tags, punctuation, or special characters.

Text Cleaning – Removing or standardizing unwanted elements in text, including punctuation, numbers, and formatting inconsistencies.

Applications of NLP – Common use cases include sentiment analysis, chatbots, machine translation, content recommendation, spam detection, and information extraction.

Challenges of NLP – Ambiguity, context-dependence, evolving language, sarcasm, cultural differences, and polysemy (words with multiple meanings).

4.8 Review Questions

1. What is Natural Language Processing, and why is it important for modern businesses?
2. Explain why human language is challenging for computers to process. Provide at least two examples of ambiguity in language.
3. What is text preprocessing, and why is it necessary before performing NLP tasks?
4. Define tokenization and describe challenges that may arise when tokenizing text.
5. Explain the purpose of stopword removal and give examples of situations where stopwords should not be removed.
6. What is lemmatization, and how does it differ from stemming? Why is lemmatization often preferred?
7. Describe how TF-IDF works and why it is useful for representing text in numerical form.

8. What are word embeddings, and how do they capture semantic relationships between words?
9. Explain how Word2Vec generates word embeddings and what role context plays in this process.
10. Why are context-dependent word representations important? Provide an example.
11. List at least five common applications of NLP in business and everyday life.
12. What are some sources of noise in real-world text data, and how can they be addressed?
13. How do vectorization techniques enable machine learning algorithms to process text data?
14. Describe the trade-offs between using simpler methods like TF-IDF and more sophisticated methods like Word2Vec.
15. Why is domain knowledge important when implementing NLP systems in a specific industry?

4.9 Lab 4: Natural Language Processing

4.9.1 Introduction

Imagine you're working as a data analyst for a popular restaurant chain, and your manager walks into your office with a challenge: "We're getting thousands of customer reviews every day across Google, Yelp, and social media. I need to know what customers really think about our food, service, and locations, but we can't possibly read them all manually. Can you help us automatically understand what customers are saying?"

This scenario perfectly illustrates why Natural Language Processing (NLP) has become one of the most valuable skills in data analytics. NLP is the technology that enables computers to understand, interpret, and analyze human language—the same language you use in emails, reviews, social media posts, and everyday conversation.

4.9.1.1 Why NLP Matters

We live in a world overflowing with text data. Every day, billions of emails are sent, millions of social media posts are published, countless customer reviews are written, and enormous amounts of business documents are created. This text contains incredibly valuable insights about customer preferences, market trends, public opinion, and business opportunities. But without NLP, this information remains locked away in a format that computers can't easily process.

In this lab, we'll work through a complete NLP pipeline using a customer review analysis scenario. You'll learn how to transform raw text into actionable business insights using

Python and machine learning.

4.9.2 Demonstration

We'll work with a synthetic dataset of customer reviews for a restaurant chain. This dataset includes reviews from various platforms with different ratings and text content. We'll use this data to demonstrate the complete NLP pipeline from raw text to business insights.

4.9.2.1 Step 1: Environment Setup and Data Creation

First, let's import the necessary libraries and create our customer review dataset:

```
# Import required libraries
import pandas as pd
import numpy as np
import matplotlib.pyplot as plt
import seaborn as sns
from sklearn.model_selection import train_test_split
from sklearn.feature_extraction.text import TfidfVectorizer,
  ↪ CountVectorizer
from sklearn.linear_model import LogisticRegression
from sklearn.naive_bayes import MultinomialNB
from sklearn.metrics import accuracy_score, classification_report,
  ↪ confusion_matrix
import re
import string
from collections import Counter
import warnings
warnings.filterwarnings('ignore')

# Set random seed for reproducibility
np.random.seed(42)
print("LAB 5: NATURAL LANGUAGE PROCESSING FUNDAMENTALS")
print("=" * 60)
```

What this code does: We import all the necessary libraries for text processing, machine learning, and data visualization. The random seed ensures our results are reproducible.

Next, we'll create a synthetic dataset that mimics real customer reviews:

```
# Create synthetic customer review dataset
print("Creating customer review dataset...")
print("=" * 40)

# Define review templates for different sentiments
```

```
positive_templates = [
    "Amazing {food}! The {service} was excellent and the {atmosphere}
     ↪ was perfect.",
    "Love this place! Great {food}, friendly {service}, and wonderful
     ↪ {atmosphere}.",
    "Outstanding {food} and fantastic {service}. Highly recommend!",
    "Delicious {food}, quick {service}, and cozy {atmosphere}. Will
     ↪ definitely return!"
]

negative_templates = [
    "Terrible {food}. The {service} was awful and the {atmosphere} was
     ↪ disappointing.",
    "Worst {food} ever! Poor {service} and terrible {atmosphere}. Never
     ↪ coming back.",
    "Disgusting {food}, rude {service}, and unpleasant {atmosphere}.
     ↪ Avoid this place!",
    "Overpriced {food}, slow {service}, and noisy {atmosphere}. Very
     ↪ disappointed."
]

neutral_templates = [
    "The {food} was okay. {service} was average and {atmosphere} was
     ↪ fine.",
    "Decent {food}, standard {service}, and typical {atmosphere}.
     ↪ Nothing special.",
    "Average {food}, normal {service}, and regular {atmosphere}. It's
     ↪ alright.",
    "The {food} was fine. {service} was okay and {atmosphere} was
     ↪ decent."
]

# Define word options for templates
food_words = ["pizza", "burger", "pasta", "salad", "steak", "chicken",
 ↪ "fish", "soup"]
service_words = ["service", "staff", "waiters", "servers", "team",
 ↪ "employees"]
atmosphere_words = ["atmosphere", "ambiance", "environment", "setting",
 ↪ "vibe", "mood"]
```

What this code does: We create template sentences for different sentiment categories and word lists to fill in the templates. This approach generates realistic-looking reviews with controlled sentiment labels.

Now let's generate the complete dataset:

```
# Generate reviews
n_reviews = 1500
reviews = []
ratings = []
sentiments = []

for i in range(n_reviews):
    # Randomly choose sentiment
    sentiment_choice = np.random.choice(['positive', 'negative',
    'neutral'], p=[0.4, 0.3, 0.3])

    if sentiment_choice == 'positive':
        template = np.random.choice(positive_templates)
        rating = np.random.choice([4, 5], p=[0.3, 0.7])
        sentiment = 'positive'
    elif sentiment_choice == 'negative':
        template = np.random.choice(negative_templates)
        rating = np.random.choice([1, 2], p=[0.6, 0.4])
        sentiment = 'negative'
    else:
        template = np.random.choice(neutral_templates)
        rating = 3
        sentiment = 'neutral'

    # Fill in template
    review_text = template.format(
        food=np.random.choice(food_words),
        service=np.random.choice(service_words),
        atmosphere=np.random.choice(atmosphere_words)
    )

    # Introduce controlled noise
    # 10% chance of sentiment mismatch
    if np.random.random() < 0.1:
        sentiment = np.random.choice(['positive', 'negative',
    'neutral'])

    # 15% chance to add extra modifier words
    if np.random.random() < 0.15:
        noise_words = ["actually", "honestly", "basically",
    "literally", "somewhat", "pretty"]
        review_text = np.random.choice(noise_words) + " " + review_text
```

```
    reviews.append(review_text)
    ratings.append(rating)
    sentiments.append(sentiment)

# Create DataFrame
review_data = pd.DataFrame({
    'review_text': reviews,
    'rating': ratings,
    'sentiment': sentiments
})

print(f"Dataset created with {len(review_data)} customer reviews")
```

Output:

```
Dataset created with 1500 customer reviews
```

Let's examine our dataset:

```
print("\n\nFirst 10 reviews:")
print(review_data.head(10))
print("\n\nDataset summary:")
print(review_data['sentiment'].value_counts())
print("\n\nRating distribution:")
print(review_data['rating'].value_counts().sort_index())
```

Output:

```
First 10 reviews:
                                         review_text  rating sentiment
0  Terrible pizza. The service was awful and the ...       1  negative
1  Love this place! Great salad, friendly employe...       5  positive
2  Decent chicken, standard service, and typical ...       3  positive
3  Average pasta, normal employees, and regular e...       3  positive
4  Worst steak ever! Poor waiters and terrible en...       1  negative
5  basically Terrible soup. The waiters was awful...       1  negative
6  Worst soup ever! Poor service and terrible atm...       1  negative
7  The salad was okay. team was average and vibe ...       3  positive
8  Outstanding chicken and fantastic team. Highly...       5  positive
9  Decent chicken, standard employees, and typica...       3  positive

Dataset summary:
sentiment
positive    569
```

```
neutral     478
negative    453
Name: count, dtype: int64

Rating distribution:
rating
1    270
2    183
3    466
4    156
5    425
Name: count, dtype: int64
```

4.9.2.2 Step 2: Text Preprocessing - Cleaning and Preparing Text

Before analyzing text data, it is essential to clean and standardize it. Raw text often contains inconsistent capitalization, punctuation, extra whitespace, and words that add little meaning, which can make analysis less accurate or even misleading. Preprocessing transforms this raw text into a consistent format that machine learning algorithms or rule-based systems can interpret reliably.

Text preprocessing typically involves several key steps. First, basic cleaning converts all text to lowercase, removes punctuation, and normalizes whitespace. This ensures that words like "Good" and "good" are treated the same and that extra spaces or symbols do not interfere with analysis. Next is tokenization, which splits text into individual words or tokens. Tokenization allows us to examine or model the text at the word level. Stopword removal is often applied to eliminate extremely common words, like "the" or "and," that do not contribute meaningful information for sentiment or topic analysis. Finally, feature extraction converts the clean text into numerical representations, such as TF-IDF vectors, which can be used by machine learning models.

The code implements these preprocessing steps. The `clean_text` function handles basic cleaning by converting text to lowercase, removing punctuation, and removing extra spaces. The `preprocess_text` function is a slightly more advanced version, using regular expressions to carefully remove punctuation while preserving word spacing. These functions ensure that the text is in a consistent, standardized form before further analysis, whether it is for rule-based scoring or machine learning models.

```
print("\n\n" + "="*60)
print("TEXT PREPROCESSING: CLEANING AND PREPARING TEXT")
print("="*60)

# Function to clean text
def clean_text(text):
    """Clean and preprocess text data"""
```

```
    # Convert to lowercase
    text = text.lower()

    # Remove punctuation
    text = text.translate(str.maketrans('', '', string.punctuation))

    # Remove extra whitespace
    text = ' '.join(text.split())

    return text

# Function for advanced text preprocessing
def preprocess_text(text):
    """Advanced text preprocessing"""
    # Convert to lowercase
    text = text.lower()

    # Remove punctuation but keep spaces
    text = re.sub(r'[^\w\s]', ' ', text)

    # Remove extra whitespace
    text = ' '.join(text.split())

    return text
```

Let's see the cleaning in action:

```
print("\nPart 1: Basic Text Cleaning")
print("-" * 30)

# Show examples of text before and after cleaning
sample_reviews = review_data['review_text'].head(5)

print("Original reviews:")
for i, review in enumerate(sample_reviews, 1):
    print(f"{i}. {review}")

print("\n\nAfter basic cleaning:")
for i, review in enumerate(sample_reviews, 1):
    cleaned = clean_text(review)
    print(f"{i}. {cleaned}")

# Apply preprocessing to all reviews
review_data['cleaned_text'] =
↪   review_data['review_text'].apply(preprocess_text)
```

Output:

```
Original reviews:
1. Terrible pizza. The service was awful and the atmosphere was
disappointing.
2. Love this place! Great salad, friendly employees, and wonderful
environment.
3. Decent chicken, standard service, and typical ambiance.
Nothing special.
4. Average pasta, normal employees, and regular environment.
It's alright.
5. Worst steak ever! Poor waiters and terrible environment.
Never coming back.

After basic cleaning:
1. terrible pizza the service was awful and the atmosphere was
disappointing
2. love this place great salad friendly employees and wonderful
environment
3. decent chicken standard service and typical ambiance nothing special
4. average pasta normal employees and regular environment its alright
5. worst steak ever poor waiters and terrible environment
never coming back
```

4.9.2.2.1 Tokenization: Breaking Text into Words

Once text is cleaned, the next step is tokenization, which breaks the text into individual words, or tokens. Tokenization allows us to analyze or model text at the word level, which is essential for sentiment analysis, word frequency analysis, and feature extraction.

In the example, the original text is: "Amazing pizza! The service was excellent and the atmosphere was perfect." A basic tokenization approach simply splits the text by spaces. This produces tokens like 'pizza!' and 'perfect.' which still include punctuation. These extra symbols can interfere with analysis because 'pizza' and 'pizza!' would be treated as different words.

Using proper preprocessing first—removing punctuation, converting to lowercase, and normalizing whitespace—produces cleaner tokens. After preprocessing, tokenization yields 'pizza' and 'perfect' without punctuation, resulting in a consistent and accurate set of words for analysis. This demonstrates the importance of combining cleaning with tokenization to prepare text effectively for sentiment scoring or machine learning.

```
print("\n\nPart 2: Tokenization - Breaking Text into Words")
print("-" * 45)
```

```
# Simple tokenization example
sample_text = "Amazing pizza! The service was excellent and the
 ↪  atmosphere was perfect."
print(f"Original text: {sample_text}")

# Basic tokenization (split by spaces)
tokens = sample_text.lower().split()
print(f"Basic tokens: {tokens}")

# Better tokenization (remove punctuation first)
cleaned_sample = preprocess_text(sample_text)
better_tokens = cleaned_sample.split()
print(f"Better tokens: {better_tokens}")
```

Output:

```
Original text: Amazing pizza! The service was excellent and the
atmosphere was perfect.
Basic tokens: ['amazing', 'pizza!', 'the', 'service', 'was',
'excellent', 'and', 'the', 'atmosphere', 'was', 'perfect.']
Better tokens: ['amazing', 'pizza', 'the', 'service', 'was',
'excellent', 'and', 'the', 'atmosphere', 'was', 'perfect']
```

Notice how proper preprocessing removes punctuation from tokens, making them cleaner for analysis.

4.9.2.2.2 Stopword Removal

After tokenization, the next step in text preprocessing is stopword removal. Stopwords are extremely common words in a language, such as "the," "and," "is," or "with," which usually do not carry meaningful information for tasks like sentiment analysis or topic modeling. Removing these words helps reduce noise and allows models to focus on the words that actually contribute to understanding the text.

In the example, the cleaned text is: "amazing pizza the service was excellent and the atmosphere was perfect". Applying stopword removal filters out common words like "the," "and," and "was," leaving a more informative set of words: "amazing pizza service excellent atmosphere perfect". These remaining words carry the key descriptive and sentiment-bearing content. By applying stopword removal to all reviews, we ensure that the processed text is concise, consistent, and better suited for machine learning or rule-based analysis.

```
print("\n\nPart 3: Stopword Removal")
print("-" * 25)
```

```
# Define common English stopwords
stopwords = {
    'i', 'me', 'my', 'myself', 'we', 'our', 'ours', 'ourselves', 'you',
     ↪ 'your', 'yours',
    'yourself', 'yourselves', 'he', 'him', 'his', 'himself', 'she',
     ↪ 'her', 'hers',
    'herself', 'it', 'its', 'itself', 'they', 'them', 'their',
     ↪ 'theirs', 'themselves',
    'what', 'which', 'who', 'whom', 'this', 'that', 'these', 'those',
     ↪ 'am', 'is', 'are',
    'was', 'were', 'be', 'been', 'being', 'have', 'has', 'had',
     ↪ 'having', 'do', 'does',
    'did', 'doing', 'a', 'an', 'the', 'and', 'but', 'if', 'or',
     ↪ 'because', 'as', 'until',
    'while', 'of', 'at', 'by', 'for', 'with', 'through', 'during',
     ↪ 'before', 'after',
    'above', 'below', 'up', 'down', 'in', 'out', 'on', 'off', 'over',
     ↪ 'under', 'again',
    'further', 'then', 'once'
}

def remove_stopwords(text):
    """Remove stopwords from text"""
    words = text.split()
    filtered_words = [word for word in words if word not in stopwords]
    return ' '.join(filtered_words)

# Example of stopword removal
print(f"Before stopword removal: {cleaned_sample}")
no_stopwords = remove_stopwords(cleaned_sample)
print(f"After stopword removal: {no_stopwords}")

# Apply stopword removal to all reviews
review_data['processed_text'] =
 ↪ review_data['cleaned_text'].apply(remove_stopwords)
```

Output:

```
Before stopword removal: amazing pizza the service was excellent
and the atmosphere was perfect
After stopword removal: amazing pizza service excellent atmosphere
perfect
```

Removing stopwords helps focus on meaningful words that carry sentiment and topic information.

4.9.2.2.3 Text Statistics Analysis

After cleaning, tokenizing, and removing stopwords, it is useful to explore some basic text statistics. Calculating metrics like word count and character count helps us understand the length and complexity of reviews across different sentiment categories. For example, positive reviews may tend to be longer, including more descriptive words, while negative or neutral reviews may be shorter or more concise. Computing the average word and character counts for each sentiment provides insight into these patterns and can guide further analysis or feature engineering.

In addition to summary statistics, examining the most common words across all reviews highlights which terms appear frequently in the dataset. Counting word frequencies can reveal the words that dominate the text, such as product names, features, or sentiment-bearing adjectives. For example, in a set of processed reviews, words like "good," "service," or "quality" may appear most often. Understanding these common words is important for both rule-based sentiment analysis, where they may be included in lexicons, and for machine learning models, where they contribute to TF-IDF or other feature representations.

```
print("\n\nPart 4: Text Statistics")
print("-" * 20)

# Calculate text statistics
review_data['word_count'] = review_data['processed_text'].apply(lambda
 ↪ x: len(x.split()))
review_data['char_count'] = review_data['processed_text'].apply(len)

print("Text statistics by sentiment:")
text_stats = review_data.groupby('sentiment')[['word_count',
 ↪ 'char_count']].mean()
print(text_stats.round(2))

# Most common words
print("\n\nMost common words across all reviews:")
all_words = ' '.join(review_data['processed_text']).split()
word_freq = Counter(all_words)
print("Top 15 most common words:")
for word, count in word_freq.most_common(15):
    print(f"  {word}: {count}")
```

Output:

```
Text statistics by sentiment:
           word_count  char_count
sentiment
negative         8.12       59.72
neutral          7.20       50.21
positive         7.42       56.39

Most common words across all reviews:
Top 15 most common words:
  employees: 264
  place: 257
  waiters: 251
  servers: 251
  ambiance: 250
  team: 247
  staff: 246
  service: 241
  vibe: 240
  average: 234
  decent: 232
  terrible: 229
  okay: 228
  fine: 228
  setting: 222
```

By combining summary statistics with word frequency analysis, it becomes possible to gain a clear understanding of the dataset. Average word and character counts reveal differences in review length across sentiment categories, while the most common words highlight the key terms that dominate the text. These insights help interpret model results, identify patterns, and inform decisions when preparing text for sentiment scoring or machine learning.

4.9.2.3 Step 3: Converting Text to Numbers with TF-IDF

Now we need to convert our text data into numerical features that machine learning models can understand. We'll use TF-IDF (Term Frequency-Inverse Document Frequency), one of the most effective methods for this conversion.

4.9.2.3.1 Understanding TF-IDF

TF-IDF combines two concepts: - Term Frequency (TF): How often a word appears in a single document - Inverse Document Frequency (IDF): How rare or common that word is across all documents

By multiplying TF and IDF, we get a score that reflects how important a word is to a specific document. Words that appear frequently in one review but not in many others receive high TF-IDF scores.

```
print("\n\n" + "="*60)
print("CONVERTING TEXT TO NUMBERS WITH TF-IDF")
print("="*60)
print("\nPart 1: Understanding TF-IDF")
print("-" * 30)
print("TF-IDF stands for Term Frequency-Inverse Document Frequency")
print("• TF (Term Frequency): How often a word appears in a document")
print("• IDF (Inverse Document Frequency): How rare/common a word is
↪   across all documents")
print("• TF-IDF = TF × IDF")
print("\n\nWords that appear frequently in a document but rarely across
↪   all documents")
print("get high TF-IDF scores (they're distinctive for that document)")
```

4.9.2.3.2 Creating TF-IDF Features

```
print("\n\nPart 2: Creating TF-IDF Features")
print("-" * 35)

# Initialize TF-IDF vectorizer
tfidf_vectorizer = TfidfVectorizer(
    max_features=1000,  # Keep top 1000 most important words
    min_df=2,           # Word must appear in at least 2 documents
    max_df=0.8,         # Word can't appear in more than 80% of
↪   documents
    ngram_range=(1, 2) # Include both single words and two-word phrases
)

# Fit and transform the text data
print("Converting text to TF-IDF features...")
X_tfidf = tfidf_vectorizer.fit_transform(review_data['processed_text'])
print(f"TF-IDF matrix shape: {X_tfidf.shape}")
print(f"Number of documents: {X_tfidf.shape[0]}")
print(f"Number of features (words/phrases): {X_tfidf.shape[1]}")

# Get feature names (the words/phrases)
feature_names = tfidf_vectorizer.get_feature_names_out()
print(f"\n\nFirst 20 features: {feature_names[:20]}")
print(f"Last 20 features: {feature_names[-20:]}")
```

Output:

```
Converting text to TF-IDF features...
TF-IDF matrix shape: (1500, 607)
Number of documents: 1500
Number of features (words/phrases): 607

First 20 features: ['actually' 'actually amazing'
 'actually average' 'actually decent'
 'actually delicious' 'actually disgusting' 'actually overpriced'
 'actually pizza' 'actually salad' 'actually soup' 'actually terrible'
 'actually worst' 'alright' 'amazing' 'amazing burger' 'amazing chicken'
 'amazing fish' 'amazing pasta' 'amazing pizza' 'amazing salad']
Last 20 features: ['waiters unpleasant' 'waiters wonderful'
 'will' 'will definitely'
 'wonderful' 'wonderful ambiance' 'wonderful atmosphere'
 'wonderful environment' 'wonderful mood' 'wonderful setting'
 'wonderful vibe' 'worst' 'worst burger' 'worst chicken' 'worst fish'
 'worst pasta' 'worst pizza' 'worst salad' 'worst soup' 'worst steak']
```

The TF-IDF feature list shows all unique words and phrases extracted from the text, but the "first" and "last" features are simply listed in alphabetical order, not by frequency or importance. While the TF-IDF matrix encodes how strongly each word or bigram represents a document, the printed feature names alone don't indicate which terms are most common or predictive. To understand which words matter most, you need to examine the actual TF-IDF values or the feature weights from a trained model.

4.9.2.3.3 Analyzing TF-IDF Scores

This step examines the TF-IDF matrix to identify which words and phrases are most and least representative across the dataset. By converting the sparse TF-IDF matrix to a dense array, we can calculate the average TF-IDF score for each feature, reflecting how distinctive it is in the collection of reviews. Words with the highest average scores, such as "fine," "okay," and "employees," appear frequently in ways that help distinguish reviews, indicating they carry more information about the text. Conversely, words or phrases with very low average scores, like "actually overpriced" or "literally delicious," appear rarely or are too evenly distributed to strongly differentiate documents. This analysis helps highlight the most influential terms that a machine learning model might rely on and provides insight into which expressions are truly informative versus those that are negligible.

```
print("\n\nPart 3: Analyzing TF-IDF Scores")
print("-" * 32)

# Convert sparse matrix to dense for analysis
X_tfidf_dense = X_tfidf.toarray()
```

```python
# Find words with highest average TF-IDF scores
mean_tfidf_scores = np.mean(X_tfidf_dense, axis=0)
word_importance = list(zip(feature_names, mean_tfidf_scores))
word_importance.sort(key=lambda x: x[1], reverse=True)

print("Top 15 most important words/phrases (highest average TF-IDF):")
for word, score in word_importance[:15]:
    print(f"  {word}: {score:.4f}")

print("\n\nLeast important words/phrases (lowest average TF-IDF):")
for word, score in word_importance[-10:]:
    print(f"  {word}: {score:.4f}")
```

Output:

```
Top 15 most important words/phrases (highest average TF-IDF):
  fine: 0.0310
  okay: 0.0310
  employees: 0.0310
  team: 0.0300
  average: 0.0300
  servers: 0.0299
  ambiance: 0.0299
  waiters: 0.0298
  staff: 0.0297
  place: 0.0295
  service: 0.0291
  decent: 0.0288
  vibe: 0.0287
  setting: 0.0275
  soup: 0.0273

Least important words/phrases (lowest average TF-IDF):
  basically average: 0.0005
  pretty average: 0.0005
  literally decent: 0.0005
  pretty disgusting: 0.0005
  actually disgusting: 0.0005
  literally delicious: 0.0005
  honestly delicious: 0.0005
  actually overpriced: 0.0005
  honestly overpriced: 0.0005
  somewhat worst: 0.0005
```

4.9.2.4 Step 4: Building Sentiment Analysis Models

Now we'll build machine learning models to automatically classify review sentiment using our TF-IDF features.

This step prepares the review data for machine learning by converting the original three-class sentiment labels (positive, neutral, negative) into a simplified binary format. Here, neutral reviews are combined with positive ones to create a "negative vs. non-negative" classification, which is common in business applications where identifying negative feedback is most critical. The TF-IDF features serve as the input data, and the binary labels become the target. The dataset is then split into training and testing sets, with 80% of reviews used to train the models and 20% reserved for evaluating their performance. This ensures the models learn patterns from the majority of the data while retaining a separate set to fairly assess predictive accuracy.

4.9.2.4.1 Preparing Data for Machine Learning

```
print("\n\n" + "="*60)
print("BUILDING SENTIMENT ANALYSIS MODELS")
print("="*60)
print("\nPart 1: Preparing Data for Machine Learning")
print("-" * 42)

# For binary classification, let's combine neutral with positive
# This is common in business applications where you want to identify
 ↪  negative vs non-negative
review_data['binary_sentiment'] = review_data['sentiment'].apply(
    lambda x: 'negative' if x == 'negative' else 'positive')

print("Binary sentiment distribution:")
print(review_data['binary_sentiment'].value_counts())

# Split data into training and testing sets
X = X_tfidf  # Our TF-IDF features
y_binary = review_data['binary_sentiment']  # 2-class problem
 ↪  (positive, negative)

# Split for binary classification
X_train, X_test, y_train_binary, y_test_binary = train_test_split(
    X, y_binary, test_size=0.2, random_state=42, stratify=y_binary)

print(f"\n\nTraining set size: {X_train.shape[0]} reviews")
print(f"Testing set size: {X_test.shape[0]} reviews")
```

Output:

```
Binary sentiment distribution:
binary_sentiment
positive    1047
negative     453
Name: count, dtype: int64

Training set size: 1200 reviews
Testing set size: 300 reviews
```

4.9.2.4.2 Building Logistic Regression Model

This section builds and evaluates a logistic regression model to classify customer reviews as either negative or non-negative (positive/neutral combined). The model is trained on the TF-IDF features from the training set and then used to predict sentiments on the test set. The output shows that the model achieves very high accuracy, correctly classifying 97% of reviews. The classification report breaks down performance for each class, reporting precision (how many predicted positives were correct), recall (how many actual positives were detected), and the F1-score (a balance of precision and recall). The results indicate that the model performs extremely well at identifying both negative and positive reviews, though the perfect-looking metrics may reflect the structured, template-based nature of the synthetic dataset rather than real-world variability.

```
print("\n\nPart 2: Building Logistic Regression Model")
print("-" * 40)

# Build logistic regression model
lr_model = LogisticRegression(random_state=42, max_iter=1000)
lr_model.fit(X_train, y_train_binary)

# Make predictions
y_pred_lr = lr_model.predict(X_test)
y_pred_proba_lr = lr_model.predict_proba(X_test)

# Calculate accuracy
lr_accuracy = accuracy_score(y_test_binary, y_pred_lr)
print(f"Logistic Regression Accuracy: {lr_accuracy:.3f}
 ↪  ({lr_accuracy*100:.1f}%)")

print("\n\nClassification Report:")
print(classification_report(y_test_binary, y_pred_lr))
```

Output:

```
Logistic Regression Accuracy: 0.970 (97.0%)
```

```
Classification Report:
              precision    recall  f1-score   support

    negative       0.96      0.95      0.95        91
    positive       0.98      0.98      0.98       209

    accuracy                           0.97       300
   macro avg       0.97      0.96      0.96       300
weighted avg       0.97      0.97      0.97       300
```

4.9.2.4.3 Analyzing Feature Importance

This step analyzes which words contribute most to the logistic regression model's predictions. By examining the model's coefficients, we can see which words strongly indicate positive or negative sentiment. Words with large positive coefficients, like "fine," "amazing," and "excellent," are most associated with positive reviews, while words with large negative coefficients, such as "terrible," "awful," and "disappointing," signal negative sentiment. The output highlights the top 10 words for each sentiment, showing which terms the model relies on most when classifying reviews. This feature-level insight helps interpret the model and understand why it makes certain predictions, making the results more transparent.

```
# Show most important features for each class
print("\n\nMost important words for sentiment classification:")
feature_importance = lr_model.coef_[0]
word_importance = list(zip(feature_names, feature_importance))
word_importance.sort(key=lambda x: abs(x[1]), reverse=True)

print("\n\nTop 10 words that indicate POSITIVE sentiment:")
positive_words = [word for word, coef in word_importance if coef >
↪  0][:10]
for word in positive_words:
    coef = next(coef for w, coef in word_importance if w == word)
    print(f"  {word}: {coef:.4f}")

print("\n\nTop 10 words that indicate NEGATIVE sentiment:")
negative_words = [word for word, coef in word_importance if coef <
↪  0][:10]
for word in negative_words:
    coef = next(coef for w, coef in word_importance if w == word)
    print(f"  {word}: {coef:.4f}")
```

Output:

```
Most important words for sentiment classification:
```

```
Top 10 words that indicate POSITIVE sentiment:
  fine: 1.8021
  okay: 1.8021
  average: 1.7741
  decent: 1.3482
  amazing: 1.2555
  excellent: 1.2555
  perfect: 1.2555
  friendly: 0.9680
  great: 0.9680
  love: 0.9680

Top 10 words that indicate NEGATIVE sentiment:
  terrible: -2.9900
  awful: -2.6047
  disappointing: -2.6047
  disappointed: -1.8042
  noisy: -1.8042
  overpriced: -1.8042
  slow: -1.8042
  very: -1.8042
  very disappointed: -1.8042
  avoid: -1.7998
```

4.9.2.4.4 Building Naive Bayes Model

This section builds and evaluates a Multinomial Naive Bayes model for classifying customer review sentiment. The model uses the TF-IDF features from the preprocessed text to learn which words are associated with positive or negative sentiment. After training on the binary-labeled dataset, the model predicts sentiment on the test set and calculates accuracy.

The output shows that the Naive Bayes model achieves 97% accuracy, identical to logistic regression in this case. The classification report breaks down performance by class: negative reviews have slightly lower recall and precision (0.95), while positive reviews are predicted almost perfectly (0.98). Overall, this demonstrates that Naive Bayes can effectively capture sentiment patterns in text, providing a simple yet powerful method for automatic review classification.

```
print("\n\nPart 3: Building Naive Bayes Model")
print("-" * 32)

# Build Naive Bayes model
nb_model = MultinomialNB()
```

```
nb_model.fit(X_train, y_train_binary)

# Make predictions
y_pred_nb = nb_model.predict(X_test)

# Calculate accuracy
nb_accuracy = accuracy_score(y_test_binary, y_pred_nb)
print(f"Naive Bayes Accuracy: {nb_accuracy:.3f}
↪   ({nb_accuracy*100:.1f}%)")

print("\n\nClassification Report:")
print(classification_report(y_test_binary, y_pred_nb))
```

Output:

```
Naive Bayes Accuracy: 0.970 (97.0%)

Classification Report:
              precision    recall  f1-score   support

    negative       0.96      0.95      0.95        91
    positive       0.98      0.98      0.98       209

    accuracy                           0.97       300
   macro avg       0.97      0.96      0.96       300
weighted avg       0.97      0.97      0.97       300
```

4.9.2.4.5 Testing Models with New Reviews

This section demonstrates how the trained sentiment analysis models can be applied to new, unseen reviews. The new reviews are first preprocessed—stopwords removed and text cleaned—then converted into TF-IDF feature vectors to match the format used during training. Both the logistic regression and Naive Bayes models make predictions on these reviews, and the predicted sentiment labels are reported along with the model confidence scores.

The output shows that for all five new reviews, both models correctly classify the sentiment, and their predictions agree in each case. Positive reviews such as "This restaurant is absolutely fantastic!" receive high confidence scores, while clearly negative reviews like "Worst restaurant ever…" are confidently labeled negative. This demonstrates that the models generalize well and can reliably classify sentiment in reviews they have not seen before, providing a practical tool for automated text analysis.

```
print("\n\n" + "="*60)
print("TESTING OUR MODEL WITH NEW REVIEWS")
```

```
print("="*60)

# Create some new test reviews
new_reviews = [
    "This restaurant is absolutely fantastic! Amazing food and
     ↪ wonderful service.",
    "Terrible experience. The food was cold and the staff was rude.",
    "The pizza was okay, nothing special but not bad either.",
    "Outstanding meal! Best pasta I've ever had. Highly recommend!",
    "Worst restaurant ever. Overpriced and disgusting food."
]

print("Testing our sentiment analysis model on new reviews:")
print("=" * 55)

# Preprocess new reviews
processed_new_reviews = [preprocess_text(remove_stopwords(review)) for
 ↪  review in new_reviews]

# Convert to TF-IDF features
new_reviews_tfidf = tfidf_vectorizer.transform(processed_new_reviews)

# Make predictions with both models
lr_predictions = lr_model.predict(new_reviews_tfidf)
lr_probabilities = lr_model.predict_proba(new_reviews_tfidf)
nb_predictions = nb_model.predict(new_reviews_tfidf)
nb_probabilities = nb_model.predict_proba(new_reviews_tfidf)

# Display results
for i, review in enumerate(new_reviews):
    print(f"\n\nReview {i+1}: \"{review}\"")
    print(f"  Logistic Regression: {lr_predictions[i]} (confidence:
     ↪  {max(lr_probabilities[i]):.3f})")
    print(f"  Naive Bayes: {nb_predictions[i]} (confidence:
     ↪  {max(nb_probabilities[i]):.3f})")

    # Check if models agree
    if lr_predictions[i] == nb_predictions[i]:
        print(f"  Models agree: {lr_predictions[i]}")
    else:
        print(f"    Models disagree!")
```

Output:

```
Review 1: "This restaurant is absolutely fantastic! Amazing food
and wonderful service."
  Logistic Regression: positive (confidence: 0.939)
  Naive Bayes: positive (confidence: 0.985)
  Models agree: positive

Review 2: "Terrible experience. The food was cold and the staff was rude."
  Logistic Regression: negative (confidence: 0.842)
  Naive Bayes: negative (confidence: 0.912)
  Models agree: negative

Review 3: "The pizza was okay, nothing special but not bad either."
  Logistic Regression: positive (confidence: 0.939)
  Naive Bayes: positive (confidence: 0.991)
  Models agree: positive

Review 4: "Outstanding meal! Best pasta I've ever had.
Highly recommend!"
  Logistic Regression: positive (confidence: 0.907)
  Naive Bayes: positive (confidence: 0.966)
  Models agree: positive

Review 5: "Worst restaurant ever. Overpriced and disgusting food."
  Logistic Regression: negative (confidence: 0.851)
  Naive Bayes: negative (confidence: 0.989)
  Models agree: negative
```

4.9.3 Practice

You work for a marketing agency that manages social media for various brands. Your client wants to understand how people feel about their brand on social media and identify the main topics people discuss. You have collected social media posts mentioning the brand and need to analyze sentiment and extract key themes.

Run this code to create and explore the social media dataset.

```
# Create social media brand analysis dataset
np.random.seed(789)  # Different seed for variety
n_posts = 1200

print("EXERCISE 1: SOCIAL MEDIA BRAND ANALYSIS")
print("=" * 45)

# Define social media post templates
positive_social_templates = [
```

```
    "Love this brand! Their {product} is amazing and {feature} works
     ↪ perfectly.",
    "Just bought {product} from this company. Excellent {feature} and
     ↪ great {quality}!",
    "Best {product} ever! The {feature} is outstanding and {quality} is
     ↪ top-notch.",
    "Highly recommend this brand! {product} has incredible {feature}
     ↪ and {quality}."
]

negative_social_templates = [
    "Disappointed with this brand. {product} has terrible {feature} and
     ↪ poor {quality}.",
    "Worst {product} ever! The {feature} doesn't work and {quality} is
     ↪ awful.",
    "Regret buying this {product}. {feature} is broken and {quality} is
     ↪ horrible.",
    "This brand is overrated. {product} has bad {feature} and cheap
     ↪ {quality}."
]

neutral_social_templates = [
    "Tried this brand's {product}. The {feature} is okay and {quality}
     ↪ is average.",
    "Got this {product} recently. {feature} works fine and {quality} is
     ↪ decent.",
    "This {product} is alright. {feature} is standard and {quality} is
     ↪ fair.",
    "Using this brand's {product}. {feature} is normal and {quality} is
     ↪ acceptable."
]

# Define word options
product_words = ["smartphone", "laptop", "headphones", "tablet",
 ↪ "smartwatch", "camera"]
feature_words = ["battery life", "screen quality", "sound", "design",
 ↪ "performance", "connectivity"]
quality_words = ["build quality", "value", "reliability", "customer
 ↪ service", "warranty", "packaging"]

# Generate social media posts
posts = []
sentiments = []
```

```
engagement_scores = []

for i in range(n_posts):
    # Choose sentiment
    sentiment_choice = np.random.choice(['positive', 'negative',
↪   'neutral'], p=[0.45, 0.25, 0.3])

    if sentiment_choice == 'positive':
        template = np.random.choice(positive_social_templates)
        engagement = np.random.normal(15, 5)  # Higher engagement for
↪   positive
        sentiment = 'positive'
    elif sentiment_choice == 'negative':
        template = np.random.choice(negative_social_templates)
        engagement = np.random.normal(25, 8)  # Highest engagement for
↪   negative (controversy)
        sentiment = 'negative'
    else:
        template = np.random.choice(neutral_social_templates)
        engagement = np.random.normal(8, 3)   # Lower engagement for
↪   neutral
        sentiment = 'neutral'

    # Fill template
    post_text = template.format(
        product=np.random.choice(product_words),
        feature=np.random.choice(feature_words),
        quality=np.random.choice(quality_words)
    )

    # Add hashtags occasionally
    if np.random.random() < 0.3:
        hashtags = ["#tech", "#review", "#brand", "#product",
↪   "#quality"]
        post_text += " " + np.random.choice(hashtags)

    posts.append(post_text)
    sentiments.append(sentiment)
    engagement_scores.append(max(0, int(engagement)))

# Create DataFrame
social_data = pd.DataFrame({
    'post_text': posts,
```

```
    'sentiment': sentiments,
    'engagement_score': engagement_scores
})

print(f"Social media dataset created with {len(social_data)} posts")
print("\n\nFirst 10 posts:")
print(social_data.head(10))
print("\n\nDataset summary:")
print(social_data['sentiment'].value_counts())
print("\n\nEngagement by sentiment:")
engagement_by_sentiment =
↪   social_data.groupby('sentiment')['engagement_score'].agg(['mean',
↪   'std'])
print(engagement_by_sentiment.round(2))
```

4.9.3.1 Lab 4 Questions

1. Dataset Overview How many social media posts are in the dataset? What are the three sentiment categories?
2. Sentiment Distribution What is the distribution of sentiment across all posts? Which sentiment is most common?
3. Engagement Analysis Which sentiment category has the highest average engagement score? Why might negative posts have high engagement?
4. Text Preprocessing Apply the text cleaning functions (`preprocess_text` and `remove_stopwords`) to the `post_text` column. Show the first 5 cleaned posts.
5. Word Analysis Calculate the most common words in the processed posts. What are the top 10 most frequent words?
6. TF-IDF Conversion Create a TF-IDF matrix for the processed posts using the same parameters as in the demonstration. How many features are generated?
7. Binary Classification Convert the sentiment labels to binary (negative vs. non-negative). Build both Logistic Regression and Naive Bayes models. Which performs better?
8. Model Testing Write 5 new social media posts about the brand and predict their sentiment using your trained models. Do the models agree on the predictions?
9. Feature Analysis Identify the top 10 words that most strongly indicate positive sentiment and the top 10 that indicate negative sentiment in your models.
10. Business Insights Based on your analysis, what recommendations would you make to the brand about their social media presence?

4.10 Conclusion

This introduction to natural language processing has covered the fundamental concepts that enable computers to work with human language. We've explored what NLP is and why it matters, the challenges that make language processing difficult, and the basic techniques for preparing text for analysis and converting it into numerical representations.

Understanding NLP starts with appreciating the complexity of human language and the challenges this creates for computers. The preprocessing steps—tokenization, cleaning, stopword removal, and lemmatization—are crucial for preparing text data for analysis. The decisions you make during preprocessing can significantly impact the performance of your NLP applications.

The choice of text representation method depends on your specific application. TF-IDF works well for many traditional NLP tasks like document classification and information retrieval. Word embeddings like Word2Vec excel at capturing semantic relationships and enabling more sophisticated language understanding.

NLP is one area where domain knowledge is particularly valuable. Understanding the language patterns, cultural context, and communication conventions of your specific domain helps you make better preprocessing decisions and interpret results more effectively. Analyzing medical text requires understanding medical terminology and abbreviations. Analyzing social media content requires familiarity with internet slang and platform-specific conventions.

When implementing NLP systems, consider the computational and storage requirements of different approaches. Simple techniques like TF-IDF are fast and require minimal resources, making them suitable for real-time applications. More sophisticated approaches like word embeddings provide better performance but require more computational resources.

Also consider the interpretability requirements of your application. TF-IDF provides clear explanations for why certain documents are considered relevant or similar. Word embeddings are more powerful but less interpretable, making it harder to explain why the system made specific decisions.

The techniques covered in this module provide the foundation for more advanced NLP applications. Modern systems build on these fundamentals to create sophisticated applications like chatbots, language translation systems, and content generation tools. As NLP technology continues to evolve rapidly, the fundamental concepts of text preprocessing and vectorization remain central to most applications.

Remember that NLP is ultimately about enabling better communication between humans and computers. The most successful NLP applications are those that understand not just the technical aspects of language processing, but also the human needs and contexts that drive language use. In future modules, we'll explore how these NLP techniques can be applied to specific business problems, showing how the preprocessing and vectorization methods you've learned here enable practical applications like sentiment analysis, document classification, and automated content generation.

4.11 References

[1] Stanford NLP Group. (2025). Natural Language Processing: Fundamentals and Applications for Beginners. https://nlp.stanford.edu/

[2] Google AI Language. (2025). Introduction to Text Processing and Understanding. https://ai.googleblog.com/

[3] OpenAI. (2025). Language Models and Natural Language Processing: A Beginner's Guide. https://openai.com/research/

[4] Hugging Face. (2025). Getting Started with Natural Language Processing. https://huggingface.co/course/

Chapter 5

Applications of NLP

5.1 Learning Outcomes

5-1: Understand how sentiment analysis determines whether text expresses positive, negative, or neutral emotions and recognizes its business applications

5-2: Explain how topic modeling automatically discovers the main themes discussed in large collections of text

5-3: Describe how named entity recognition identifies important people, places, and organizations mentioned in documents

5-4: Recognize how these NLP applications build on the text preprocessing techniques from the previous module

5.2 Introduction

Picture this scenario: You're scrolling through your company's latest product reviews on Amazon, and you notice something interesting. While most reviews mention similar features—battery life, screen quality, customer service—the tone varies dramatically. Some customers are thrilled with their purchase, others are frustrated, and many fall somewhere in between. As a product manager, you need to understand not just what customers are talking about, but how they feel about it and which specific issues matter most.

This challenge plays out millions of times every day across the business world. Social media managers need to quickly identify when customers are upset about their brand. Market researchers want to understand what topics people discuss most about their industry. Customer service teams need to automatically route angry customers to senior representatives while handling routine questions with chatbots. News organizations want to automatically identify the key people and companies mentioned in breaking stories.

What connects all these scenarios is the need for natural language processing applications that can understand the meaning, emotion, and important details hidden in human language. While the previous module taught you the fundamentals of preparing text for analysis, this module explores three powerful applications that businesses use every day to extract real value from text data.

These aren't theoretical concepts—they're practical tools that companies like Amazon, Netflix, and Google use to process millions of documents and make better business decisions. Sentiment analysis helps businesses understand customer emotions at scale. Topic modeling reveals the hidden themes in large collections of text. Named entity recognition automatically extracts important people, places, and organizations from documents. Together, these techniques transform overwhelming amounts of text into actionable business insights.

5.3 Sentiment Analysis: Understanding How People Feel

Imagine you're managing customer service for a popular restaurant chain, and you receive hundreds of online reviews every week. Some reviews say "The food was absolutely amazing and the service was perfect!" while others complain "Terrible experience, cold food and rude staff." As a human, you immediately understand that the first review expresses positive feelings while the second expresses negative feelings. Sentiment analysis teaches computers to make these same distinctions automatically.

Sentiment analysis is the process of automatically determining the emotional tone behind text—whether someone is expressing positive, negative, or neutral feelings about a topic. This capability has become essential for businesses trying to understand customer satisfaction, monitor brand reputation, and respond appropriately to customer feedback in our digital world.

The power of sentiment analysis becomes clear when you consider the scale of modern communication. A large company might receive thousands of customer emails, social media mentions, and product reviews every day. Reading through all this feedback manually would take weeks, but sentiment analysis can process it in minutes, automatically flagging the most urgent negative feedback while identifying positive trends worth celebrating.

5.3.1 How Sentiment Analysis Works

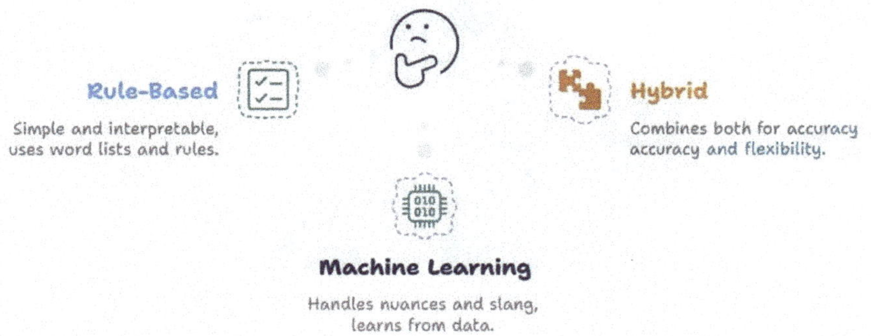

At its core, sentiment analysis is about teaching computers to recognize emotions in text. Just like humans can tell when a sentence expresses happiness, anger, or disappointment, sentiment analysis systems learn to associate certain words and phrases with positive, negative, or neutral feelings. Words like "excellent," "amazing," and "love" generally indicate positive sentiment, while "terrible," "awful," and "hate" usually signal negative sentiment. These systems can process thousands of documents at once and pick up subtle patterns that would be difficult for a human to notice.

There are two main approaches to sentiment analysis: rule-based methods and machine learning methods. Rule-based sentiment analysis works by using predefined dictionaries of words labeled with sentiment scores, combined with rules to handle context. For example, a simple rule might say that the word "good" is positive, but the phrase "not good" reverses the sentiment to negative. Rule-based systems can also account for intensifiers ("really good" is more positive than "good") and negations ("not bad" expresses mild positive sentiment). These systems are straightforward and interpretable, which makes it easy to see why a certain sentence is classified as positive or negative.

Machine learning–based sentiment analysis takes a different approach. Instead of relying on fixed rules, it learns patterns from large datasets where human experts have labeled text with sentiments. By analyzing thousands of examples, the system learns which words, phrases, and sentence structures correspond to positive, negative, or neutral emotions. It can detect subtle expressions like slang, sarcasm, or compound phrases that might confuse simple rule-based systems. For instance, it can recognize that "sick" in “This movie is sick!” is positive slang, while “I feel sick after watching this movie” is clearly negative.

In practice, many sentiment analysis systems combine both approaches. Rule-based methods provide clear, interpretable rules for straightforward cases, while machine learning methods handle more nuanced language patterns. Together, these techniques allow modern sentiment analysis systems to accurately understand and classify the emotional tone of text.

5.3.2 Levels of Sentiment Analysis

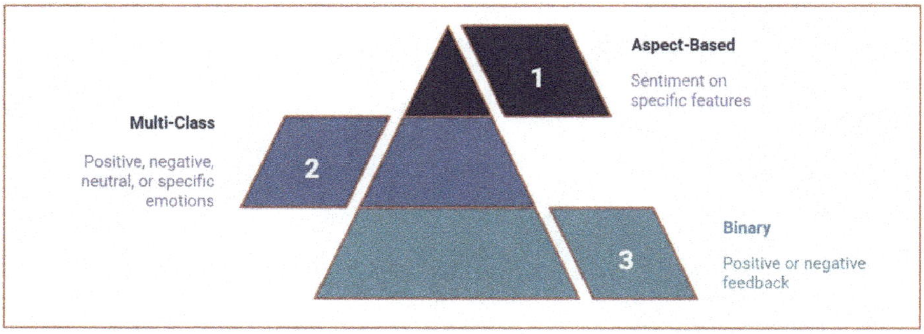

The simplest form of sentiment analysis classifies text as either positive or negative. This binary approach works well for many business applications where you need clear directional feedback. A retail company might use binary sentiment analysis to automatically categorize customer reviews, quickly identifying products that receive consistently negative feedback and need attention.

Multi-class sentiment analysis extends beyond positive and negative to include neutral sentiment and sometimes more specific emotions like anger, joy, sadness, or excitement. This provides more nuanced understanding of customer emotions and enables more targeted business responses. A customer service team might use multi-class sentiment analysis to automatically route support tickets—angry customers get routed to senior representatives, while neutral inquiries can be handled by automated systems or junior staff.

Aspect-based sentiment analysis represents the most sophisticated approach, analyzing sentiment toward specific features or aspects of a product or service. Instead of just determining overall sentiment, these systems can identify that a customer loves their phone’s camera quality (positive sentiment toward camera) but hates the battery life (negative sentiment toward battery). This granular feedback helps businesses prioritize which specific issues to address first.

5.3.3 Real-World Business Applications

Brand monitoring represents one of the most common applications of sentiment analysis. Companies use these systems to track mentions of their brand across social media, news articles, and review sites, automatically identifying when sentiment shifts negative so they can respond quickly to potential reputation issues.

A coffee shop chain might use sentiment analysis to monitor social media mentions across all their locations. When sentiment at a particular location becomes consistently negative, the system automatically alerts management, enabling rapid intervention to address service issues before they escalate into broader reputation problems. This proactive approach helps maintain brand reputation and customer satisfaction.

Customer feedback analysis helps companies understand satisfaction levels and identify areas for improvement without manually reading through thousands of survey responses or reviews. An e-commerce platform might use sentiment analysis to automatically analyze product reviews, identifying which products receive consistently positive feedback (candidates for promotion) and which receive negative feedback (candidates for removal or improvement).

Market research applications use sentiment analysis to understand public opinion about different brands, products, or topics. Companies can track how sentiment toward their brand compares to competitors and identify opportunities to differentiate themselves. An automotive manufacturer might analyze customer sentiment toward their vehicles versus competitors across different aspects like reliability, design, and value, using this competitive intelligence to inform marketing strategies and product development.

Social media management has been transformed by sentiment analysis. Instead of manually monitoring every mention of their brand, companies can automatically identify the most urgent negative feedback that requires immediate response while celebrating positive mentions that could be amplified through marketing efforts.

5.3.4 Challenges and Practical Considerations

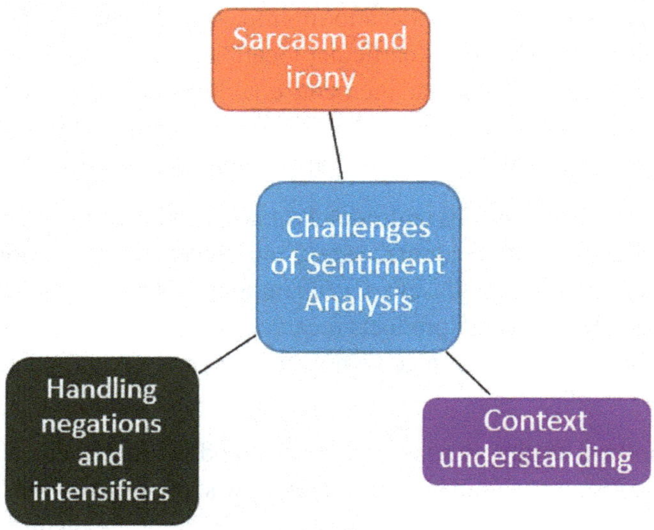

Sarcasm and irony represent ongoing challenges for sentiment analysis systems. The phrase "Great, another software update that breaks everything" expresses negative sentiment despite containing the positive word "great." Detecting this requires understanding context, tone, and often cultural knowledge that can be difficult for computers to master.

Context dependency means that the same words can express different sentiments in different situations. "This movie is a disaster" clearly expresses negative sentiment about a film, but "This disaster movie is amazing" expresses positive sentiment. Effective sentiment analysis systems must consider the broader context to make accurate determinations.

Cultural and linguistic variations affect how sentiment is expressed across different communities and languages. What constitutes polite criticism in one culture might be considered harsh in another. Businesses operating globally must ensure their sentiment analysis systems are trained on data that reflects the linguistic and cultural patterns of their target audiences.

Despite these challenges, sentiment analysis has become an essential tool for businesses seeking to understand customer emotions and opinions at scale. The key to successful implementation lies in understanding the limitations of the technology, choosing appropriate applications, and combining automated analysis with human oversight for critical decisions.

5.4 Topic Modeling

Imagine you're analyzing 5,000 customer reviews for your company's products, and you need to understand the main themes customers are discussing. Reading through each review individually would take weeks, but you need insights quickly to guide product development decisions. Topic modeling provides an automated solution by discovering the hidden themes that run through large collections of text without requiring you to specify what to look for in advance.

Topic modeling is like having an intelligent research assistant who can read through thousands of documents and tell you, "Here are the main themes people are discussing: product quality, customer service, shipping speed, and pricing. Here's which documents focus on each theme and how much attention each topic receives overall." The computer discovers these themes automatically by analyzing patterns in how words appear together across documents.

This capability has become invaluable for businesses dealing with large amounts of text data. Companies use topic modeling to analyze customer feedback, social media conversations, employee surveys, research papers, and news coverage. The algorithm identifies clusters of words that frequently appear together, revealing the underlying topics that people are discussing most.

5.4.1 Understanding How Topic Modeling Works

The fundamental insight behind topic modeling is that documents usually discuss multiple related themes, and each theme can be characterized by certain words that appear frequently when people write about it. When you write a restaurant review, you might discuss the food quality, service speed, atmosphere, and value for money. Topic modeling recognizes that documents often contain multiple topics and tries to identify what those topics are.

Think about analyzing restaurant reviews. You might discover topics like "food quality" (characterized by words like delicious, tasty, bland, overcooked), "service" (characterized by words like waiter, friendly, slow, attentive), "atmosphere" (characterized by words like cozy, noisy, romantic, crowded), and "value" (characterized by words like expensive, cheap, worth, overpriced). Topic modeling algorithms discover these natural groupings automatically by analyzing which words tend to appear together across many reviews.

The process works by examining word co-occurrence patterns across your entire document collection. Words that frequently appear together in the same documents are likely to belong to the same topic. For example, words like "battery," "charging," "power," and "duration" might cluster together to form a topic about device battery life, while words like "screen," "display," "bright," and "resolution" might form a topic about screen quality.

5.4.2 How Topic Modeling Algorithms Work

The most popular approach to topic modeling is called Latent Dirichlet Allocation, or LDA. Despite the intimidating name, the core concept is intuitive: LDA assumes that each document discusses multiple topics, and each topic can be characterized by certain words that appear frequently when discussing it.

LDA works by starting with a random assignment of words to topics, then iteratively improving these assignments by considering which words tend to appear together and which topics tend to appear together in documents. Over many iterations, coherent topics emerge that represent meaningful themes in your text collection.

For example, if you're analyzing news articles, LDA might discover topics like "politics" (characterized by words like election, candidate, vote, policy), "sports" (characterized by words like game, team, score, player), and "technology" (characterized by words like software, computer, innovation, digital). Each article would be described as a mixture of these topics—a sports article might be 80% sports topic, 15% business topic (if discussing team finances), and 5% politics topic (if mentioning government sports policies).

An alternative approach uses clustering techniques to group similar documents together based on their content. This method converts documents into numerical representations using the TF-IDF techniques you learned in the previous module, then applies clustering algorithms to group similar documents. Documents that use similar vocabulary and discuss related concepts end up in the same cluster, effectively creating topic-based groupings.

The advantage of clustering approaches is their simplicity and interpretability. The disadvantage is that they assume each document belongs to exactly one topic, while in reality, documents often discuss multiple themes. LDA's ability to represent documents as mixtures of topics often provides more realistic and useful results.

5.4.3 Practical Applications of Topic Modeling

Customer feedback analysis represents one of the most valuable applications of topic modeling. Instead of manually reading through thousands of reviews to understand customer concerns, topic modeling can automatically identify themes like "shipping problems," "product quality issues," "customer service experiences," and "pricing concerns." This insight guides product development, customer service improvements, and marketing strategies.

A streaming service might use topic modeling to analyze viewer comments and discover topics like "content recommendation accuracy," "video quality issues," "user interface problems," and "subscription pricing concerns." Each topic would be represented by a cluster of related words, and each comment would be associated with one or more topics based on its content. This analysis helps the company prioritize which issues to address first and understand how different problems affect different user segments.

Content organization benefits significantly from topic modeling. News websites use topic modeling to automatically categorize articles and recommend related content to readers. Instead of manually tagging each article with categories, the system can automatically identify that an article discusses topics like "international politics," "economic policy," and "trade relations," then recommend other articles that discuss similar topics.

Market research applications leverage topic modeling to analyze social media conversations, news coverage, and industry reports. Companies can track how discussion topics evolve over time, identify emerging trends, and understand how their brand is perceived relative to competitors. A smartphone manufacturer might analyze social media discussions to discover that conversations about their brand focus on topics like "camera quality," "battery life," and "software updates," while conversations about competitors focus on different themes.

Human resources departments use topic modeling to analyze employee feedback, exit interviews, and internal communications to understand workplace concerns and identify areas for improvement. Rather than manually categorizing employee feedback, topic modeling can automatically identify themes like "work-life balance," "career development opportunities," "management communication," and "compensation concerns."

5.4.4 Getting Good Results from Topic Modeling

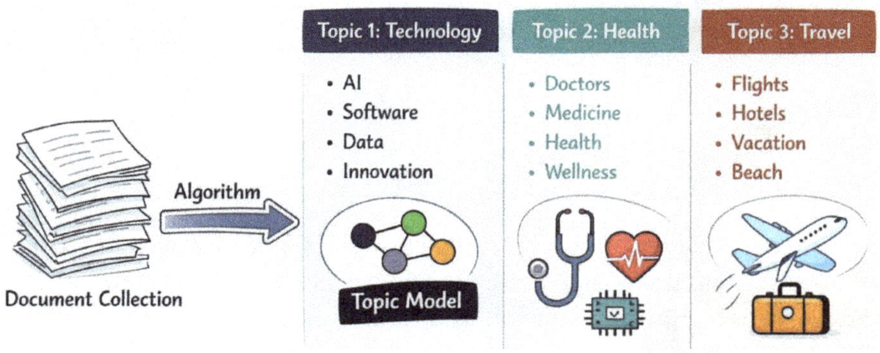

The success of topic modeling depends heavily on proper text preprocessing using the techniques from the previous module. Removing irrelevant words, handling different word forms appropriately, and cleaning the text data all significantly impact the quality of discovered topics.

Choosing the right number of topics represents one of the most important decisions in topic modeling. Too few topics result in overly broad themes that aren't useful for decision-making. Too many topics create overly specific themes that don't provide meaningful insights. Most practitioners experiment with different numbers of topics and evaluate which produces the most interpretable and useful results.

The quality of your input data also matters enormously. Topic modeling works best when you have a substantial collection of documents (typically hundreds or thousands) that discuss related but varied themes. If your documents are too similar, the algorithm won't find meaningful distinctions. If they're too different, the topics might be too broad to be useful.

Interpreting topic modeling results requires human judgment and domain expertise. The algorithm provides clusters of words that tend to appear together, but humans must interpret what these clusters mean and whether they represent meaningful business themes. This interpretation step is crucial for translating algorithmic output into actionable business insights.

5.5 Named Entity Recognition

Imagine you're a journalist covering a breaking news story, and you need to quickly identify all the people, companies, and locations mentioned in hundreds of news articles and social media posts. Or picture yourself as a legal assistant who needs to extract all the party names, dates, and monetary amounts from a stack of contracts. Named Entity Recognition, commonly called NER, automates these tasks by identifying and classifying important entities mentioned in text.

NER systems work like intelligent highlighters that can read through documents and automatically mark all the important names, places, companies, dates, and other specific information. This capability transforms unstructured text into structured data that can be easily searched, analyzed, and integrated with databases and other business systems.

The power of NER becomes apparent when dealing with large volumes of text where manual extraction would be impractical or impossible. A financial services company might use NER to extract company names and financial figures from thousands of earnings reports. A healthcare organization might use NER to identify medications and medical conditions from patient records. A customer service team might use NER to automatically extract customer names and product information from support emails.

5.5.1 Understanding What Entities Are

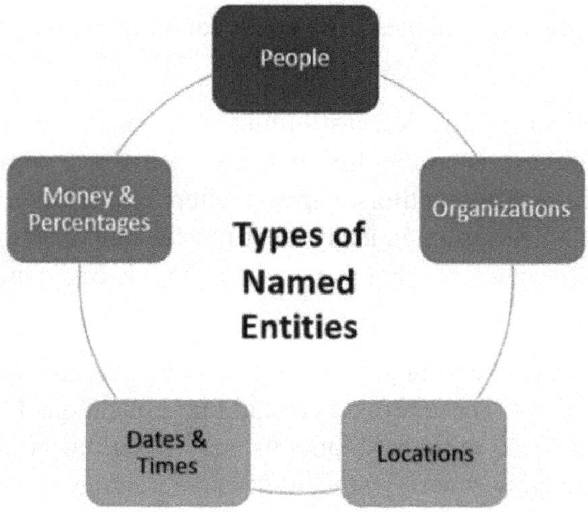

Entities are specific, real-world objects that can be identified with proper names. They represent the "who," "what," "where," and "when" of text content. Unlike general nouns like "company" or "person," entities refer to specific instances like "Apple Inc." or "John Smith." This specificity makes entities particularly valuable for information extraction and business analysis.

The importance of entities becomes clear when you consider how much business-critical information is embedded in everyday text. Customer emails mention specific products, competitors, and dates. News articles discuss particular companies, people, and locations. Legal documents reference specific parties, amounts, and deadlines. Social media posts mention brands, places, and events. NER systems can automatically extract this structured information, enabling analysis that would otherwise require extensive manual effort.

Consider a customer service email that says, "I ordered the iPhone 15 Pro from your San Francisco store on December 10th, but it hasn't arrived yet. Can you check with FedEx about the delivery status?" A human customer service representative immediately identifies the key information: product (iPhone 15 Pro), location (San Francisco store), date (December 10th), and shipping company (FedEx). NER systems can automatically extract this same information, enabling automated routing, database updates, and response generation.

5.5.2 Types of Entities and Their Uses

NER systems typically recognize several standard categories of entities. Person names include both full names and references to individuals, which proves essential for customer relationship management applications where you need to track mentions of specific people across documents and communications. A sales team might use NER to automatically extract customer names from email communications and update their CRM system.

Organization names include companies, institutions, government agencies, and other formal entities. This category is crucial for business intelligence applications where you need to track mentions of competitors, partners, suppliers, or customers. A market research team might use NER to automatically identify which companies are mentioned most frequently in industry news, helping them track competitive dynamics and market trends.

Location entities encompass everything from specific addresses to cities, states, countries, and geographic regions. These prove essential for applications like supply chain management, where you need to track shipments and operations across different locations, or marketing analysis, where you want to understand geographic patterns in customer feedback.

Date and time entities include specific dates, times, and duration expressions. These prove essential for timeline analysis, event extraction, and compliance applications where timing is crucial. A legal firm might use NER to automatically extract all dates mentioned in contracts, helping them track deadlines and important milestones.

Monetary entities include currency amounts, financial figures, and economic indicators, which are vital for financial analysis and business intelligence applications. An investment firm might use NER to automatically extract financial figures from earnings reports and news articles, enabling automated analysis of company performance.

5.5.3 How NER Systems Learn

Modern NER systems use machine learning approaches trained on large collections of text where entities have been manually labeled by human experts. The training process involves showing the system thousands of examples of text where entities have been correctly identified and labeled.

For example, the system might see sentences like “Apple Inc. reported strong quarterly earnings” where “Apple Inc.” is labeled as an organization, or “John Smith visited Paris last Tuesday” where “John Smith” is labeled as a person, “Paris” as a location, and “last Tuesday” as a date.

The system learns to associate certain patterns with specific entity types. It might learn that words appearing before “Inc.” or “Corp.” are likely to be organization names, that capitalized words following titles like "Mr." or "Dr." are likely to be person names, or that phrases containing month names and numbers are likely to be dates.

Context plays a crucial role in entity recognition. The word "Apple" could refer to the fruit or the technology company, and NER systems learn to use surrounding words to make this distinction. In the sentence "I bought an Apple computer," the word "computer" provides context suggesting "Apple" refers to the company. In "I ate an apple for lunch," the context suggests the fruit.

5.5.4 Business Applications of NER

Customer relationship management systems benefit enormously from NER capabilities. By automatically extracting customer names, company names, and contact information from emails, support tickets, and sales communications, businesses can maintain more complete and accurate customer databases while reducing manual data entry errors.

A software company might use NER to automatically extract customer names and company names from support tickets, enabling their system to automatically link tickets to existing customer records and provide support representatives with relevant account history. This improves response times and ensures consistent service quality.

Financial services applications use NER to extract key information from earnings reports, news articles, and regulatory filings. By automatically identifying company names, financial figures, and dates, analysts can quickly process large volumes of financial documents and identify trends that require attention.

Healthcare applications leverage NER to extract medical information from patient records, research papers, and clinical notes. Systems can automatically identify medications, dosages, medical conditions, and treatment procedures, enabling better patient care coordination and medical research while reducing the risk of errors.

Legal applications use NER to process contracts, case documents, and regulatory texts. By automatically extracting party names, dates, monetary amounts, and legal references, law firms can more efficiently review large document collections and identify relevant information for cases.

Media and content applications use NER to automatically tag news articles, social media posts, and other content with relevant entities. This enables better content organization, more accurate search results, and improved content recommendation systems. A news organization might automatically tag articles with the people, companies, and locations mentioned, helping readers find related articles and editors track coverage patterns.

5.5.5 Practical Considerations

The accuracy of NER systems depends on the quality of training data and how well it matches your specific domain. Systems trained on general news text might not perform well on specialized technical documents, highlighting the importance of domain-specific training when possible.

Ambiguity represents an ongoing challenge for NER systems. The same text might refer to different entities depending on context. "Washington" could refer to the state, the city, or George Washington. "Jordan" could be a person's name or a country. Effective NER systems use context clues to resolve these ambiguities, but they're not always successful.

Privacy and compliance considerations become important when using NER to extract personal information from documents. Organizations must ensure that their use of NER complies with relevant privacy regulations and that extracted personal information is handled appropriately.

Despite these challenges, NER has become an essential tool for businesses seeking to extract structured information from unstructured text at scale. The key to successful implementation lies in understanding the limitations of the technology, choosing appropriate applications, and maintaining human oversight for critical decisions.

5.6 Key Terms

Sentiment Analysis – The process of automatically determining the emotional tone of text, classifying it as positive, negative, or neutral.

Rule-Based Sentiment Analysis – A method that uses predefined dictionaries of sentiment-labeled words and rules to determine sentiment.

Machine Learning–Based Sentiment Analysis – A method that trains models on labeled text data to learn patterns of sentiment automatically.

Binary Sentiment Analysis – Classifying text into two categories: positive or negative.

Multi-Class Sentiment Analysis – Classifying text into more than two categories, often including neutral and specific emotions.

Aspect-Based Sentiment Analysis – Determining sentiment toward specific features or aspects of a product or service rather than overall sentiment.

Topic Modeling – An unsupervised technique that identifies the main themes or topics within a large collection of text.

Latent Dirichlet Allocation (LDA) – A popular topic modeling algorithm that assumes each document is a mixture of multiple topics and identifies word patterns to infer topics.

Document Clustering – Grouping similar documents based on content using numerical representations such as TF-IDF vectors.

Named Entity Recognition (NER) – The process of identifying and classifying key entities in text, such as people, organizations, locations, dates, and monetary values.

Entity – A specific, real-world object or concept mentioned in text, e.g., "Apple Inc.", "Paris," or "December 10th."

Entity Types – Categories of entities recognized by NER, commonly including Person, Organization, Location, Date/Time, and Monetary.

Context Dependency – The principle that the meaning or sentiment of a word can change depending on surrounding text.

Sarcasm and Irony – Linguistic challenges where the literal meaning of words differs from the intended sentiment.

Business Applications of NLP – Real-world uses of NLP techniques in areas such as customer feedback analysis, brand monitoring, market research, content organization, healthcare, finance, and legal processing.

Preprocessing Dependency – The idea that successful NLP applications rely on proper text preprocessing (tokenization, cleaning, stopword removal, lemmatization) to ensure accurate analysis.

Domain Expertise – Knowledge of specific industry terminology, language patterns, and communication norms, crucial for interpreting NLP outputs effectively.

5.7 Review Questions

1. What is sentiment analysis, and why is it important for businesses?
2. Describe the differences between rule-based and machine learning–based sentiment analysis.
3. Explain the difference between binary, multi-class, and aspect-based sentiment analysis. Provide examples of when each might be used.
4. How can sentiment analysis help companies monitor brand reputation or analyze customer feedback?

5. What challenges do sarcasm, irony, and context dependency pose for sentiment analysis systems?
6. Define topic modeling and explain how it can help businesses understand large collections of text.
7. How does Latent Dirichlet Allocation (LDA) identify topics in documents?
8. Compare document clustering with LDA for topic discovery. What are the advantages and limitations of each?
9. Describe practical business applications of topic modeling. Give at least three examples.
10. What is named entity recognition (NER), and what types of entities does it commonly identify?
11. How does context help NER systems correctly identify entities like "Apple" as a company versus a fruit?
12. Give examples of business applications for NER in industries such as customer service, finance, healthcare, or legal services.
13. Why is proper text preprocessing critical for successful NLP applications like sentiment analysis, topic modeling, and NER?
14. How does domain expertise improve the accuracy and usefulness of NLP applications?
15. What are key considerations when implementing NLP systems in a business setting (e.g., trade-offs, accuracy, speed, interpretability)?

5.8 Lab 5A: Sentiment Analysis

5.8.1 Introduction

Imagine you're working as a data analyst for a major hotel chain. Every day, thousands of customers leave reviews on travel websites, social media, and feedback forms. Your manager asks you a critical question: "How do our customers really feel about our service, and which locations need immediate attention?"

Reading through thousands of reviews manually would take weeks, but sentiment analysis can provide answers in minutes. Sentiment analysis is the process of automatically determining whether text expresses positive, negative, or neutral opinions. It's one of the most practical applications of natural language processing in business today.

Consider these real customer reviews:

> "The staff was incredibly helpful and the room was spotless! Best hotel experience ever!"

"Terrible service, dirty rooms, and overpriced. Never staying here again."

"The location was convenient, but the wifi was slow."

A human can easily identify the first as positive, the second as negative, and the third as mixed. But how can we teach computers to make these same judgments automatically?

There are two main approaches to sentiment analysis:

Rule-Based Methods use predefined lists of positive and negative words (lexicons) combined with rules about language patterns. These methods are transparent and explainable but may miss context and sarcasm.

Machine Learning Methods learn patterns from examples of text labeled with sentiments. These methods can capture complex patterns but require training data and are less interpretable.

Understanding both rule-based and machine learning approaches gives you flexibility to choose the right method for different business situations and data constraints.

5.8.2 Demonstration

We'll analyze customer feedback for a hotel chain to understand guest satisfaction and identify areas for improvement. Our dataset includes reviews from multiple sources: website reviews, email feedback, social media posts, and survey responses.

Let's start by importing libraries and creating a comprehensive, realistic customer feedback dataset that reflects real-world challenges:

```
# Import required libraries
import pandas as pd
import numpy as np
import matplotlib.pyplot as plt
import seaborn as sns
from sklearn.model_selection import train_test_split
from sklearn.feature_extraction.text import TfidfVectorizer
from sklearn.linear_model import LogisticRegression
from sklearn.ensemble import RandomForestClassifier
from sklearn.svm import SVC
from sklearn.metrics import accuracy_score, classification_report,
↪ confusion_matrix
import re
import string
from collections import Counter, defaultdict
import warnings
warnings.filterwarnings('ignore')

# Set random seed for reproducibility
```

```
np.random.seed(42)

print("LAB 6: ADVANCED SENTIMENT ANALYSIS - REALISTIC VERSION")
print("=" * 60)
```

5.8.2.1 Step 1: Creating Realistic Customer Feedback Dataset

The key to realistic sentiment analysis is creating data that reflects real-world complexity, ambiguity, and noise.

```
print("Creating realistic customer feedback dataset...")
print("=" * 50)

# Define realistic feedback templates with mixed sentiments and
 ↪ ambiguity
mixed_positive_templates = [
    "Overall good {product}, though the {feature} could be better.
     ↪ {service} was helpful.",
    "Decent {product} with some issues. {feature} was okay but
     ↪ {service} exceeded expectations.",
    "Happy with the {product} despite minor problems with {feature}.
     ↪ {service} was professional.",
    "Good {product} for the price. {feature} needs improvement but
     ↪ {service} was excellent.",
    "Satisfied with {product}. {feature} was average, {service} made up
     ↪ for it."
]

mixed_negative_templates = [
    "Disappointed with {product}. {feature} was terrible but {service}
     ↪ tried to help.",
    "Poor {product} overall. {feature} didn't work properly, though
     ↪ {service} was polite.",
    "Not impressed with {product}. {feature} was awful despite decent
     ↪ {service}.",
    "Unsatisfied with {product}. {feature} failed multiple times,
     ↪ {service} was unhelpful.",
    "Bad experience with {product}. {feature} was broken, {service}
     ↪ couldn't fix it."
]

sarcastic_templates = [
    "Oh great, another {product} with 'amazing' {feature}. {service}
     ↪ was just fantastic.",
```

```
    "Sure, the {product} is 'perfect' if you enjoy broken {feature} and
     ↪ slow {service}.",
    "Absolutely 'love' how the {product} {feature} never works and
     ↪ {service} doesn't care.",
    "What a 'wonderful' {product}. {feature} is 'excellent' and
     ↪ {service} is 'top-notch'.",
    "Really 'enjoying' this {product}. {feature} is 'flawless' and
     ↪ {service} is 'amazing'."
]

contextual_templates = [
    "The {product} was fine until {feature} stopped working during my
     ↪ important meeting. {service} helped eventually.",
    "First time using this {product}. {feature} seems complicated but
     ↪ {service} walked me through it.",
    "Been using this {product} for years. {feature} used to be great
     ↪ but now it's declining. {service} says it's normal.",
    "Compared to my old {product}, this one's {feature} is different.
     ↪ {service} explained the changes.",
    "My colleague recommended this {product}. {feature} works as
     ↪ advertised, {service} was responsive."
]

# Add realistic noise and complexity
noise_words = ["actually", "basically", "literally", "honestly",
 ↪ "obviously", "apparently", "supposedly"]
hedge_words = ["somewhat", "kind of", "sort of", "pretty much", "more
 ↪ or less", "I guess"]
intensifiers = ["really", "very", "extremely", "absolutely", "totally",
 ↪ "completely"]

# Generate comprehensive dataset with realistic complexity
n_feedback = 2000
feedback_texts = []
true_sentiments = []
sentiment_scores = []
sources = []
complexity_levels = []

# Create realistic feedback with noise and ambiguity
for i in range(n_feedback):
    # Choose sentiment category with realistic distribution
    sentiment_choice = np.random.choice([
```

```
        'clear_positive', 'mixed_positive', 'neutral',
          ↪ 'mixed_negative', 'clear_negative', 'sarcastic'
    ], p=[0.20, 0.25, 0.20, 0.20, 0.10, 0.05])

    # Generate feedback based on sentiment with realistic complexity
    if sentiment_choice == 'clear_positive':
        template = "Great {product}! {feature} is excellent and
↪   {service} was outstanding."
        sentiment = 'positive'
        score = np.random.uniform(0.6, 0.9)
        complexity = 'low'
    elif sentiment_choice == 'mixed_positive':
        template = np.random.choice(mixed_positive_templates)
        sentiment = 'positive'
        score = np.random.uniform(0.2, 0.6)
        complexity = 'high'
    elif sentiment_choice == 'neutral':
        template = "The {product} is okay. {feature} is average and
↪   {service} was standard."
        sentiment = 'neutral'
        score = np.random.uniform(-0.2, 0.2)
        complexity = 'medium'
    elif sentiment_choice == 'mixed_negative':
        template = np.random.choice(mixed_negative_templates)
        sentiment = 'negative'
        score = np.random.uniform(-0.6, -0.2)
        complexity = 'high'
    elif sentiment_choice == 'clear_negative':
        template = "Terrible {product}! {feature} is awful and
↪   {service} was horrible."
        sentiment = 'negative'
        score = np.random.uniform(-0.9, -0.6)
        complexity = 'low'
    else:  # sarcastic
        template = np.random.choice(sarcastic_templates)
        sentiment = 'negative'  # Sarcasm is typically negative
        score = np.random.uniform(-0.8, -0.4)
        complexity = 'very_high'

    # Add contextual complexity for some reviews
    if np.random.random() < 0.3:
        template = np.random.choice(contextual_templates)
        complexity = 'high'
```

```
    # Fill template with hotel-specific terms
    products = ["hotel", "room", "service", "experience", "stay",
↪   "accommodation"]
    features = ["location", "cleanliness", "staff attitude",
↪   "amenities", "value", "comfort"]
    services = ["front desk", "housekeeping", "restaurant", "wifi",
↪   "parking", "concierge"]

    feedback_text = template.format(
        product=np.random.choice(products),
        feature=np.random.choice(features),
        service=np.random.choice(services)
    )

    # Add realistic noise words
    if np.random.random() < 0.4:
        noise_word = np.random.choice(noise_words + hedge_words +
↪   intensifiers)
        words = feedback_text.split()
        insert_pos = np.random.randint(1, len(words))
        words.insert(insert_pos, noise_word)
        feedback_text = ' '.join(words)

    # Add typos and informal language occasionally
    if np.random.random() < 0.1:
        feedback_text = feedback_text.replace("good",
↪   "gud").replace("great", "gr8")

    source = np.random.choice([
        'Website Review', 'Email Feedback', 'Social Media', 'Support
         ↪  Ticket',
        'Survey Response', 'Phone Feedback'
    ])

    feedback_texts.append(feedback_text)
    true_sentiments.append(sentiment)
    sentiment_scores.append(score)
    sources.append(source)
    complexity_levels.append(complexity)

# Create DataFrame
feedback_data = pd.DataFrame({
```

```
    'feedback_text': feedback_texts,
    'true_sentiment': true_sentiments,
    'sentiment_score': sentiment_scores,
    'source': sources,
    'complexity': complexity_levels
})

print(f"Dataset created with {len(feedback_data)} customer feedback
↪  entries")
print("\nFirst 10 feedback entries:")
print(feedback_data.head(10))

print("\nDataset summary:")
print(feedback_data['true_sentiment'].value_counts())

print("\nComplexity distribution:")
print(feedback_data['complexity'].value_counts())

print("\nSource distribution:")
print(feedback_data['source'].value_counts())
```

Output:

```
Dataset created with 2000 customer feedback entries

First 10 feedback entries:
                                       feedback_text  ... complexity
0  Satisfied with stay. cleanliness was average, ...  ...       high
1  Great accommodation! more or less cleanliness ...  ...        low
2  Great experience! amenities is completely exce...  ...        low
3  First time using this experience. location see...  ...       high
4  Great experience! value is excellent and resta...  ...        low
5  First time using this room. amenities seems co...  ...       high
6  Great room! value is excellent and housekeepin...  ...        low
7  The hotel was somewhat fine until amenities st...  ...       high
8  The experience was obviously fine until cleanl...  ...       high
9  Been using this hotel for years. value really ...  ...       high

Dataset summary:
true_sentiment
positive    887
negative    701
neutral     412
Name: count, dtype: int64
```

```
Complexity distribution:
complexity
high         1204
low           446
medium        275
very_high      75
Name: count, dtype: int64

Source distribution:
source
Social Media       351
Website Review     341
Survey Response    341
Email Feedback     335
Support Ticket     324
Phone Feedback     308
Name: count, dtype: int64
```

5.8.2.2 Step 2: Rule-Based Sentiment Analysis

In the previous step, we used a simple approach that looked at individual words and labeled them as positive or negative. While that works for basic cases, real language is more complex. People use stronger and weaker words, add emphasis, use negation (like "not good"), and sometimes even express sarcasm. A more advanced rule-based system helps us handle these situations more realistically.

To improve our model, we will build an enhanced sentiment lexicon. A lexicon is simply a dictionary of words paired with sentiment scores. Instead of treating all positive or negative words the same, we assign different strengths to each word. For example, the word "excellent" expresses a stronger positive feeling than "okay," so it receives a higher score. Similarly, "terrible" is more negative than "bad," so it gets a lower score.

We begin by creating two dictionaries: one for positive words and one for negative words. Each word is assigned a numerical value between -1 and 1. Strong positive words are closer to 1, strong negative words are closer to -1, and weaker words fall somewhere in between. This allows the model to capture not just direction (positive or negative), but also intensity.

Next, we introduce intensifiers. These are words like "very," "extremely," or "slightly" that change the strength of a sentiment. For example, "very good" should be more positive than "good," while "slightly bad" should be less negative than "bad." We store these words along with multipliers that adjust the sentiment score accordingly.

We also define a set of negation words such as "not," "never," and "don't." Negation is important because it can completely reverse meaning. For instance, "not good" should be interpreted as negative, even though "good" is normally positive. Including negation helps the model avoid common mistakes.

Finally, we include a simple list of sarcasm indicators. These are phrases like "yeah right" or "oh great" that often signal the opposite of what the words literally mean. Detecting sarcasm is difficult, even for advanced models, but adding a few basic indicators can still improve performance in obvious cases.

After defining these components, we print out the number of words and rules in each category. This gives us a quick check that our enhanced lexicon has been created successfully and is ready to use in the next step of our sentiment analysis.

```
print("\n" + "="*60)
print("RULE-BASED SENTIMENT ANALYSIS")
print("="*60)

print("STEP 1: Creating Enhanced Sentiment Lexicons")
print("-" * 35)

# Enhanced sentiment lexicons with more nuanced scoring
positive_words = {
    # Strong positive words
    'excellent': 1.0, 'amazing': 1.0, 'fantastic': 1.0, 'outstanding':
     ↪ 1.0, 'incredible': 1.0,
    'perfect': 1.0, 'wonderful': 0.9, 'great': 0.8, 'awesome': 0.9,
     ↪ 'brilliant': 0.9,

    # Moderate positive words
    'good': 0.6, 'nice': 0.5, 'fine': 0.4, 'okay': 0.3, 'decent': 0.4,
    'happy': 0.7, 'pleased': 0.6, 'satisfied': 0.6, 'love': 0.9,
     ↪ 'like': 0.5,
    'recommend': 0.7, 'impressed': 0.7, 'helpful': 0.6, 'professional':
     ↪ 0.6,

    # Weak positive words
    'acceptable': 0.3, 'adequate': 0.3, 'reasonable': 0.4, 'fair': 0.3
}

negative_words = {
    # Strong negative words
    'terrible': -1.0, 'awful': -1.0, 'horrible': -1.0, 'disgusting':
     ↪ -1.0, 'hate': -1.0,
    'worst': -1.0, 'appalling': -1.0, 'dreadful': -1.0, 'atrocious':
     ↪ -1.0,
```

```
    # Moderate negative words
    'bad': -0.8, 'poor': -0.7, 'disappointing': -0.7, 'frustrated':
     ↪ -0.7, 'annoyed': -0.6,
    'upset': -0.6, 'dissatisfied': -0.7, 'unhappy': -0.6, 'dislike':
     ↪ -0.5, 'problem': -0.5,

    # Weak negative words
    'issues': -0.4, 'concerns': -0.4, 'complaints': -0.5, 'lacking':
     ↪ -0.5
}

# Enhanced intensity modifiers
intensifiers = {
    'very': 1.5, 'extremely': 1.8, 'incredibly': 1.7, 'absolutely':
     ↪ 1.6,
    'really': 1.3, 'quite': 1.2, 'pretty': 1.1, 'rather': 1.1,
    'somewhat': 0.8, 'slightly': 0.7, 'a bit': 0.7, 'kind of': 0.8,
    'sort of': 0.8, 'more or less': 0.7
}

# Enhanced negation detection
negation_words = {
    'not', 'no', 'never', 'nothing', 'nobody', 'nowhere', 'neither',
     ↪ 'nor',
    'dont', "don't", 'doesnt', "doesn't", 'didnt', "didn't", 'wont',
     ↪ "won't",
    'wouldnt', "wouldn't", 'cant', "can't", 'couldnt', "couldn't",
     ↪ 'shouldnt', "shouldn't",
    'but', 'however', 'although', 'though', 'despite'
}

# Sarcasm indicators (simple detection)
sarcasm_indicators = {
    'oh great', 'sure', 'yeah right', 'absolutely', 'perfect',
     ↪ 'wonderful',
    'fantastic', 'amazing', 'excellent'
}

print(f"Positive words in lexicon: {len(positive_words)}")
print(f"Negative words in lexicon: {len(negative_words)}")
print(f"Intensity modifiers: {len(intensifiers)}")
print(f"Negation words: {len(negation_words)}")
```

Output:

```
============================================================
RULE-BASED SENTIMENT ANALYSIS
============================================================
STEP 1: Creating Enhanced Sentiment Lexicons
----------------------------------------
Positive words in lexicon: 28
Negative words in lexicon: 23
Intensity modifiers: 14
Negation words: 29
```

Now that we have built our enhanced lexicons and rules, we apply them to actually score and classify text. This part of the lab takes each feedback comment and calculates a sentiment score that reflects not only the words used, but also modifiers, negations, and even simple sarcasm patterns.

First, the text is preprocessed. This means it is converted to lowercase; contractions are expanded (e.g., "don't" → "do not"), punctuation is removed, and extra spaces are cleaned up. This ensures that words are recognized correctly when we compare them to our sentiment lexicons.

Next, we detect potential sarcasm. The code looks for patterns like "yeah right" or words in quotes, which often indicate the opposite sentiment from what the words literally say. Sarcasm is challenging to detect perfectly, but even this basic check can improve the model's understanding of tricky sentences.

The main scoring function works word by word:

1. Each word is checked against the positive and negative lexicons.
2. If a word has an intensity modifier before it (like "very" or "slightly"), the sentiment score is adjusted accordingly.
3. Negations (like "not" or "never") are detected in the three words preceding a sentiment word. If found, the score is reversed and slightly reduced.
4. If sarcasm is detected and the word is positive, the score is reversed to account for sarcastic praise.
5. All word scores in the text are averaged to create a single sentiment score between -1 (very negative) and +1 (very positive).

Finally, this numeric score is converted into a category: "positive," "negative," or "neutral," using slightly stricter thresholds to reduce misclassification of neutral or borderline statements.

After applying this enhanced rule-based scoring to all feedback entries, we check accuracy by comparing predicted sentiment to the true sentiment labels.

```
print("\nSTEP 2: Implementing Enhanced Rule-Based Scoring")
print("-" * 40)
```

```
def preprocess_text_for_rules(text):
    """Enhanced preprocessing for rule-based analysis"""
    # Convert to lowercase
    text = text.lower()

    # Handle contractions
    contractions = {
        "won't": "will not", "can't": "cannot", "n't": " not",
        "'re": " are", "'ve": " have", "'ll": " will", "'d": " would"
    }
    for contraction, expansion in contractions.items():
        text = text.replace(contraction, expansion)

    # Remove punctuation but keep spaces
    text = re.sub(r'[^\w\s]', ' ', text)

    # Remove extra whitespace
    text = ' '.join(text.split())

    return text

def detect_sarcasm(text):
    """Simple sarcasm detection"""
    text_lower = text.lower()

    # Check for quotes around positive words (often sarcastic)
    if "'" in text or '"' in text:
        for word in ['great', 'perfect', 'wonderful', 'amazing',
         ↪ 'excellent']:
            if f"'{word}'" in text_lower or f'"{word}"' in text_lower:
                return True

    # Check for sarcasm patterns
    sarcasm_patterns = ['oh great', 'sure,', 'yeah right', 'just
↪   fantastic']
    for pattern in sarcasm_patterns:
        if pattern in text_lower:
            return True

    return False

def enhanced_rule_based_sentiment_score(text):
```

```
    """Enhanced sentiment scoring with better context handling"""
    # Preprocess text
    processed_text = preprocess_text_for_rules(text)
    words = processed_text.split()

    # Check for sarcasm
    is_sarcastic = detect_sarcasm(text)

    total_score = 0
    word_count = 0

    i = 0
    while i < len(words):
        word = words[i]
        score = 0
        multiplier = 1

        # Check for intensity modifiers before the current word
        if i > 0 and words[i-1] in intensifiers:
            multiplier = intensifiers[words[i-1]]

        # Check for sentiment words
        if word in positive_words:
            score = positive_words[word] * multiplier
        elif word in negative_words:
            score = negative_words[word] * multiplier

        # Enhanced negation detection (look back 3 words)
        negated = False
        for j in range(max(0, i-3), i):
            if words[j] in negation_words:
                negated = True
                break

        if negated and score != 0:
            score = -score * 0.8  # Reverse and slightly reduce
↪   intensity

        # Handle sarcasm (reverse positive sentiment)
        if is_sarcastic and score > 0:
            score = -score * 0.6

        if score != 0:
```

```
                total_score += score
                word_count += 1

            i += 1

        # Normalize score
        if word_count > 0:
            final_score = total_score / word_count
            # Clip to [-1, 1] range
            final_score = max(-1, min(1, final_score))
        else:
            final_score = 0

        return final_score

    def classify_sentiment_from_score(score):
        """Convert numerical score to sentiment category with adjusted
         ↪ thresholds"""
        if score > 0.15:  # Slightly higher threshold for positive
            return 'positive'
        elif score < -0.15:  # Slightly lower threshold for negative
            return 'negative'
        else:
            return 'neutral'

    # Apply enhanced rule-based analysis
    print("Applying enhanced rule-based sentiment analysis...")
    feedback_data['rule_based_score'] = feedback_data['feedback_text'].
     ↪ apply(enhanced_rule_based_sentiment_score)
    feedback_data['rule_based_sentiment'] = feedback_data[
     ↪ 'rule_based_score'].apply(classify_sentiment_from_score)

    # Calculate accuracy
    rule_based_accuracy = accuracy_score(feedback_data['true_sentiment'],
     ↪ feedback_data['rule_based_sentiment'])
    print(f"Enhanced rule-based accuracy: {rule_based_accuracy:.3f}
     ↪ ({rule_based_accuracy*100:.1f}%)")

    print("\nEnhanced Rule-based Classification Report:")
    print(classification_report(feedback_data['true_sentiment'],
     ↪ feedback_data['rule_based_sentiment']))
```

Output:

```
STEP 2: Implementing Enhanced Rule-Based Scoring
----------------------------------------
Applying enhanced rule-based sentiment analysis...
Enhanced rule-based accuracy: 0.562 (56.2%)

Enhanced Rule-based Classification Report:
              precision    recall  f1-score   support

    negative       1.00      0.62      0.77       701
     neutral       0.17      0.23      0.19       412
    positive       0.60      0.67      0.63       887

    accuracy                           0.56      2000
   macro avg       0.59      0.51      0.53      2000
weighted avg       0.65      0.56      0.59      2000
```

The output shows that the enhanced rule-based sentiment model achieved an overall accuracy of 0.562 (56.2%). This means the system correctly classified a little over half of all feedback items. While this level of accuracy may seem modest, it is typical for rule-based approaches. Natural language is highly nuanced, and fixed rules often struggle to capture sarcasm, context, and subtle tone differences that influence sentiment.

The classification report provides a more detailed breakdown of performance across each sentiment category using precision, recall, and F1-scores. For negative sentiment, the model achieved a precision of 1.00 and a recall of 0.62. This indicates that when the model predicts a post as negative, it is almost always correct (no false positives). However, it fails to identify a portion of actual negative posts, meaning some negative content is missed.

For neutral sentiment, performance is significantly weaker, with a precision of 0.17 and a recall of 0.23. This reflects the inherent difficulty of identifying neutral language. Neutral posts often contain words that overlap with mildly positive or negative expressions, making it challenging for simple rule-based systems to distinguish them accurately.

For positive sentiment, the model performs moderately well, with a precision of 0.60 and a recall of 0.67. This suggests the system is fairly effective at recognizing positive language, although there is still room for improvement. Overall, the results highlight that rule-based systems can provide a useful baseline but are limited in handling the complexity of real-world text, particularly for ambiguous or neutral sentiment.

5.8.2.3 Step 3: Machine Learning Sentiment Analysis

In the previous step, we relied on hand-crafted rules to score sentiment. While rule-based methods can capture obvious patterns, they struggle with the subtleties of real language, like context, unusual word combinations, or sentences that don't use our predefined lexicons. Machine learning approaches can learn these patterns directly from labeled data, allowing for more flexible and often more accurate sentiment predictions.

Before training a model, we preprocess the text to preserve the most meaningful information while cleaning it up. This includes converting text to lowercase, expanding contractions (so "don't" becomes "do not"), and removing most punctuation. Unlike rule-based preprocessing, we carefully preserve sentiment signals like important word sequences, because machine learning models can learn from these patterns.

Next, we transform the text into numerical features using TF-IDF vectorization. TF-IDF, which stands for Term Frequency–Inverse Document Frequency, measures how important a word is in a document relative to the entire dataset. This approach allows the model to focus on words that are significant for sentiment classification rather than very common words like "the" or "and."

We also fine-tune the vectorizer parameters to create a more realistic scenario. The parameter `max_features` is set to 1500, which limits the total number of features to the most important 1500 words or phrases. The parameter `min_df` is set to 3, which ignores words that appear in fewer than three documents, removing rare terms that could add noise. The parameter `max_df` is set to 0.7, which ignores words that appear in more than 70 percent of the documents, filtering out overly common words. The `ngram_range` is set to (1, 2), so the model considers both single words and word pairs, allowing it to capture short phrases like "not good." Finally, `stop_words` is set to 'english', which removes common words that do not contribute meaningfully to sentiment analysis.

After transforming the text, we split the dataset into training and testing sets using stratified sampling. This ensures that each sentiment category is proportionally represented in both sets, helping the model learn and evaluate more fairly.

```
print("\n" + "="*60)
print("MACHINE LEARNING SENTIMENT ANALYSIS")
print("="*60)

# Enhanced preprocessing for machine learning
def preprocess_text_for_ml(text):
    """Enhanced preprocessing that preserves important sentiment
     ↪ signals"""
    text = text.lower()

    # Handle contractions properly
    contractions = {
        "won't": "will not", "can't": "cannot", "n't": " not",
        "'re": " are", "'ve": " have", "'ll": " will", "'d": " would"
    }
    for contraction, expansion in contractions.items():
        text = text.replace(contraction, expansion)
```

```
    # Remove punctuation but preserve some sentiment indicators
    text = re.sub(r'[^\w\s]', ' ', text)
    text = ' '.join(text.split())
    return text

feedback_data['processed_text'] =
↪   feedback_data['feedback_text'].apply(preprocess_text_for_ml)

# Create TF-IDF features with realistic parameters
tfidf_vectorizer = TfidfVectorizer(
    max_features=1500,  # Reduced from 2000 to increase difficulty
    min_df=3,           # Increased to filter out rare words
    max_df=0.7,         # Reduced to filter out very common words
    ngram_range=(1, 2), # Keep bigrams for context
    stop_words='english'
)

X_tfidf =
↪   tfidf_vectorizer.fit_transform(feedback_data['processed_text'])
y = feedback_data['true_sentiment']

# Split data with stratification
X_train, X_test, y_train, y_test = train_test_split(
    X_tfidf, y, test_size=0.25, random_state=42, stratify=y  # Larger
↪   test set
)

print(f"Training set size: {X_train.shape[0]} feedback entries")
print(f"Testing set size: {X_test.shape[0]} feedback entries")
print(f"Feature dimensions: {X_train.shape[1]} TF-IDF features")
```

Output:

```
============================================================
MACHINE LEARNING SENTIMENT ANALYSIS
============================================================
Training set size: 1500 feedback entries
Testing set size: 500 feedback entries
Feature dimensions: 799 TF-IDF features
```

The printed output shows that the training set contains 1500 feedback entries. This portion of the data is used for the model to learn patterns and relationships in the text. The testing set contains 500 feedback entries, which are held out to evaluate how well the model generalizes to unseen data.

The feature dimensions after TF-IDF vectorization amount to 799. This means that each feedback entry is represented as a 799-dimensional vector, with each dimension corresponding to the importance of a specific word or phrase. Together, this preprocessing and feature creation step prepares the dataset for training machine learning classifiers that can detect sentiment more accurately than simple rule-based approaches, even when the language is complex or nuanced.

With the TF-IDF features ready, different machine learning models can be trained to classify sentiment. Using multiple models allows for comparison of approaches and helps determine which performs best for this type of text data. Each model is trained on the same training set and evaluated on the same testing set to ensure a fair comparison.

5.8.2.3.1 Model 1: Logistic Regression

Logistic Regression is a classic algorithm for classification. It works by finding the best linear boundary that separates different sentiment classes based on the TF-IDF features. Here, we set parameters to make the model realistic and stable:

- `max_iter=2000` ensures the model has enough iterations to converge.
- `C=0.5` controls regularization to prevent overfitting.
- `solver='lbfgs'` supports multiclass classification for our three sentiment categories (positive, neutral, negative).

After training, we predict sentiment for the test set and calculate accuracy and a classification report. The accuracy tells us the percentage of correct predictions overall. The classification report breaks down performance by class, showing precision (how many predicted positives were actually positive), recall (how many actual positives were correctly predicted), and F1-score (a balanced metric combining precision and recall).

5.8.2.3.2 Model 2: Random Forest

Random Forest is an ensemble method that combines many decision trees. Each tree makes a prediction, and the final class is decided by majority vote. This method can capture more complex patterns in the data. Parameters are chosen to reduce overfitting and improve generalization:

- `n_estimators=50` limits the number of trees to reduce computation.
- `max_depth=10` restricts tree depth so the model doesn't memorize training data.
- `min_samples_split=10` and `min_samples_leaf=5` further prevent overfitting by requiring enough data to make splits.

As with Logistic Regression, we predict test set labels and examine accuracy and the classification report. Random Forest often performs well when relationships are nonlinear or when individual words interact in complex ways.

5.8.2.3.3 Model 3: Support Vector Machine (SVM)

SVM is another powerful classification method that finds the optimal boundary separating classes in high-dimensional space. We use a linear kernel because our TF-IDF features are already high-dimensional. Parameters are chosen to be realistic:

- `C=0.3` controls regularization strength, balancing margin size and misclassification.
- `max_iter=1000` limits computation while allowing convergence.

SVM is particularly effective when classes are well-separated in feature space and can handle the sparse, high-dimensional nature of TF-IDF vectors.

```
# Model 1: Logistic Regression with realistic parameters
print("1. Logistic Regression Model:")
from sklearn.linear_model import LogisticRegression

lr_model = LogisticRegression(
    random_state=42,
    max_iter=2000,
    C=0.5,
    solver="lbfgs"   # multiclass-capable
)

lr_model.fit(X_train, y_train)
y_pred_lr = lr_model.predict(X_test)

from sklearn.metrics import accuracy_score, classification_report
lr_accuracy = accuracy_score(y_test, y_pred_lr)

print(f"Accuracy: {lr_accuracy:.3f} ({lr_accuracy*100:.1f}%)")
print("\nClassification Report:")
print(classification_report(y_test, y_pred_lr))

# Model 2: Random Forest with realistic parameters
print("\n2. Random Forest Model:")
rf_model = RandomForestClassifier(
    n_estimators=50,     # Reduced from 100
    max_depth=10,        # Limited depth to prevent overfitting
    min_samples_split=10, # Increased to prevent overfitting
    min_samples_leaf=5,   # Increased to prevent overfitting
    random_state=42
)
rf_model.fit(X_train, y_train)
y_pred_rf = rf_model.predict(X_test)
rf_accuracy = accuracy_score(y_test, y_pred_rf)
```

```
print(f"Accuracy: {rf_accuracy:.3f} ({rf_accuracy*100:.1f}%)")
print("\nClassification Report:")
print(classification_report(y_test, y_pred_rf))

# Model 3: Support Vector Machine with realistic parameters
print("\n3. Support Vector Machine Model:")
svm_model = SVC(
    kernel='linear',
    C=0.3,              # Increased regularization
    random_state=42,
    max_iter=1000       # Limited iterations
)
svm_model.fit(X_train, y_train)
y_pred_svm = svm_model.predict(X_test)
svm_accuracy = accuracy_score(y_test, y_pred_svm)

print(f"Accuracy: {svm_accuracy:.3f} ({svm_accuracy*100:.1f}%)")
print("\nClassification Report:")
print(classification_report(y_test, y_pred_svm))
```

Output:

```
1. Logistic Regression Model:
Accuracy: 0.828 (82.8%)

Classification Report:
              precision    recall  f1-score   support

    negative       0.86      0.77      0.81       175
     neutral       1.00      0.69      0.82       103
    positive       0.76      0.94      0.84       222

    accuracy                           0.83       500
   macro avg       0.87      0.80      0.82       500
weighted avg       0.85      0.83      0.83       500

2. Random Forest Model:
Accuracy: 0.824 (82.4%)

Classification Report:
              precision    recall  f1-score   support

    negative       0.98      0.69      0.81       175
```

```
     neutral       1.00      0.69      0.82       103
    positive       0.72      0.99      0.83       222

    accuracy                           0.82       500
   macro avg       0.90      0.79      0.82       500
weighted avg       0.87      0.82      0.82       500

3. Support Vector Machine Model:
Accuracy: 0.830 (83.0%)

Classification Report:
              precision    recall  f1-score   support

    negative       1.00      0.70      0.82       175
     neutral       1.00      0.69      0.82       103
    positive       0.72      1.00      0.84       222

    accuracy                           0.83       500
   macro avg       0.91      0.80      0.83       500
weighted avg       0.88      0.83      0.83       500
```

For each model, the printed output includes accuracy, which represents the percentage of correctly predicted sentiment labels. This provides a quick sense of overall model performance. In addition, the classification report offers a detailed breakdown by class, showing precision, recall, and F1-score. This information helps identify which sentiment categories the model predicts well and which are more challenging. For example, neutral sentiment is often more difficult to classify than strongly positive or negative feedback.

By comparing the results across Logistic Regression, Random Forest, and SVM, we can determine which model best balances accuracy and robustness, supporting informed choices for real-world sentiment analysis. When all approaches are compared, the rule-based system achieves 56.2 percent accuracy. While it is effective at capturing obvious positive and negative words, it struggles with subtle language, negation, and neutral feedback. In contrast, the machine learning models perform substantially better. Logistic Regression achieves 82.8 percent accuracy, Random Forest 82.4 percent, and SVM 83.0 percent. These models are able to learn patterns directly from the data, handle complex word combinations, and generalize more effectively to new feedback, making them more reliable for practical sentiment classification tasks.

To compare all the sentiment analysis approaches, we can summarize the accuracy of each model on the test set.

```
print("\nMODEL COMPARISON")
print("-" * 30)
```

```
models = {
    "Rule-based": rule_based_accuracy,
    "Logistic Regression": lr_accuracy,
    "Random Forest": rf_accuracy,
    "SVM": svm_accuracy
}

for name, acc in models.items():
    print(f"{name:<20} {acc:.3f}")
```

Output:

```
MODEL COMPARISON
------------------------------
Rule-based           0.562
Logistic Regression  0.828
Random Forest        0.824
SVM                  0.830
```

This comparison highlights an important lesson: rule-based methods can be useful for quick or interpretable solutions, but machine learning approaches typically provide more accurate and robust sentiment classification in real-world scenarios. The machine learning models are better able to learn patterns from data, handle complex word combinations, and generalize effectively to new feedback.

5.8.3 Practice

You work for an e-commerce company that sells electronics. The company wants to understand customer sentiment about their products to improve customer satisfaction and identify potential issues. You have access to product reviews from the company website.

Run this code to create and explore a realistic product review dataset.

5.8.3.1 Lab 5A Questions

1. How many total social media posts are in the dataset? How many posts are labeled as positive, negative, and neutral?

2. Which product type (e.g., smartphone, laptop, etc.) appears most frequently in the dataset? Which appears least frequently?

3. How many unique features (e.g., battery life, design, etc.) are mentioned in the dataset, and how frequently does each appear?

4. Display the first 10 posts. Identify one example each of a positive, negative, and neutral post.
5. Apply a rule-based sentiment scoring function to all posts. Store the results in a new column called `rule_based_score`.
6. Convert the numeric scores into categorical sentiment labels (positive, negative, neutral). Store these in a column called `rule_based_sentiment`.
7. Compare the rule-based predictions with the actual sentiment labels. What is the overall accuracy of the rule-based model?
8. Display five example posts where the rule-based sentiment matches the true sentiment and five where it does not match. What patterns do you observe in the mismatches?
9. Preprocess the post text (cleaning and stopword removal) and store the results in a column called `processed_text`.
10. Apply TF-IDF vectorization using appropriate parameters. How many features are generated?
11. Split the dataset into training and testing sets using a 75/25 split. How many posts are in each set?
12. Train three machine learning models: Logistic Regression, Naive Bayes, and Support Vector Machine (SVM). After training, evaluate each model on the test set and report the accuracy scores to assess how well each model predicts sentiment.
13. Compare the performance of the machine learning models with the rule-based approach. Which method performs best? Why?
14. Identify the top 10 words most strongly associated with positive sentiment and the top 10 associated with negative sentiment based on your model.
15. Based on your analysis, what recommendations would you make to the brand regarding their social media strategy and customer engagement?

5.9 Lab 5B: Topic Modeling and LDA

5.9.1 Introduction

Imagine you work for a large e-commerce company and your manager hands you 10,000 customer reviews from the past month. She asks, "What are customers talking about? What are the main themes in these reviews?" Reading through each review would take weeks, but you need insights today to guide product improvements and marketing strategies.

This is exactly the problem that topic modeling solves. Topic modeling is like having an intelligent research assistant who can read through thousands of documents and tell you: "Here are the main themes people are discussing: product quality, shipping speed, customer service, and pricing. Here's which documents focus on each theme and how much attention each topic receives overall."

Topic modeling is an automated technique that discovers hidden themes, or topics, in large collections of text documents. Unlike sentiment analysis, which determines whether text is positive or negative, topic modeling identifies the subjects people are actually discussing. The key insight is that documents usually cover multiple related themes, and each theme can be characterized by certain words that frequently appear together. For example, when writing a restaurant review, you might discuss food quality, service speed, atmosphere, and value for money. Topic modeling recognizes these natural groupings automatically.

Topic modeling has numerous real-world applications. In customer feedback analysis, it can automatically categorize thousands of reviews into themes such as shipping issues, product quality, or customer service. News websites use it to organize content and recommend related articles. In market research, it helps analyze social media conversations to identify emerging trends and brand perception. HR departments can leverage topic modeling to understand employee feedback themes like work-life balance, career development, or compensation.

This technique is crucial for data analytics because it helps unlock insights from large amounts of unstructured text data. Instead of manually reading thousands of documents, analysts can discover hidden patterns that were previously unknown, scale their analysis to process vast amounts of text in minutes rather than weeks, guide decision-making by understanding what customers, employees, or stakeholders are really talking about, track how discussion topics evolve over time, and prioritize actions by focusing on the most frequently discussed issues.

5.9.2 Demonstration

We'll analyze customer reviews for a fictional electronics retailer to discover what topics customers discuss most frequently. Our dataset includes reviews for various products like smartphones, laptops, headphones, and tablets.

5.9.2.1 Step 1: Setting Up Our Environment and Data

In this step, we are setting up our Python environment and creating a realistic dataset of customer reviews to demonstrate topic modeling techniques. This is important because before analyzing real text data, we need to understand how to properly structure our data and ensure we have the necessary libraries and tools for topic modeling.

```
# Import required libraries
import pandas as pd
```

```
import numpy as np
import matplotlib.pyplot as plt
import seaborn as sns
from sklearn.feature_extraction.text import TfidfVectorizer,
 ↪ CountVectorizer
from sklearn.decomposition import LatentDirichletAllocation
from sklearn.cluster import KMeans
from sklearn.metrics import silhouette_score
import warnings
warnings.filterwarnings('ignore')

# Set random seed for reproducibility
np.random.seed(42)

# Create synthetic customer review data
review_templates = {
    'battery_life': [
        "The battery life on this device is amazing, lasts all day",
        "Battery drains too quickly, needs charging multiple times
         ↪ daily",
        "Great battery performance, can use for hours without
         ↪ charging",
        "Poor battery life, dies within a few hours of use",
        "Excellent battery duration, perfect for long trips"
    ],
    'screen_quality': [
        "The display is crystal clear with vibrant colors",
        "Screen quality is poor, colors look washed out",
        "Beautiful bright display, perfect for watching videos",
        "Display has dead pixels and poor brightness",
        "Amazing screen resolution, very sharp and clear"
    ],
    'customer_service': [
        "Customer support was helpful and resolved my issue quickly",
        "Terrible customer service, waited hours for response",
        "Support team was knowledgeable and friendly",
        "Customer service representatives were rude and unhelpful",
        "Excellent support experience, problem solved immediately"
    ],
    'shipping_delivery': [
        "Fast shipping, arrived earlier than expected",
        "Slow delivery, took weeks to arrive",
        "Package arrived on time and well protected",
```

```
        "Shipping was delayed and package was damaged",
        "Quick delivery, excellent packaging"
    ],
    'price_value': [
        "Great value for money, worth every penny",
        "Overpriced for what you get, not worth it",
        "Reasonable price point for the quality",
        "Too expensive, similar products cost much less",
        "Excellent value, high quality at fair price"
    ]
}

# Generate 500 reviews
reviews = []
topics = []
for i in range(500):
    # Randomly select a topic
    topic = np.random.choice(list(review_templates.keys()))
    # Randomly select a template from that topic
    review = np.random.choice(review_templates[topic])
    # Add some variation
    if np.random.random() > 0.7:  # 30% chance to combine topics
        second_topic = np.random.choice(list(review_templates.keys()))
        second_review =
 ↪  np.random.choice(review_templates[second_topic])
        review = review + ". " + second_review

    reviews.append(review)
    topics.append(topic)

# Create DataFrame
review_data = pd.DataFrame({
    'review_text': reviews,
    'true_topic': topics  # We'll use this to evaluate our results
})

print("Customer Review Dataset Overview:")
print("=" * 50)
print(f"Number of reviews: {len(review_data)}")
print(f"Average review length:
 ↪  {review_data['review_text'].str.len().mean():.1f} characters")
print("\nFirst 5 reviews:")
for i in range(5):
```

```
    print(f"{i+1}. {review_data['review_text'].iloc[i]}")

print("\nTrue topic distribution:")
print(review_data['true_topic'].value_counts())
```

Output:

```
Customer Review Dataset Overview:
==================================================
Number of reviews: 500
Average review length: 63.4 characters

First 5 reviews:
1. Shipping was delayed and package was damaged
2. The battery life on this device is amazing, lasts all day
3. Excellent support experience, problem solved immediately.
Shipping was delayed and package was damaged
4. Reasonable price point for the quality
5. Beautiful bright display, perfect for watching videos

True topic distribution:
customer_service     115
shipping_delivery    104
battery_life         101
screen_quality        95
price_value           85
Name: count, dtype: int64
```

5.9.2.2 Step 2: Text Preprocessing for Topic Modeling

Before we can uncover the main topics in our product reviews, it's important to clean and standardize the text to remove noise and prepare it for analysis. Raw text often contains inconsistencies such as mixed capitalization, punctuation, numbers, and extra spaces, all of which can interfere with topic modeling. To address this, we first convert all text to lowercase so that words like "Phone" and "phone" are treated the same. We then remove punctuation, symbols, and numbers, since these elements usually do not contribute meaningfully to identifying topics. Finally, any extra spaces created during cleaning are removed to keep the text consistent, ensuring our algorithm focuses on the meaningful words that will reveal the hidden themes.

```
import re
from sklearn.feature_extraction.text import ENGLISH_STOP_WORDS

def preprocess_text(text):
```

```
    """Clean and preprocess text for topic modeling"""
    # Convert to lowercase
    text = text.lower()

    # Remove special characters and digits
    text = re.sub(r'[^a-zA-Z\s]', '', text)

    # Remove extra whitespace
    text = ' '.join(text.split())

    return text

# Apply preprocessing
review_data['cleaned_text'] =
↪   review_data['review_text'].apply(preprocess_text)

print("Text Preprocessing Results:")
print("=" * 40)
print("Original vs Cleaned Examples:")
for i in range(3):
    print(f"\nOriginal: {review_data['review_text'].iloc[i]}")
    print(f"Cleaned:  {review_data['cleaned_text'].iloc[i]}")
```

Output:

```
Text Preprocessing Results:
========================================
Original vs Cleaned Examples:

Original: Shipping was delayed and package was damaged
Cleaned:  shipping was delayed and package was damaged

Original: The battery life on this device is amazing, lasts all day
Cleaned:  the battery life on this device is amazing lasts all day

Original: Excellent support experience, problem solved immediately.
Shipping was delayed and package was damaged
Cleaned:  excellent support experience problem solved immediately
shipping was delayed and package was damaged
```

Once the text is cleaned, we create a document-term matrix using TF-IDF (Term Frequency-Inverse Document Frequency). TF-IDF helps highlight the words that are most important in each review while downplaying very common words that appear across many reviews. In building this matrix, we limit the vocabulary to the top 100 words to focus on the most relevant terms, remove common English stop words, and exclude words that appear in fewer than two reviews or more than 80% of reviews.

```
# Create document-term matrix using TF-IDF
print("\nCreating document-term matrix...")
vectorizer = TfidfVectorizer(
    max_features=100,  # Keep top 100 words
    stop_words='english',  # Remove common English words
    min_df=2,  # Word must appear in at least 2 documents
    max_df=0.8  # Word must appear in less than 80% of documents
)

# Fit and transform the text data
doc_term_matrix = vectorizer.fit_transform(review_data['cleaned_text'])
feature_names = vectorizer.get_feature_names_out()

print(f"Document-term matrix shape: {doc_term_matrix.shape}")
print(f"Vocabulary size: {len(feature_names)}")
print(f"Top 20 words in vocabulary: {list(feature_names[:20])}")
```

Output:

```
Creating document-term matrix...
Document-term matrix shape: (500, 92)
Vocabulary size: 92
Top 20 words in vocabulary: ['amazing', 'arrive', 'arrived', 'battery',
'beautiful', 'bright', 'brightness', 'charging', 'clear', 'colors',
'cost', 'crystal', 'customer', 'daily', 'damaged', 'day', 'dead',
'delayed', 'delivery', 'device']
```

This code creates a document-term matrix from your cleaned review text using the TF-IDF method. The matrix represents each document (review) as a vector of word importance scores, allowing the topic modeling algorithm to work with numerical data instead of raw text. The printed output tells us several things: the shape (500, 92) shows there are 500 reviews and 92 unique words in the vocabulary after filtering; the vocabulary size confirms there are 92 words retained for analysis; and the top 20 words give a snapshot of the most significant words that appear across the dataset. This helps you understand which words the algorithm will use to detect underlying topics.

5.9.2.3 Step 3: Latent Dirichlet Allocation (LDA) Topic Modeling

With the text data cleaned and transformed into a document-term matrix, we now apply Latent Dirichlet Allocation (LDA) to uncover the underlying topics in our customer reviews. LDA is a statistical model that identifies patterns in how words appear together across documents, allowing it to discover common themes without us having to read every review.

To make this idea easier to understand, think of each document as a recipe and each topic as a type of cuisine. For example, you might have Italian, Mexican, or Japanese cuisines, and each one is defined by a set of common ingredients.

A single recipe usually isn't limited to just one cuisine—it might be mostly Italian but include some elements of another style. In the same way, LDA assumes that each document is a mixture of topics. A customer review might mostly focus on battery life but also include comments about price or customer service.

At the same time, each topic is made up of a group of words that tend to appear together. For instance, a "battery" topic might include words like battery, charging, power, and hours, while a "customer service" topic might include support, help, response, and service.

LDA works by analyzing all the documents and uncovering: - the main topics that exist in the dataset - the key words associated with each topic - how strongly each topic appears in each document

This is what we mean by a "mixture of topics" (documents contain multiple themes) and a "mixture of words" (topics are defined by groups of related words).

```
print("LATENT DIRICHLET ALLOCATION (LDA) TOPIC MODELING")
print("=" * 60)

# Apply LDA with 5 topics (we know there should be 5 from our data
 ↪  generation)
n_topics = 5
lda_model = LatentDirichletAllocation(
    n_components=n_topics,
    random_state=42,
    max_iter=100,
    learning_method='batch'
)

# Fit the model
lda_model.fit(doc_term_matrix)

print(f"LDA Model trained with {n_topics} topics")
print(f"Log likelihood: {lda_model.score(doc_term_matrix):.2f}")
```

Output:

```
LATENT DIRICHLET ALLOCATION (LDA) TOPIC MODELING
============================================================
LDA Model trained with 5 topics
```

```
Log likelihood: -5874.89
```

Once trained, LDA provides a list of topics, each represented by its most significant words. For instance, one topic might include words like “smartphone,” “battery,” and “camera,” while another might highlight “laptop,” “performance,” and “speed.” Examining these top words helps us interpret what each topic represents in terms of real-world themes or product features.

```
# Display topics and their top words
def display_topics(model, feature_names, n_top_words=8):
    """Display topics with their top words"""
    topics = []
    for topic_idx, topic in enumerate(model.components_):
        top_words_idx = topic.argsort()[-n_top_words:][::-1]
        top_words = [feature_names[i] for i in top_words_idx]
        topics.append(top_words)
        print(f"\nTopic {topic_idx + 1}:")
        print(f"Top words: {', '.join(top_words)}")
    return topics

print("\nDiscovered Topics:")
print("-" * 30)
lda_topics = display_topics(lda_model, feature_names)
```

Output:

```
Discovered Topics:
------------------------------


Topic 1:
Top words: unhelpful, rude, representatives, excellent,
service, customer, took, weeks

Topic 2:
Top words: colors, support, quickly, team, knowledgeable,
friendly, vibrant, crystal

Topic 3:
Top words: arrived, reasonable, point, similar, products,
expensive, cost, performance

Topic 4:
Top words: life, battery, dies, quick, packaging, overpriced,
use, worth
```

```
Topic 5:
Top words: waited, terrible, response, damaged, delayed, service,
brightness, pixels
```

After identifying the topics, we can also assign each review to the topic it most likely belongs to. This allows us to see representative examples of reviews for each topic, giving concrete insight into how the topics manifest in actual customer feedback.

```
# Get topic assignments for each document
doc_topic_probs = lda_model.transform(doc_term_matrix)

# Assign each document to its most likely topic
doc_topic_assignments = doc_topic_probs.argmax(axis=1)

# Show example documents for each topic
print("\nExample Reviews for Each Topic:")
print("-" * 40)
for topic_num in range(n_topics):
    topic_docs = review_data[doc_topic_assignments == topic_num]
    print(f"\nTopic {topic_num + 1} Examples:")
    for i, (idx, row) in enumerate(topic_docs.head(2).iterrows()):
        print(f"  {i+1}. {row['review_text']}")

# Calculate topic distribution
topic_counts =
↪ pd.Series(doc_topic_assignments).value_counts().sort_index()
print(f"\nTopic Distribution:")
for i, count in enumerate(topic_counts):
    percentage = (count / len(review_data)) * 100
    print(f"Topic {i+1}: {count} reviews ({percentage:.1f}%)")
```

Output:

```
Example Reviews for Each Topic:
----------------------------------------


Topic 1 Examples:
  1. Customer service representatives were rude and unhelpful
  2. Slow delivery, took weeks to arrive. Package arrived on time
  and well protected

Topic 2 Examples:
  1. Battery drains too quickly, needs charging multiple times daily.
  Excellent value, high quality at fair price
  2. Customer support was helpful and resolved my issue quickly.
```

```
  Reasonable price point for the quality

Topic 3 Examples:
  1. Reasonable price point for the quality
  2. Reasonable price point for the quality

Topic 4 Examples:
  1. The battery life on this device is amazing, lasts all day
  2. Beautiful bright display, perfect for watching videos

Topic 5 Examples:
  1. Shipping was delayed and package was damaged
  2. Excellent support experience, problem solved immediately.
  Shipping was delayed and package was damaged

Topic Distribution:
Topic 1: 85 reviews (17.0%)
Topic 2: 115 reviews (23.0%)
Topic 3: 107 reviews (21.4%)
Topic 4: 105 reviews (21.0%)
Topic 5: 88 reviews (17.6%)
```

This code takes the LDA model we trained and assigns each review to a topic based on the patterns it learned in the document-term matrix. First, it calculates the probability that each review belongs to each topic. Then, each review is assigned to the topic with the highest probability, which is considered the review's main theme. The printed examples show actual reviews for each topic, giving a sense of what kinds of comments are grouped together. For instance, Topic 1 might capture reviews about customer service, Topic 4 about battery life and device features, and so on. Finally, the topic distribution counts how many reviews were assigned to each topic and what percentage of the total dataset that represents. This gives an overview of which topics are most common and helps identify the main areas of concern or interest in the customer feedback.

5.9.2.4 Step 4: Clustering-Based Topic Modeling

In this step, we compare LDA with a clustering-based approach using K-Means, which groups reviews based on similarity rather than relying on a probabilistic topic model. By applying K-Means to the TF-IDF matrix, we partition the reviews into a fixed number of clusters so that reviews within the same cluster are more similar to each other than to reviews in other clusters. This allows us to explore the main themes in the dataset from a different perspective and see how patterns of word similarity can reveal groupings that may align with or differ from the topics identified by LDA.

```
print("\n\nCLUSTERING-BASED TOPIC MODELING")
print("=" * 50)

# Apply K-Means clustering to the TF-IDF matrix
kmeans = KMeans(n_clusters=n_topics, random_state=42, n_init=10)
cluster_assignments = kmeans.fit_predict(doc_term_matrix)

# Calculate silhouette score to evaluate clustering quality
silhouette_avg = silhouette_score(doc_term_matrix, cluster_assignments)
print(f"K-Means clustering completed")
print(f"Silhouette Score: {silhouette_avg:.3f}")
```

Output:

```
CLUSTERING-BASED TOPIC MODELING
==================================================
K-Means clustering completed
Silhouette Score: 0.163
```

The silhouette score helps us understand how well the clustering worked by measuring how similar each review is to its own cluster compared to other clusters. The score ranges from -1 to 1:

- Values close to 1 mean the clusters are very well separated and clearly defined
- Values around 0 mean the clusters overlap and are not very distinct
- Negative values mean many points may be assigned to the wrong cluster

In practice, a silhouette score above 0.5 is considered strong, around 0.25–0.5 is moderate, and below 0.25 is relatively weak.

In our case, the score is 0.163, which is quite low. This suggests that while the model is forming clusters, the boundaries between them are not very clear. This often happens with text data because reviews can discuss multiple topics at once, making it harder for K-Means to create clean, well-separated groups.

```
# Get top words for each cluster
def get_cluster_top_words(doc_term_matrix, cluster_assignments,
↪   feature_names, n_top_words=8):
    """Get top words for each cluster"""
    cluster_topics = []
    for cluster_num in range(n_topics):
        # Get documents in this cluster
        cluster_docs = doc_term_matrix[cluster_assignments ==
↪   cluster_num]

        # Calculate mean TF-IDF scores for words in this cluster
```

```
        mean_scores = cluster_docs.mean(axis=0).A1

        # Get top words
        top_word_indices = mean_scores.argsort()[-n_top_words:][::-1]
        top_words = [feature_names[i] for i in top_word_indices]
        cluster_topics.append(top_words)

        print(f"\nCluster {cluster_num + 1}:")
        print(f"Top words: {', '.join(top_words)}")

    return cluster_topics

print("\nDiscovered Clusters:")
print("-" * 30)
cluster_topics = get_cluster_top_words(doc_term_matrix,
 ↪  cluster_assignments, feature_names)
```

Output:

```
Discovered Clusters:
------------------------------

Cluster 1:
Top words: battery, use, life, hours, charging, dies, poor, performance

Cluster 2:
Top words: support, team, friendly, knowledgeable, issue, helpful,
resolved, immediately

Cluster 3:
Top words: quality, display, colors, clear, delivery, screen,
price, worth

Cluster 4:
Top words: service, customer, rude, unhelpful, representatives,
terrible, response, waited

Cluster 5:
Top words: shipping, arrived, package, fast, earlier, expected,
damaged, delayed
```

This code identifies the most important words for each cluster discovered by K-Means. For each cluster, it selects the reviews assigned to that cluster and calculates the average TF-IDF score for each word across those reviews. The words with the highest average scores are considered the most representative of that cluster. The output lists these top words for each cluster, providing insight into the themes captured by the clustering approach. For example, one cluster might focus on battery and performance issues, another on customer support experiences, and another on product quality and display. This helps us understand the main topics in each group without reading every review, and allows comparison with the topics identified by LDA.

We can also look at example reviews from each cluster to see how the topics manifest in real customer feedback:

```
# Show example documents for each cluster
print("\nExample Reviews for Each Cluster:")
print("-" * 40)
for cluster_num in range(n_topics):
    cluster_docs = review_data[cluster_assignments == cluster_num]
    print(f"\nCluster {cluster_num + 1} Examples:")
    for i, (idx, row) in enumerate(cluster_docs.head(2).iterrows()):
        print(f"  {i+1}. {row['review_text']}")

# Calculate cluster distribution
cluster_counts =
↪ pd.Series(cluster_assignments).value_counts().sort_index()
print(f"\nCluster Distribution:")
for i, count in enumerate(cluster_counts):
    percentage = (count / len(review_data)) * 100
    print(f"Cluster {i+1}: {count} reviews ({percentage:.1f}%)")
```

Output:

```
Example Reviews for Each Cluster:
----------------------------------------


Cluster 1 Examples:
  1. The battery life on this device is amazing, lasts all day
  2. Battery drains too quickly, needs charging multiple times daily.
  Excellent value, high quality at fair price

Cluster 2 Examples:
  1. Customer support was helpful and resolved my issue quickly.
  Reasonable price point for the quality
  2. Support team was knowledgeable and friendly

Cluster 3 Examples:
  1. Reasonable price point for the quality
  2. Beautiful bright display, perfect for watching videos
```

```
Cluster 4 Examples:
  1. Terrible customer service, waited hours for response
  2. Excellent support experience, problem solved immediately.
  Terrible customer service, waited hours for response

Cluster 5 Examples:
  1. Shipping was delayed and package was damaged
  2. Excellent support experience, problem solved immediately.
  Shipping was delayed and package was damaged

Cluster Distribution:
Cluster 1: 107 reviews (21.4%)
Cluster 2: 68 reviews (13.6%)
Cluster 3: 194 reviews (38.8%)
Cluster 4: 63 reviews (12.6%)
Cluster 5: 68 reviews (13.6%)
```

This code shows example reviews for each cluster generated by K-Means and summarizes how many reviews belong to each cluster. By printing a few sample reviews per cluster, we can see how the themes indicated by the top words actually appear in real customer feedback—for instance, one cluster may focus on battery life, another on customer support, and another on shipping issues. The cluster distribution then quantifies how many reviews fall into each cluster and what percentage of the dataset that represents, giving a clear picture of which topics are most common and how customer feedback is grouped.

5.9.2.5 Step 5: Comparing Methods and Choosing Optimal Number of Topics

In this step, we are testing different numbers of topics to determine the optimal configuration for our dataset. Choosing the right number of topics is important because it directly affects the quality and interpretability of the results; too few topics may oversimplify the themes, while too many can create overlapping or unclear groupings. By evaluating multiple options, we can select a topic count that best captures the main themes in the customer reviews.

```
print("\n\nFINDING OPTIMAL NUMBER OF TOPICS")
print("=" * 50)

# Test different numbers of topics
topic_range = range(2, 8)
lda_scores = []
silhouette_scores = []

for n_topics_test in topic_range:
```

```
    # Test LDA
    lda_test = LatentDirichletAllocation(
        n_components=n_topics_test,
        random_state=42,
        max_iter=50
    )
    lda_test.fit(doc_term_matrix)
    lda_scores.append(lda_test.score(doc_term_matrix))

    # Test K-Means
    kmeans_test = KMeans(n_clusters=n_topics_test, random_state=42,
 ↪  n_init=10)
    cluster_labels = kmeans_test.fit_predict(doc_term_matrix)
    silhouette_scores.append(silhouette_score(doc_term_matrix,
 ↪  cluster_labels))

# Display results
print("Topic Number Evaluation:")
print("-" * 30)
print(f"{'Topics':<8} {'LDA Score':<12} {'Silhouette':<12}")
print("-" * 32)
for i, n_topics_test in enumerate(topic_range):
    print(f"{n_topics_test:<8} {lda_scores[i]:<12.2f}
     ↪  {silhouette_scores[i]:<12.3f}")

# Find optimal numbers
best_lda_idx = np.argmax(lda_scores)
best_silhouette_idx = np.argmax(silhouette_scores)

print(f"\nOptimal number of topics:")
print(f"LDA (highest log-likelihood):
 ↪  {list(topic_range)[best_lda_idx]} topics")
print(f"K-Means (highest silhouette):
 ↪  {list(topic_range)[best_silhouette_idx]} topics")
```

Output:

```
FINDING OPTIMAL NUMBER OF TOPICS
==================================================
Topic Number Evaluation:
------------------------------
Topics   LDA Score    Silhouette
--------------------------------
2        -5756.91     0.072
```

```
3         -5859.82     0.107
4         -5861.88     0.140
5         -5874.89     0.163
6         -5871.29     0.184
7         -5844.08     0.221

Optimal number of topics:
LDA (highest log-likelihood): 2 topics
K-Means (highest silhouette): 7 topics
```

This code tests different numbers of topics to find the optimal configuration for both LDA and K-Means. For each number of topics in the range of 2 to 7, it trains an LDA model and calculates its log-likelihood score, which measures how well the model explains the data, and it also applies K-Means clustering and calculates the silhouette score, which measures how well-defined the clusters are. The results are displayed in a table showing LDA scores and silhouette scores for each topic count. The optimal number of topics is then selected based on the highest score for each method: LDA suggests 2 topics because that maximizes the log-likelihood, while K-Means suggests 7 clusters because that maximizes the silhouette score. This comparison helps guide the choice of topic numbers depending on the method used and ensures the topics or clusters are meaningful and well-separated.

5.9.3 Practice

You work for a digital media company that publishes news articles across multiple categories. Your manager wants to understand what topics are trending in your article database to guide editorial decisions and content strategy. You have a dataset of 400 news articles that need to be analyzed for topic discovery.

Run this code to create and explore the news article dataset.

```
# Create news article dataset
np.random.seed(123)

# News article templates by category
article_templates = {
    'technology': [
        "New smartphone features artificial intelligence capabilities
         ↪ and advanced camera technology",
        "Software company releases innovative app with machine learning
         ↪ algorithms",
        "Tech startup develops breakthrough in cloud computing and data
         ↪ storage solutions",
        "Cybersecurity experts warn about new threats in digital
         ↪ infrastructure",
```

```
        "Social media platform introduces privacy features and user
         ↪  control options"
    ],
    'sports': [
        "Basketball team wins championship game with outstanding player
         ↪  performance",
        "Football season begins with exciting matches and record
         ↪  attendance",
        "Olympic athletes prepare for upcoming games with intensive
         ↪  training programs",
        "Tennis tournament features international players competing for
         ↪  grand prize",
        "Soccer league announces new rules and player transfer
         ↪  policies"
    ],
    'business': [
        "Stock market shows positive trends with technology sector
         ↪  leading gains",
        "Company reports quarterly earnings exceeding analyst
         ↪  expectations significantly",
        "Merger announcement between major corporations creates
         ↪  industry consolidation",
        "Startup receives venture capital funding for expansion and
         ↪  growth plans",
        "Economic indicators suggest recovery in manufacturing and
         ↪  retail sectors"
    ],
    'health': [
        "Medical researchers discover new treatment for chronic disease
         ↪  conditions",
        "Healthcare system implements digital solutions for patient
         ↪  care improvement",
        "Nutrition study reveals benefits of balanced diet and regular
         ↪  exercise",
        "Mental health awareness campaign promotes wellness and support
         ↪  resources",
        "Pharmaceutical company develops innovative drug for rare
         ↪  medical conditions"
    ],
    'environment': [
        "Climate change report shows impact on global weather patterns
         ↪  and ecosystems",
        "Renewable energy project generates clean power for thousands
         ↪  of households",
```

```
        "Conservation efforts protect endangered species and natural
         ↪ habitats",
        "Pollution reduction initiative improves air quality in urban
         ↪ areas",
        "Sustainable agriculture practices help farmers reduce
         ↪ environmental impact"
    ]
}

# Generate 400 articles
articles = []
true_categories = []
for i in range(400):
    # Randomly select a category
    category = np.random.choice(list(article_templates.keys()))
    # Randomly select a template
    article = np.random.choice(article_templates[category])

    # 20% chance to create mixed-topic articles
    if np.random.random() > 0.8:
        second_category =
 ↪  np.random.choice(list(article_templates.keys()))
        second_article =
 ↪  np.random.choice(article_templates[second_category])
        article = article + ". " + second_article

    articles.append(article)
    true_categories.append(category)

# Create DataFrame
news_data = pd.DataFrame({
    'article_text': articles,
    'true_category': true_categories
})

print("News Article Dataset Overview:")
print("=" * 50)
print(f"Number of articles: {len(news_data)}")
print(f"Average article length:
 ↪  {news_data['article_text'].str.len().mean():.1f} characters")

print("\nFirst 5 articles:")
for i in range(5):
```

```
    print(f"{i+1}. {news_data['article_text'].iloc[i]}")

print("\nTrue category distribution:")
print(news_data['true_category'].value_counts())

# Preprocess the text
news_data['cleaned_text'] =
 ↪  news_data['article_text'].apply(preprocess_text)

# Create document-term matrix
news_vectorizer = TfidfVectorizer(
    max_features=150,
    stop_words='english',
    min_df=3,
    max_df=0.7
)

news_doc_term_matrix =
 ↪  news_vectorizer.fit_transform(news_data['cleaned_text'])
news_feature_names = news_vectorizer.get_feature_names_out()

print(f"\nDocument-term matrix shape: {news_doc_term_matrix.shape}")
print(f"Vocabulary size: {len(news_feature_names)}")
```

5.9.3.1 Lab 5B Questions

1. **Dataset Overview**: How many articles are in the dataset, and what is the average length of an article in characters?

2. **Content Analysis**: Examine the first five articles. Identify which category each article likely belongs to based on its content. Compare your guess to the true_category column.

3. **Preprocessing Understanding**: What preprocessing steps were applied to the article_text before creating the document-term matrix? Why are these steps important for topic modeling?

4. **Matrix Structure**: After preprocessing, what is the shape of the document-term matrix? What do the rows and columns represent?

5. **Vocabulary Analysis**: How many unique words (features) are retained in the TF-IDF vocabulary, and how were the words filtered (e.g., minimum or maximum document frequency)?

6. **Word Relevance**: Display the top 10 words in the vocabulary. Which words

seem most relevant to technology articles? To sports articles?

7. **LDA Implementation**: Using LDA with 5 topics, train a topic model on the news document-term matrix. What is the log-likelihood score, and what does it indicate about the model fit?

8. **Topic Interpretation**: For each topic discovered by LDA, list the top 8 words. How do these words help you interpret the topic?

9. **Document Assignment**: Assign each article to the most likely LDA topic. Pick one topic and list two example articles that belong to it. Explain why they fit that topic.

10. **Topic Distribution**: Calculate the distribution of articles across the 5 LDA topics. Which topic has the most articles, and which has the fewest?

11. **Clustering Comparison**: Apply K-Means clustering with 5 clusters to the TF-IDF matrix. What is the silhouette score, and what does it tell you about the clustering quality?

12. **Cluster Analysis**: For each cluster, list the top 8 words based on average TF-IDF scores. How do these compare to the LDA topics?

13. **Method Evaluation**: Assign articles to clusters and examine two example articles per cluster. Do the clusters align with the true article categories?

14. **Comparative Analysis**: Compare LDA and K-Means results. Which method seems better at separating articles into meaningful topics for this dataset? Explain your reasoning.

15. **Mixed Topics Challenge**: Some articles contain mixed topics (two categories). How might this affect the results of both LDA and clustering? Suggest one way to handle mixed-topic articles in topic modeling.

5.10 Conclusion

This exploration of NLP applications has introduced you to three powerful techniques that businesses use every day to extract value from text data. We've seen how sentiment analysis reveals the emotional tone behind customer feedback, how topic modeling discovers the main themes in large document collections, and how named entity recognition extracts important people, places, and organizations from unstructured text.

The key insight to remember is that these applications build directly on the text preprocessing techniques you learned in the previous module. Sentiment analysis relies on proper text cleaning and tokenization to accurately detect emotional cues. Topic modeling depends on effective preprocessing to discover meaningful themes rather than noise. Named entity recognition requires careful text preparation to identify entities accurately in context.

Successful implementation of these NLP applications requires understanding your specific business needs and choosing the right tool for each job. Sentiment analysis works best when you need to understand customer emotions and opinions. Topic modeling excels when you want to discover what themes people discuss most in large text collections. Named entity recognition shines when you need to extract specific factual information from documents.

The choice of approach often involves trade-offs between accuracy, speed, and interpretability. Simple keyword-based approaches might be sufficient for well-defined problems, while more complex machine learning models might be necessary for nuanced applications. The most successful implementations combine automated analysis with human oversight, using technology to scale human judgment rather than replace it entirely.

Domain expertise remains crucial for successful NLP applications. Understanding the language patterns, terminology, and communication conventions of your specific industry helps you make better decisions about which techniques to apply and how to interpret results. Medical applications require understanding of medical terminology, legal applications need familiarity with legal language, and social media analysis requires understanding of informal communication patterns.

As you continue to explore NLP applications, remember that the goal is to solve real business problems and create value for users. The most successful applications are those that genuinely improve how people work with information, make decisions, and understand their customers. Focus on creating solutions that enhance human capabilities rather than simply automating existing processes.

The techniques you've learned in this module—sentiment analysis, topic modeling, and named entity recognition—represent some of the most immediately practical applications of NLP in business today. They provide a foundation for understanding how language processing can create real business value and prepare you for even more sophisticated applications as the field continues to advance.

Looking ahead, these NLP techniques will continue to evolve and improve, offering new opportunities for businesses to understand their customers, optimize their operations, and make better decisions based on text data. The foundation you've built in understanding both basic preprocessing and practical applications prepares you to adapt to new developments and apply these powerful techniques effectively in your own work.

5.11 References

[1] Stanford NLP Group. (2025). Natural Language Processing Applications: From Sentiment to Entity Recognition. https://nlp.stanford.edu/

[2] IBM Research. (2025). Sentiment Analysis in Business: Applications and Best Practices. https://research.ibm.com/

[3] Google AI Language. (2025). Topic Modeling and Information Extraction: Practical Business Applications. https://ai.googleblog.com/

[4] MIT Technology Review. (2025). Named Entity Recognition for Business Intelligence: Use Cases and Implementation. https://www.technologyreview.com/

Chapter 6

Practical Implementation of ML and NLP

6.1 Learning Outcomes

6-1: Understand how individual ML and NLP models integrate into business systems and the new challenges this creates

6-2: Analyze how ML and NLP models support business decision-making processes and identify appropriate use cases

6-3: Explain how conversational AI systems combine multiple ML and NLP models into integrated applications

6-4: Evaluate the role of human oversight in AI-powered business systems and recognize when automated decisions are appropriate

6.2 Introduction

Imagine you are the head of digital transformation at a growing retail company. Over the past year, your team has built several impressive machine learning models: a customer churn prediction model with 85% accuracy, a sentiment analysis system that classifies 90% of product reviews correctly, and a recommendation engine that performs well in testing. Your executives are excited and want to deploy these models into real business operations right away.

As you start planning, you quickly realize that moving from successful models to successful business systems is not straightforward. How can you ensure the churn model doesn't unfairly target certain customer segments? How do you integrate sentiment analysis into a customer service workflow that handles thousands of inquiries per day? How do you prevent the recommendation engine from making inappropriate suggestions?

This scenario highlights a key challenge in implementing machine learning and NLP: transitioning from individual models that perform well in testing to integrated business systems that work fairly, reliably, and responsibly in the real world. In earlier chapters, you learned how to build and evaluate models—predicting outcomes, classifying text, and measuring performance. In practice, these models rarely operate alone. They are part of larger systems that automate decisions, guide users, and influence real outcomes.

This chapter shows how the models and techniques you've learned come together in practical business applications. We will explore how bias can appear when models encounter real-world data, how conversational AI systems combine multiple models into integrated applications, and how text summarization and generation tools support decision-making while requiring careful human oversight.

Most importantly, you will see how the evaluation principles and responsible practices you've already learned apply when models move from development environments into systems that affect customers, employees, and business outcomes.

6.3 From Models to Business Systems

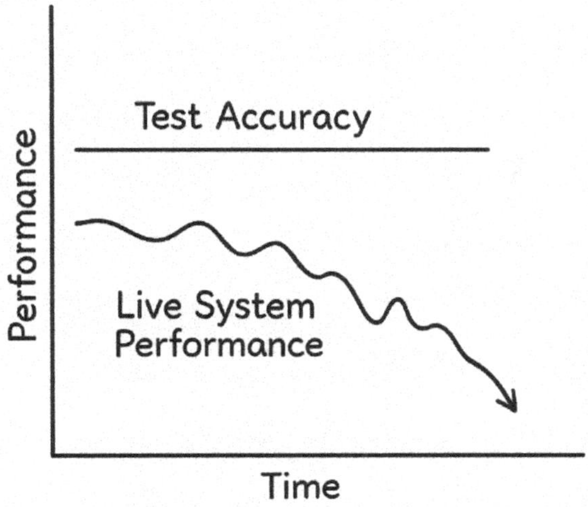

Throughout this course, you've learned to build and evaluate individual machine learning models. You've trained regression models to predict numerical outcomes, built classification systems to categorize data, processed text with NLP techniques, and measured performance using metrics like accuracy, precision, and recall. These skills provide the foundation for applied machine learning, but real business applications require integrating these individual models into larger systems that operate reliably at scale.

The transition from models to systems introduces new complexities that go beyond algorithmic performance. A customer churn prediction model that achieves 85% accuracy in testing might perform differently when deployed on live customer data that includes new patterns the training data didn't capture. A sentiment analysis model that works well on product reviews might struggle when applied to customer service emails that use different language patterns and express different types of concerns.

6.3.1 Understanding System-Level Challenges

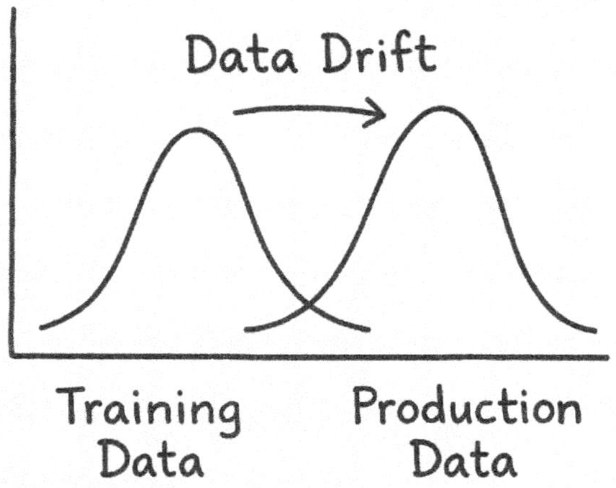

When individual models become part of business systems, they encounter challenges that don't exist in controlled testing environments. Data drift occurs when the real-world data the system encounters differs from the training data used to build the models. Customer behavior changes over time, new products are introduced, market conditions shift, and external events create patterns that weren't present in historical data.

Consider a recommendation system trained on pre-pandemic shopping data. When deployed during the pandemic, it might struggle to make good recommendations because customer preferences and shopping patterns changed dramatically. The individual recommendation algorithms might be technically sound, but the system fails because the underlying assumptions about customer behavior no longer hold.

Integration complexity emerges when multiple models must work together within business workflows. A customer service system might combine intent classification models, sentiment analysis models, named entity recognition systems, and response generation models. Each individual model might perform well in isolation, but their combined performance depends on how well they work together and how errors from one model affect the others.

Performance monitoring becomes more complex when models operate within business systems. Traditional metrics like accuracy and F1 score remain important, but businesses also need to track system-level metrics like response time, user satisfaction, business impact, and fairness across different user groups. A chatbot might have high accuracy in understanding customer intents but still fail if it takes too long to respond or if customers find the interactions frustrating.

6.3.2 Business Context and Model Performance

The business context in which models operate significantly affects their real-world performance and impact. A fraud detection model that achieves 95% accuracy might seem excellent, but if it generates too many false positives, it could frustrate legitimate customers and increase customer service costs. The same model might be perfectly acceptable for initial screening if human reviewers verify flagged transactions, but inappropriate for automated blocking of customer accounts.

Stakeholder expectations and constraints shape how models are deployed and evaluated. Marketing teams might prioritize models that increase customer engagement, even if they're less accurate than alternatives. Compliance teams might require models that can provide clear explanations for their decisions, even if this reduces performance. Customer service teams might need models that fail gracefully and provide helpful error messages when they encounter situations they can't handle.

Business processes and workflows determine how models integrate with existing operations. A hiring recommendation system must fit into existing HR workflows, integrate with applicant tracking systems, and support the decision-making processes that hiring managers already use. The most technically sophisticated model is useless if it doesn't align with how the business actually operates.

6.3.3 Success Metrics Beyond Model Performance

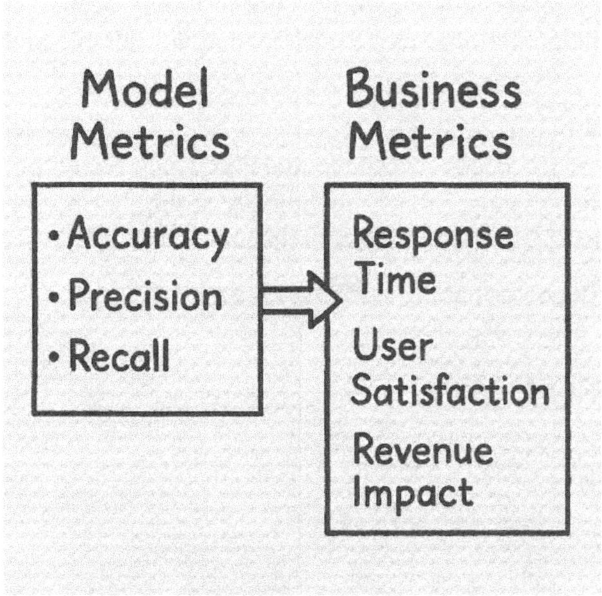

Successful deployment of ML and NLP systems requires measuring success at multiple levels. Technical performance metrics like accuracy, precision, and recall remain important for understanding how well individual models work. But business success requires additional metrics that capture user experience, business impact, and operational efficiency.

User experience metrics measure how well the system serves its intended users. For a customer service chatbot, this might include metrics like conversation completion rate, user satisfaction scores, and the percentage of conversations that require human handoff. For a recommendation system, it might include click-through rates, conversion rates, and user engagement metrics.

Business impact metrics connect system performance to business outcomes. A customer churn prediction system should be evaluated based on how well it helps the business retain customers, not just how accurately it predicts churn. A content recommendation system should be measured by its impact on user engagement and business revenue, not just by algorithmic performance metrics.

Operational efficiency metrics track how well the system integrates into business operations. This includes metrics like system uptime, response time, maintenance costs, and the amount of human oversight required. A system that requires constant manual intervention might not be viable even if it performs well technically.

6.4 ML and NLP Models in Business Decision-Making

Machine learning and NLP models only create value when they are used to support real business decisions. These models influence actions such as who gets approved, prioritized, flagged, or denied. As a result, model quality is not just about technical performance, but about whether the model produces decisions that are reliable and appropriate in real-world settings.

Designing models for business use means thinking beyond accuracy. Models must fit into existing workflows, support the needs of stakeholders, and operate within organizational goals and constraints. A model that is technically strong but poorly integrated can lead to confusion, misuse, or unintended consequences.

One of the most important risks in decision-making systems is bias.

6.4.1 Bias

Bias occurs when models systematically produce worse or unfair outcomes for certain groups. This usually happens because of data and modeling choices, not because of intent. If training data is incomplete, unbalanced, or reflects historical inequalities, models will learn and repeat those patterns. For example, a model trained on past hiring or lending decisions may disadvantage certain groups because past decisions were biased, not because those groups are less qualified.

Bias can also be hidden during evaluation. A model may appear accurate overall while performing poorly for specific demographic groups. When performance is only measured in aggregate, these differences remain invisible, even though they directly affect real decisions.

Addressing bias uses the same skills required to build effective business models. Improving data quality, balancing training samples, selecting features carefully, and evaluating performance across groups all help ensure that models support better and more consistent decisions. In business settings, a model is only successful if it leads to decisions that are not just accurate, but also dependable and fair.

6.5 Conversational AI as an Integrated NLP Pipeline

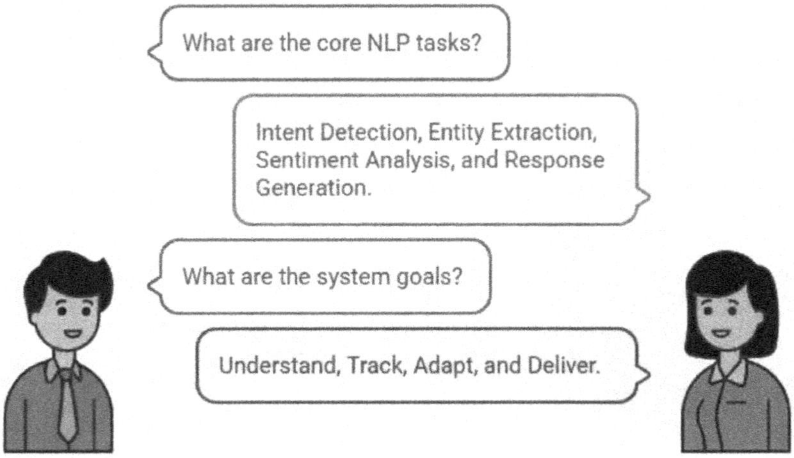

The chatbots and virtual assistants that customers interact with every day aren't single models—they're sophisticated systems that combine multiple machine learning and NLP models working together. Understanding conversational AI through the lens of the NLP techniques you've learned helps you see how individual models integrate into complex, interactive applications.

A customer service chatbot combines intent classification (supervised learning), named entity recognition (NER), sentiment analysis, and response generation. Each component uses techniques you've already learned, but their integration creates new challenges around maintaining context, handling errors gracefully, and providing coherent user experiences.

6.5.1 Intent Classification as Supervised Learning

When a customer types "I want to return my order," the chatbot's first task is intent classification—determining what the customer wants to accomplish. This is fundamentally a supervised learning problem using the classification techniques. The system analyzes the customer's message and predicts which of many possible intents (return request, order status inquiry, complaint, etc.) best matches their needs.

Training intent classification models requires labeled datasets where customer messages are paired with their intended meanings. This follows the same supervised learning process you learned: collect training data, extract features from text using preprocessing techniques, train classification models, and evaluate performance using metrics like precision and recall.

The text preprocessing techniques you learned—tokenization, stopword removal, and lemmatization—directly apply to preparing customer messages for intent classification.

The TF-IDF and word embedding techniques you studied provide ways to convert customer messages into numerical features that classification algorithms can process.

Performance evaluation for intent classification uses the same metrics you learned for classification problems. High precision means that when the system predicts a specific intent, it's usually correct. High recall means that the system successfully identifies most instances of each intent. The F1 score balances these considerations, which is particularly important when different intents require different types of responses.

6.5.2 Entity Extraction and Context Management

Once the system understands the customer's intent, it needs to extract specific information from their message. If a customer says "I want to return the blue sweater I ordered last week," the system needs to identify "blue sweater" as a product and "last week" as a time reference. This is named entity recognition (NER).

Entity extraction in conversational AI faces additional challenges because conversations span multiple messages. When a customer follows up with "When will I get my refund?", the system needs to understand that "refund" refers to the return request from the previous message. This requires maintaining conversation context across multiple exchanges.

Context management combines the entity recognition techniques you learned with memory systems that track information across conversation turns. The system maintains a conversation state that includes previously extracted entities, the current conversation topic, and any actions taken so far. This context helps interpret ambiguous references and maintain coherent conversations.

Error handling becomes crucial when entity extraction fails or produces uncertain results. The system might ask clarifying questions ("Which order are you referring to?") or provide options for the customer to choose from. These error handling strategies use the same principles you learned for dealing with uncertain model predictions.

6.5.3 Sentiment Analysis for Response Adaptation

Conversational AI systems use sentiment analysis to adapt their responses to the customer's emotional state. A frustrated customer complaining about a defective product should receive a different type of response than a neutral customer asking about shipping times. This applies the sentiment analysis techniques you learned to real-time conversation management.

Sentiment detection in conversations requires analyzing not just individual messages but the overall emotional trajectory of the conversation. A customer might start neutral but become frustrated if their issue isn't resolved quickly. The system needs to detect these emotional changes and adapt its responses accordingly.

Response adaptation based on sentiment involves selecting appropriate response templates, adjusting language formality, and determining when to escalate to human agents. A customer expressing anger might receive more empathetic language and faster escalation to human support, while a satisfied customer might receive standard automated responses.

The evaluation challenges you learned for sentiment analysis—handling sarcasm, context dependency, and cultural variations—become even more complex in conversational settings where context spans multiple messages and emotional states can change rapidly.

6.5.4 Response Generation and Quality Control

The final component of conversational AI is generating appropriate responses based on the understood intent, extracted entities, detected sentiment, and conversation context. This combines template-based approaches with the text generation techniques that are becoming increasingly sophisticated.

Template-based response generation uses predefined response templates that are filled in with specific information extracted from the conversation. For a return request, the system might use a template like "I can help you return your [PRODUCT]. Your return authorization number is [NUMBER]." This approach ensures consistent, accurate responses but can feel robotic.

Neural response generation uses text generation techniques to create more natural, contextually appropriate responses. These systems can generate responses that feel more conversational and adapt to the specific context of each interaction. However, they require careful quality control to ensure accuracy and appropriateness.

Quality control for conversational AI involves monitoring conversation success rates, user satisfaction, and the accuracy of information provided. The evaluation techniques you learned—precision, recall, and human evaluation—apply to assessing response quality. Additionally, conversation-level metrics like task completion rate and user satisfaction provide insights into overall system performance.

6.6 Text Summarization and Generation as Decision Support Tools

Text summarization and text generation are used in business to help people work faster, not to replace their judgment. These systems support decision-making by reducing the time it takes to read large amounts of information or to produce routine written content. The final decisions still belong to humans.

Summarization systems are used when people are overwhelmed with information. Executives, analysts, and managers often need to review long reports, customer feedback, or research documents. A summarization system reads these materials and produces a shorter version that highlights the main points, allowing decision-makers to understand the situation quickly before deciding what action to take.

Different types of summarizations serve different needs. Extractive summarization pulls key sentences directly from documents and works well for factual or regulatory materials where exact wording matters. Abstractive summarization rewrites information in a concise form and is better suited for high-level overviews, such as executive briefings that combine insights from multiple sources.

Text generation systems are used to produce large amounts of routine business writing. Companies use them to draft marketing content, customer emails, internal reports, and status updates. These systems help maintain consistent tone and structure while reducing the time employees spend on repetitive writing tasks. Humans typically review and edit this content before it is finalized or sent.

Because these systems influence communication and understanding, they must be used carefully. AI-generated summaries or text can include errors, omit important details, or introduce bias. For this reason, organizations rely on human review processes to verify accuracy, ensure appropriate tone, and catch mistakes before the content is used in decisions or shared externally.

The most effective systems are designed with humans in the loop. AI handles the first draft or summary, and people check, correct, and approve the output. This approach allows organizations to benefit from speed and scale while keeping accountability and judgment where they belong—with humans.

6.7 The Capstone Message: Responsible Implementation

Throughout this course, you've learned to build predictive models, process natural language, evaluate system performance, and deploy AI applications in business contexts. These technical skills provide the foundation for creating valuable AI systems, but the most important lesson transcends any specific technique or algorithm: the core responsibility of applied machine learning is choosing appropriate models, evaluating them honestly, and using them to support—not replace—human judgment.

This responsibility remains constant whether you're building a simple regression model to predict sales, implementing a sophisticated NLP system to analyze customer feedback, or deploying a conversational AI system to handle customer service inquiries. The scale and complexity may vary, but the fundamental principles of responsible AI development and deployment apply universally.

6.7.1 Connecting Technical Skills to Business Impact

The predictive modeling techniques provide powerful tools for understanding patterns in data and making informed predictions about future outcomes. But their business value depends on how well they're integrated into decision-making processes that account for uncertainty, changing conditions, and human expertise.

A customer churn prediction model is only valuable if it helps the business take effective action to retain customers. This requires not just accurate predictions, but also understanding which customers are most valuable to retain, what interventions are most likely to be successful, and how to balance automated outreach with human relationship management.

The NLP techniques enable businesses to extract insights from vast amounts of text data that would be impossible to process manually. But their impact depends on how well they're integrated into workflows that combine automated analysis with human interpretation and action.

Sentiment analysis of customer reviews becomes valuable when it helps product teams prioritize improvements, customer service teams identify urgent issues, and marketing teams understand customer perceptions. The technical capability to classify sentiment is just the starting point—the business value comes from acting on these insights effectively.

6.7.2 Evaluation as an Ongoing Responsibility

The evaluation techniques you learned—measuring accuracy, precision, recall, and other performance metrics—represent more than just technical exercises. They provide the foundation for ongoing accountability and improvement in AI systems that affect real people and business outcomes.

Regular performance monitoring helps ensure that AI systems continue to work effectively as conditions change. Customer behavior evolves, market conditions shift, and new patterns emerge that weren't present in training data. Systematic evaluation helps identify when models need updating, retraining, or replacement.

Fairness evaluation ensures that AI systems treat all users appropriately and don't inadvertently discriminate against particular groups. This requires extending the evaluation techniques you learned to measure performance across different demographic groups and identify disparities that might indicate bias.

Business impact evaluation connects technical performance to real-world outcomes. A model that maintains high accuracy but fails to deliver business value needs to be reconsidered, just as a model that delivers business value despite modest technical performance might be worth maintaining and improving.

6.7.3 Human Judgment as the Ultimate Safeguard

The most sophisticated AI systems remain tools that augment human capabilities rather than replace human judgment. The businesses that succeed with AI are those that thoughtfully integrate automated capabilities with human oversight, creativity, and ethical reasoning.

Human oversight provides the context, empathy, and ethical reasoning that AI systems currently lack. A customer service chatbot can handle routine inquiries efficiently, but human agents remain essential for complex problems, emotional situations, and cases that require creative problem-solving or ethical judgment.

Domain expertise helps ensure that AI systems are applied appropriately and that their outputs are interpreted correctly. A financial analyst using AI-generated market summaries brings knowledge about market dynamics, regulatory requirements, and business strategy that helps put automated insights into proper context.

Accountability and responsibility ultimately rest with the humans who design, deploy, and use AI systems. Technical capabilities create possibilities, but human judgment determines how those capabilities are used and whether they create positive outcomes for businesses and society.

6.8 Key Terms

Model Integration – The process of combining individual ML or NLP models into larger business systems that operate reliably in real-world workflows.

Data Drift – Changes in real-world data over time that differ from the data used to train a model, potentially affecting performance.

Integration Complexity – Challenges that arise when multiple models must work together within business processes or systems.

System-Level Performance Metrics – Metrics that evaluate AI systems beyond individual model performance, including user satisfaction, response time, business impact, and fairness.

Bias in AI Models – Systematic errors that produce unfair outcomes for certain groups, often stemming from imbalanced or unrepresentative training data.

Human Oversight – Involvement of humans in monitoring, validating, and intervening in AI systems to ensure ethical, reliable, and fair outcomes.

Conversational AI – AI systems like chatbots and virtual assistants that combine multiple NLP and ML models to interact with humans in natural language.

Intent Classification – A supervised learning task in conversational AI that predicts the purpose of a user's input (e.g., return request, complaint, inquiry).

Entity Extraction – Using NLP to identify and classify key pieces of information in text, such as products, dates, or locations, within a conversation.

Context Management – Maintaining and updating conversation state to interpret user inputs correctly across multiple interactions.

Response Generation – Producing appropriate outputs in conversational AI, either via template-based methods or neural text generation.

Sentiment Adaptation – Adjusting AI responses based on detected emotions or tone of user inputs to improve user experience.

Text Summarization – Automatically condensing long documents or datasets into concise versions while retaining key information; can be extractive or abstractive.

Text Generation – Using AI to produce written content, such as emails, reports, or marketing copy, often requiring human review.

Business Impact Metrics – Measures that link AI system performance to tangible business outcomes, such as customer retention, revenue, or efficiency improvements.

Operational Efficiency Metrics – Measures that assess how effectively an AI system fits into business operations, including uptime, response speed, and manual intervention requirements.

Responsible AI Implementation – Applying AI systems in a way that prioritizes fairness, accountability, transparency, and alignment with human decision-making.

Evaluation Across Demographics – Assessing AI system performance for different groups to identify disparities and ensure fairness.

Human-in-the-Loop (HITL) – A design approach where humans review and validate AI outputs to maintain quality, accountability, and ethical standards.

6.9 Review Questions

1. What are the main challenges when integrating individual ML or NLP models into larger business systems?
2. How does data drift affect model performance in real-world applications? Provide an example.
3. Explain integration complexity in systems that combine multiple models. Why can models that perform well individually fail when combined?
4. What are system-level performance metrics, and why are they important beyond traditional accuracy or precision?
5. Define bias in AI models and describe strategies to detect and mitigate it in business applications.
6. Why is human oversight critical when deploying ML and NLP systems in business?

7. Describe the components of a conversational AI system and how they work together.
8. How does intent classification work, and what role does text preprocessing play in it?
9. Explain entity extraction and context management in conversational AI. Why are they important for maintaining coherent interactions?
10. How is sentiment analysis used in conversational AI to adapt system responses?
11. Compare template-based response generation with neural response generation. What are the advantages and challenges of each?
12. What is the purpose of text summarization and text generation in business decision-making? How do humans remain involved?
13. How should AI system performance be evaluated to ensure both technical accuracy and real-world business value?
14. Explain the concept of human-in-the-loop (HITL) and why it is essential for responsible AI implementation.
15. How do domain expertise and business context influence the effectiveness of ML and NLP systems?
16. Describe how operational efficiency and user experience metrics contribute to evaluating AI systems.
17. What are the key principles of responsible AI deployment in business settings?

6.10 Conclusion

The field of machine learning and NLP continues to evolve rapidly, with new techniques, tools, and applications emerging regularly. The foundation you've built in this course—understanding core concepts, evaluation principles, and responsible practices—prepares you to adapt to these changes and continue learning throughout your career.

The specific algorithms and tools you've learned will continue to improve and evolve, but the fundamental principles of data quality, model evaluation, bias detection, and human oversight will remain relevant. These principles provide a stable foundation for navigating technological change and making good decisions about when and how to adopt new AI capabilities.

Critical thinking about AI applications—understanding their capabilities and limitations, recognizing potential risks and benefits, and maintaining appropriate skepticism about automated solutions—becomes increasingly important as AI systems become more prevalent and sophisticated.

The most successful practitioners of applied machine learning are those who combine technical competence with business understanding, ethical reasoning, and commitment to continuous learning. They use AI to solve real problems and create genuine value while maintaining human judgment and oversight that ensure these powerful tools serve human needs effectively.

As you continue your journey in applied machine learning, remember that the goal is not to build the most sophisticated AI system possible, but to create solutions that genuinely improve business outcomes and human experiences. The techniques you've learned provide the tools to achieve this goal, but success ultimately depends on how thoughtfully and responsibly you apply them.

6.11 References

[1] MIT Sloan Management Review. (2025). From Models to Systems: Deploying Machine Learning in Business Operations. https://sloanreview.mit.edu/

[2] Harvard Business Review. (2025). Responsible AI in Practice: Bias Detection and Human Oversight in Business Applications. https://hbr.org/

[3] Stanford HAI. (2025). Conversational AI Systems: Integrating Multiple ML and NLP Models for Business Applications. https://hai.stanford.edu/

[4] McKinsey & Company. (2025). AI Decision Support Systems: Text Generation and Summarization in Business Context. https://www.mckinsey.com/

www.ingramcontent.com/pod-product-compliance
Lightning Source LLC
Chambersburg PA
CBHW061354240926
51846CB00007B/1405
* 9 7 8 1 9 6 9 2 3 3 3 9 5 *